HALF BAKED HARVEST
EVERY DAY

HALF BAKED HARVEST

recipes for balanced, flexible, feel-good meals

EVERY DAY

Tieghan Gerard

CLARKSON POTTER/PUBLISHERS
NEW YORK

To my loving and kind HBH community, this book is for you all. Thank you for inspiring me to continue to create. I hope this collection of recipes brings new, delicious ideas to your kitchen.

CONTENTS

introduction

If you've been around for a while, you know I come from a big family. Crazy as it may be, my family recently grew, and I'm now one of EIGHT kids! My littlest brother, Oslo, arrived in 2020, and he is the greatest thing that came out of that whole year. While most of my siblings are scattered all over the place now, I'm still up in the mountains of Colorado. I live in a renovated log horse barn steps away from our separate studio barn, where I cook and shoot photos and generally stay busy. A lot of days, I'm on my feet all day cooking and testing new recipes. Other days, I race against the setting sun to get photographs of the finished dishes. And then there are the days I huddle in front of my pizza oven to keep cozy while catching up on emails and calls.

I do all this with my family just next door, which I love. They LOVE food, always have, and they are what started my cooking and keep me cooking—if only because they are constantly hungry! My little sister, Asher, and my brothers (whenever they roll through town) are constantly popping into the studio looking for something to eat. Somehow, no matter how busy I am, I can't resist stopping what I'm doing to make them their favorite foods—that's just what you do for the people you love!

But when my schedule overfills and stress sets in, taking care of myself is usually the first thing to go. And I bet the same is true for you. But it doesn't have to be! No matter what else is going on, we all need to eat—every single day.

Food is, quite literally, fuel for life. So sometimes you need a quick sheet pan meal thrown together from whatever's on hand, while other times you can leisurely enjoy both the cooking process and the meal. Sometimes you crave a clean, light, nutrient-packed dish, while other times you just want a big plate of something comforting. For me, the days are all different, but one thing is constant: I always want to be sure my loved ones and I are eating well.

To me, "eating well" means not only sustaining your body but also giving yourself what you feel you need. I am definitely NOT an expert on any sort of healthy eating. What I have learned, though, is that I care about how food makes me feel, but I don't want to spend a lot of time stressing about it. I want to know where my food came from, what's in it, and who made it. I want to feel good about what I eat without sacrificing flavor or overcomplicating the process. And that's the approach I take in my cooking every single day: I aim to make food that is delicious, usually healthy, sometimes decadent, and always satisfying.

what "balance" means to me

We're always hearing about the importance of "balanced meals." I don't disagree, but if you're looking for rules and regulations on health, I'm afraid you're in the wrong place. I'm not a nutritionist, and I would never want to tell you how you "should" be eating. For me, feel-good food is not about calorie-counting or restriction. But it IS about lots of flavor and satisfaction. That means cooking with plenty of good fat, reducing sugar when possible—or using natural sweeteners like honey, dates, and maple syrup—and, most important, using non-processed ingredients that are whole and real. The other piece I feel is equally important is to give my body what it wants. Some days that's a heaping plate of hearty,

well-seasoned, yummy vegetables, and some days it's a bowl of cheesy, buttery, gooey noodles. That's what balance is for me.

I set out to create a book that embodies the way I eat. I also wanted to give you guys more of what you've been asking for: the "healthy-ish" recipes I usually share on the blog at the start of each year. You—and I—want to eat those sorts of meals throughout the year, too, so I wanted to share more of them here. But my biggest hope is no matter what you're looking for on any particular day, you will find something here that works for you. Whatever you're feeling, that you can flip through the pages and find something super satisfying. And, of course, that some of these recipes will be on repeat in your kitchen!

I've organized the recipes by types of meals and ingredients. Some dishes are lightened-up versions of old favorites. Others are heavy on superfoods. If you're all about clean living, that's here. And if you just NEED chocolate cake, that's here, too. (Spoiler alert: it's really good . . .) Whenever possible, I've indicated where you can make a choice of ingredients. There's tons of flexibility here, and you should feel empowered to make the decision that works for you. I do a lot of cooking "research" on my family—some of my most popular recipes have come from Creighton's insane imagination or whatever Red is craving. They are all picky in their own ways, and believe it or not, so am I. So it's very important for my recipes to be flexible and fun. Maybe the way I prepared a dish isn't exactly how you want to eat it that day—that's okay! You can leave out the cheese, use gluten-free pasta, add in more greens, or do whatever else sounds good. I've also given multiple options for how to cook some things, especially when it comes to the slow cooker and pressure cooker, since I know we don't all have them (but those of us who do LOVE them).

Cinnamon Sugar Knots, page 49

Coconut Cake with Chocolate Frosting, page 265

To make this book as easy and fun to use as possible, I included some icons to help you navigate what's here. Look for the following categories throughout the book so you can see what a recipe has to offer at a glance:

30 30 Minutes or Less: You'll be able to whip this up in a snap!

1 One-Pan: The recipe requires you to use only one pan, skillet, or sheet pan (these are some of my favorites!).

P Pantry Ingredients: If you have a well-stocked pantry, you already have everything you need.

DF Dairy-Free: The way I've written the recipe is without any dairy products.

GF Gluten-Free: Same as dairy-free! The way I've written the recipe is without any gluten products.

SF Refined Sugar–Free: While the recipe may include some natural sugars or sweeteners, it doesn't have any refined sugar.

V Vegetarian: No meat (obviously).

Additionally, depending on some ingredient choices you may make, many recipes can easily be made dairy-free, gluten-free, or vegetarian. There's a recipe in this book for every palate and craving and occasion and mood. Wherever you are today, right now, you'll find something in here that's exactly what you need and want. My goal is simple: for you to feel GOOD when you eat these dishes!

ingredients

When it comes to food, quality means more to me than pretty much anything else. I won't bore you with an exhaustive list of the basic ingredients to stock up on (you can find those on my blog or in one of my other cookbooks). However, I do want to share some info on items where there are a lot of options that might be confusing, and let you know the selections I turn to over and over again.

eggs

We keep twelve chickens between my house and the studio. That means I pretty much always have fresh eggs on hand. If you're shopping in a grocery store, you'll find a million different words on the packaging—what do they all mean?! In my opinion, the best egg is organic, pasture-raised or free-range, and certified humane. Vital Farms and Kirkland are reliable brands. All of my recipes call for large eggs.

butter

Butter makes everything better—that's just a fact. I use it throughout this book, but in moderation, and only when needed.

I always, always prefer salted butter. That's what I use in all of the recipes in this book. If you prefer unsalted, that's fine—you just may need to add more salt to your finished dish.

I prefer to use organic, European-style butter, which is at least 82 percent butterfat, whereas most American-style butter is only 80 percent. That extra fat makes for a yellower, smoother butter that tastes richer. In addition, European-style is often cultured, which gives it a slightly tangy taste, and is probiotic. Whichever style you choose probably won't make a huge impact on the outcome of your dish, though; it's most noticeable when the butter plays a big role. The brands I like are Straus Family Creamery, Kerrygold, Vermont Creamery, and Land O'Lakes Extra Creamy.

milk, cream, and yogurt

Some people prefer not to eat dairy, and I totally get that. Wherever possible, the recipes here call for the milk of your choice: whole or skim cow's milk or goat's milk, or almond, oat, soy, or whatever else you prefer. I use goat milk because, well, I have goats! You can easily find it in most grocery stores now; Meyenberg is a good brand. I like it because it's less processed than some cow's milk, and it's easier for a lot of people to digest. I also love the flavor, which is a little tangier—but you won't notice that in recipes, only if you're drinking it straight.

I often use coconut milk in place of heavy cream, and I'll usually call for either/or throughout this book. When I say coconut milk, I ALWAYS mean the unsweetened full-fat canned version—I like the texture it adds, plus I think it has the best flavor. Native Forest is my favorite brand. Just give the can a good shake before you crack it open, or if yours won't shake, stir it to reincorporate the cream into the liquid before using it.

When it comes to yogurt, I like full-fat plain Greek yogurt for everything. Fage and Greek Gods are my favorite brands. They've got a great creaminess and a nice tang that makes it a perfect sub for sour cream, crème fraîche, and mayonnaise.

cheese

You probably know this about me already . . . I LOVE cheese. Like, really love it. There's plenty of it in these recipes. You should always feel free to use as much or as little as you like, and if you just prefer not to eat cheese, it can be left out of a lot of dishes, too.

But if you do opt in, you gotta get the good stuff for maximum YUM. Cheese is, of course, made from milk, so just like milk, depending on the animal it comes from, some cheese might be easier to digest than others. If lactose can be issue for you, try goat's or sheep's milk cheese, which has less lactose (though it's not lactose-free).

I usually prefer to shred and grate cheese myself. Sometimes pre-shredded, packaged cheese contains added ingredients.

READING LABELS

To be sure you're bringing home only the good stuff, I recommend checking out the labels of the products you buy. Be wary of any weird, exceptionally long words—I like to be able to pronounce the names of everything I'm putting into my body! In general, the first ingredient should be what the food actually is. For example, with ketchup you'll want to see tomatoes listed as the first ingredient. Always avoid ingredient lists that are miles long.

Keep an eye out for added sugars. These will be listed a lot of different ways: concentrated fruit or vegetable juice, corn sweetener, molasses, syrup, fructose, maltose, sucrose . . . basically anything that ends in "ose."

Also, look for good fats. I prefer products made with avocado oil and olive oil rather than canola oil.

No matter what, don't opt out of full-fat versions because you think the low-fat version is "better" for you. It's not! Unnatural additives usually take the place of the removed fat. You don't want to be eating these additives . . . trust me.

QUICK NOTES

Mozzarella: Fresh mozzarella contains a lot of water, which will end up in your food if you use it on top of, say, a pizza. That's why I call for low-moisture whole-milk mozzarella any time the cheese will be melted. The package will be labeled this way!

Parmesan: Without a doubt, Parm is my favorite cheese to grate! I think it makes pretty much everything better, so you will see it used in many recipes here. I also love to save Parmesan rinds to add extra flavor to my soups and tomato sauces; just drop it in while the dish is simmering and then discard it before serving. If you're looking for a nondairy option, nutritional yeast is a great substitute—I've found it to have the closest flavor to Parmesan. It won't melt, but it does the trick!

salt

Salt is something our bodies need to stay healthy. For the recipes in this book, unless otherwise specified, I use fine pink Himalayan salt. In addition to being pretty (yes, it really is pink!), this type of salt contains many minerals. It's thought to be the least processed form of sea salt. Redmond Real Salt is another great option, and since it comes from the Great Salt Lake in Utah, it has a low carbon footprint for those living in the United States. If kosher salt is what you know and love, that's all good, too. You'll just want to use a little bit more than what I call for, since it's not quite as fine. A good rule of thumb no matter what? Taste your food before you add salt!

meat and fish

All of the chicken recipes here work with thighs or breasts. Use what you like! If you're cooking thighs, the timing is a bit more forgiving, as they don't dry out as fast as white meat.

Red meat gets a bad rap sometimes, but, for me, it's really important for balanced eating. It's a great source of iron and nutrients and supports healthy brain function. I prefer to stick to grass-fed beef, since it's natural for cows to eat grass, versus grain-fed. And grass-fed beef generally contains less monounsaturated (bad) fat but more omega fatty acids—and those are GOOD!

When it comes to ground beef, I opt for 80% lean and 20% fat.

You'll see bacon in several recipes here. If bacon is not for you, you can either swap it for prosciutto or simply leave it out. I always look for organic bacon that says "no sugar added" on the packaging.

I usually buy uncured, which has no added sodium nitrates or nitrites.

For fish, both wild-caught and farm-raised can be good choices, depending on a number of factors. You always want to opt for the most sustainable and ethical choice, which often just means asking your fishmonger or checking with sources such as seafoodwatch.org.

oils

I use extra-virgin olive oil . . . in almost everything. My favorites are Brightland 100% Extra-Virgin Heirloom Olive Oil and Cobram Estate Extra-Virgin Olive Oil. That said, I also like to have avocado oil on hand for when I'm cooking something at a high temperature. It doesn't smoke and burn as quickly as olive oil. I use

Thrive Market or Primal Kitchen avo oil. These two oils are also great because they contain healthy fats.

Having an oil mister on hand can help you to better control the amount you're using.

I also like organic virgin or unrefined coconut oil. Those words just mean the oil has undergone the least amount of processing, and therefore it will have the greatest number of antioxidants and anti-inflammatory benefits. Dr. Bronner's and Nutiva are both great brands.

stock or broth

Whether you pick up stock or broth, both will work in recipes in the same way. Technically, stock is made more from bones and broth more from meat. Either way, when using store-bought, I always opt for low-sodium so I can control the taste of the dish myself. Pacific Foods is my favorite brand.

pasta

For many dishes that involve noodles, I will usually call for a specific shape or size. If you have it, great! If you don't, I promise—pretty much anything will work. But for pasta, you should feel free to use whatever type you prefer, whether it's egg, whole-wheat, spinach, semolina, chickpea, cauliflower, brown rice, or anything else! Pasta and noodles are an ingredient that's flexible. Banza and Lotus Foods make great non-wheat versions.

flour

All-purpose flour is great, and it reliably gives you a light and fluffy outcome, especially in baking. Sometimes you just need it . . . but other times, you can use something slightly healthier and still reach a similar outcome. Brands I love across the board are Bob's Red Mill, King Arthur, and Whole Foods 365 Organic. Here are some of the other flours used throughout these recipes:

Almond: Just ground-up almonds, almond flour doesn't usually have a strong almond flavor.

Arrowroot: Arrowroot powder (sometimes called "flour") is a replacement for cornstarch—it thickens or crisps in the same way—but with a more neutral flavor. It's great for those with corn sensitivities.

Coconut: I like coconut flour in baked goods because of its fine texture. In large amounts, it might add a hint of coconut flavor.

Oat: Simply ground-up oats, oat flour does impart flavor, which is a reason to use it. It's on the heartier end, closer to whole-wheat flour.

Rye: All rye flours have great flavor, but I use dark rye. As far as flour goes, it has high nutrition content—fiber, antioxidants, minerals, vitamins—as well as health benefits: it can help lower your cholesterol, it's low on the glycemic index . . . should I keep going?

Whole-wheat and whole-wheat pastry: This is a bit healthier than all-purpose, as it's made with the whole grain. It's denser, darker, and heartier. Whole-wheat pastry flour is a finer, lighter version, which is helpful in baking.

Almond flour, arrowroot powder, and coconut flour are gluten-free. Oat flour is gluten-free as long as it's labeled that way. But your best bet for making a gluten-free swap for all-purpose would be to use an equal amount of the brand Cup4Cup.

sweeteners

With few exceptions (you KNOW me and desserts!), I try not to add refined sugar to my dishes. In its place, you'll find plenty of honey and maple syrup. I like to use raw honey because it hasn't been heated or pasteurized, so it has the most antioxidants, vitamins, and other nutrients. If it's an option for you, locally made honey, made with local pollen, might even help you fight allergies! And I always go with pure maple syrup because that's all it is—maple!—no other sugar has been added.

That said, refined sugar does have its time and place. In these instances, I don't believe in artificial sweeteners like stevia and aspartame. I will always specify granulated (white) sugar or light or dark brown. For brown sugar, most recipes are pretty forgiving if you want to use whichever type you have on hand.

chocolate

As far as I'm concerned, chocolate is KEY to balanced eating. I love the Colorado-based brand Chocolove, which melts really nicely. The 77% is my favorite. And I am a big fan of Hu 70%, which is vegan and paleo.

seeds, nuts, and nut butters

A little protein, a little crunch . . . you're going to want to have a lot of these on hand! Trust me, you won't be sorry. My favorites: almonds, cashews, flaxseeds, hazelnuts, peanuts, pecans, pepitas, (pumpkin seeds), pine nuts, sesame seeds, sunflower seeds, and walnuts (which are super high in omegas).

I also love cooking with almond butter, cashew butter, peanut butter, and tahini. Look for packaging that says "no sugar added." Artisana is one of my favorite nut butter brands.

herbs and spices

I absolutely LOVE cooking with fresh herbs, and I recommend having as many on hand as possible. My go-to herbs are basil, cilantro, dill, and thyme. I also like parsley and oregano. If I call for cooking with fresh herbs that you don't have on hand, you can use dried; for every 1 tablespoon fresh, use 1 teaspoon dried. (If they're just for garnishing, though, skip the herbs altogether!)

My go-to spices: black pepper, cardamom, cayenne, chili powder, chipotle chile powder, cinnamon, cumin, garlic powder, nutmeg, onion powder, smoked paprika, and turmeric.

spicy things

I also LOVE crushed red pepper flakes. In many recipes I will give a range for the quantity—use as much or as little spice as you like! Same goes for hot sauce (I like Frank's RedHot), gochujang (I like Mother in Law's), sambal oelek, and harissa.

other condiments and sauces

Mayonnaise: I like the kind made with avocado oil, which has healthier fats than canola oil. Vegan mayonnaise is also good. Primal Kitchen is my go-to.

Vinegars: SO much flavor. I keep apple cider (great for gut health), balsamic, champagne, red wine, and rice vinegars handy at all times.

Soy sauce: Always, always low-sodium. I often opt for tamari instead, a type of soy sauce that is naturally gluten-free (as long as it's labeled that way). For all of my recipes, you can use these interchangeably.

Fish sauce: I would say fish sauce is my holy grail product in the kitchen. I always go for Red Boat!

Miso: This salty paste is made from fermented soybeans and has tons of minerals, vitamins, and gut-health benefits. I usually opt for white or yellow by Miso Master.

Ketchup: Organic and unsweetened are key here. I get mine from Primal Kitchen.

Marinara sauce: I recommend Rao's, which can be found at most grocery stores. The flavor is spot-on and delicious, and it's made with ingredients that I'd actually put into a classic marinara sauce myself.

breakfast

sheet pan french toast

with whipped lemon ricotta and juicy berries

PREP 10 MINUTES
COOK 20 MINUTES
TOTAL 30 MINUTES
SERVES 4 TO 6

When I was growing up, the weekends were either for pancakes or Dad's cinnamon toast. Mom made special monkey bread on Christmas, but otherwise breakfast was just bagels or cereal. After I took over the family cooking, my brother Creighton asked for French toast. I'm honestly not sure where he'd ever tried it before, but I looked it up and made a pretty basic version. Everyone loved it . . . loved it so much that every single piece disappeared the second I took it out of the skillet. I admit, it was pretty good. But also? I stood over the stove for at least an hour flipping French toast when what I really wanted to be doing was eating it! Enter this recipe, with no flipping necessary but the same delicious outcome! This oven-baked French toast is pretty close to a classic pan-fried version, but you'll get to sit down and eat it faster. The whipped lemon ricotta and sweet berries at the end are the perfect finishing touches.

BERRIES

2 cups fresh berries of your choice, sliced if large

2 tablespoons raw honey

Flaky sea salt

FRENCH TOAST

Extra-virgin olive oil, for greasing

4 large eggs

2 cups milk of your choice

3 tablespoons salted butter, melted

1 tablespoon pure vanilla extract

1 tablespoon raw honey

1 teaspoon ground cinnamon

¼ teaspoon freshly grated nutmeg

½ teaspoon fine pink Himalayan salt

1 brioche loaf, soft whole-grain loaf, or challah, cut into generous 1-inch-thick slices

WHIPPED LEMON RICOTTA

1 cup whole-milk ricotta cheese

1 tablespoon raw honey

2 teaspoons lemon zest

Raw honey or pure maple syrup, for serving

1. Preheat the oven to 425°F. Grease a baking sheet.

2. **MAKE THE BERRIES.** In a medium bowl, toss together the berries, honey, and a pinch of flaky salt. Let sit for 15 to 20 minutes.

3. **MEANWHILE, MAKE THE FRENCH TOAST.** In a medium bowl, whisk together the eggs, milk, melted butter, vanilla, honey, cinnamon, nutmeg, and salt. Dip one slice of bread into the egg mixture and turn it to coat. Remove, allowing any excess to drip off. Place the coated bread on the prepared baking sheet. Repeat with the remaining slices.

4. Bake the French toast for 10 minutes, then use a spatula to flip the slices. Bake until lightly golden, about 10 minutes more.

5. **MEANWHILE, MAKE THE WHIPPED RICOTTA.** Place the ricotta in a food processor and process until smooth and creamy, about 1 minute. Add the honey and lemon zest and pulse to combine.

6. Place one or two slices of French toast on each plate. Dollop with the whipped ricotta and spoon the berries and their juices over the top. Drizzle with more honey, if desired. Serve.

whole-wheat popovers
with maple apple butter

PREP 10 MINUTES
COOK 40 MINUTES
TOTAL 50 MINUTES
MAKES 6 POPOVERS
OR 12 MINI POPOVERS

The first Thanksgiving we lived in Colorado, I was in eighth grade. We had recently moved and were still starting our new lives here—just my parents, brothers, and I were celebrating, as my little siblings, Asher and Oslo, hadn't joined us yet. But one key memory from that day was that it was the first time I made popovers, and they were by far the biggest hit of the day. I think those popovers might be THE thing that convinced my mom I could really do this whole cooking thing. Ever since, I always bake them for Thanksgiving—it's tradition now. They are my mom's (and now Asher's) favorite part of the Thanksgiving meal. These look impressive, but they're super simple to make. Don't be afraid to fill your pan; they will literally pop straight up rather than spill over the sides. Apple butter plus salted butter on a popover is so good, but you have to serve them hot. Nothing is better!

2 tablespoons plus 6 teaspoons salted butter, plus more, at room temperature, for serving

1½ cups whole milk, at room temperature

3 large eggs, at room temperature

1 cup whole-wheat pastry flour

½ cup all-purpose flour

1 teaspoon fine pink Himalayan salt

Maple Apple Butter (recipe follows) or store-bought apple butter, at room temperature, for serving

1. Preheat the oven to 450°F with a rack positioned in the lower third of the oven.

2. In a small skillet over medium heat or using the microwave, melt 2 tablespoons of the butter. In a medium bowl, vigorously whisk together the milk and eggs until frothy, about 1 minute. Add the melted butter, both flours, and the salt, and whisk to combine. It's okay if there are some small lumps.

3. Place 1 teaspoon of the remaining butter in each cup of a 6-cup standard popover pan. (Alternatively, you can use a 12-cup muffin tin to make mini popovers, using ½ teaspoon butter per cup.) Transfer the pan to the oven for 2 to 3 minutes to melt the butter and heat the pan.

4. Carefully remove the popover pan from the oven and tilt it in a circular motion to coat the cups with butter. Divide the batter evenly among the popover cups, filling each three-quarters of the way.

5. Bake for 20 minutes. Do not open the oven—your popovers might deflate. Then reduce the oven temperature to 350°F and bake until the popovers are puffed, golden, and crisp, 15 to 20 minutes more.

6. To serve, split the warm popovers in half and spread them with more butter and the apple butter.

maple apple butter
MAKES ABOUT 4 CUPS

4 pounds apples, preferably Honeycrisp, cored and diced (about 10 cups)

1¼ cups apple cider

½ cup pure maple syrup, plus more as needed

1 teaspoon pure vanilla extract

2 teaspoons ground cinnamon or 1 or 2 cinnamon sticks

½ teaspoon freshly grated nutmeg

¼ teaspoon ground cloves

Pinch of fine pink Himalayan salt

Preheat the oven to 425°F. In a high-speed blender, working in batches as needed, combine the apples with the apple cider and blend until smooth. Transfer the mixture to a 9 × 13-inch baking dish. Add the maple syrup, vanilla, cinnamon, nutmeg, cloves, and salt and stir to combine. Roast for 30 to 35 minutes. Give the apple butter a stir, and reduce the oven temperature to 350°F. Continue roasting, stirring every 30 minutes, for 1 to 1½ hours more, until the apple butter is thick and golden brown. Taste and add more maple syrup as needed. Discard the cinnamon stick(s), if using. Let the apple butter cool. Store refrigerated in airtight glass jars for up to 1 month.

pumpkin streusel coffee cake

with cinnamon butter

PREP 10 MINUTES

COOK 1 HOUR

TOTAL 1 HOUR 10 MINUTES, PLUS COOLING TIME

MAKES 1 (9 × 5-INCH) LOAF

Okay, let's talk about coffee cake. I understand that's what it's called because you're supposed to have it WITH coffee, but I've always found it bizarre that there's no coffee IN it. I am a literal person, so I had to add coffee to my coffee cake! And it works so well with the mix of warming spices here: cinnamon, nutmeg, ginger, and cloves. Fall flavors are my favorite, but I try to wait until October to start baking with pumpkin. This is one of the first recipes I make every autumn because it's just so delicious. You'll find surprise bursts of brown sugar in some bites, but it's subtle enough that you definitely won't feel a sugar high, which makes this coffee cake the best breakfast or all-day snack.

CAKE

¼ cup melted coconut oil, plus more for greasing

½ cup pure maple syrup

2 large eggs, at room temperature

2 teaspoons pure vanilla extract

1 cup pumpkin puree

½ cup brewed coffee

2½ cups whole-wheat pastry flour

2 teaspoons baking powder

½ teaspoon baking soda

2 tablespoons ground flaxseed

2 teaspoons ground cinnamon

½ teaspoon freshly grated nutmeg

¼ teaspoon ground ginger

¼ teaspoon ground cloves

1 teaspoon fine pink Himalayan salt

STREUSEL

3 tablespoons whole-wheat pastry flour

2 tablespoons dark brown sugar

1½ teaspoons ground cinnamon

2 tablespoons cold salted butter, cubed

CINNAMON BUTTER

4 tablespoons (½ stick) salted butter, at room temperature

2 tablespoons pure maple syrup

½ teaspoon ground cinnamon

Pinch of fine pink Himalayan salt

1. Preheat the oven to 350°F. Grease a 9 × 5-inch loaf pan.

2. **MAKE THE CAKE.** In a large bowl, whisk together the coconut oil, maple syrup, eggs, and vanilla. Add the pumpkin and coffee and whisk until smooth. Add the flour, baking powder, baking soda, flaxseed, cinnamon, nutmeg, ginger, cloves, and salt. Stir until just combined.

3. **MAKE THE STREUSEL.** In a medium bowl, combine the flour, brown sugar, and cinnamon. Add the butter and use your fingers to pinch the butter into the flour mixture until a crumble forms.

4. Add half of the batter to the prepared pan. Evenly sprinkle the streusel over the batter, then add the remaining batter over the top. Bake until a toothpick inserted into the center of the cake comes out clean, 50 to 60 minutes. Cover the cake with foil after 30 minutes if the top is browning too much.

5. **MEANWHILE, MAKE THE CINNAMON BUTTER.** In a small bowl, stir together the butter, maple syrup, cinnamon, and salt.

6. Remove the cake from the oven and let cool in the pan for at least 10 minutes. Slice and serve warm or at room temperature smeared with cinnamon butter. Store any leftovers in an airtight container at room temperature for up to 5 days.

better-than-the-box
blueberry lemon poppyseed muffins

PREP 15 MINUTES
COOK 25 MINUTES
TOTAL 40 MINUTES
MAKES 18 MUFFINS

When it comes to muffins, I am very particular. As a kid I'd make the Wild Blueberry Muffin boxed mix from Betty Crocker. You know, the one that comes with the can of berries packed in syrup? I would bake them on Friday afternoons after school for my younger brother Red. The muffins came out so moist and had the best blueberry flavor, most likely due to those syrup-soaked blueberries, which, while sugary, sure were good. I've tried for years to re-create those muffins from scratch, and while I haven't made an identical match, these are close. A little fancier, I suppose, and surely healthier, as they're made with whole, real ingredients, but they're just as easy and DELICIOUS. The secret is using a mix of fresh blueberries and blueberry jam to add both texture and moisture to each muffin. Honey keeps things sweet, and a light, lemony glaze on top is the real icing on the . . . muffin. So much better than anything from a box.

MUFFINS

½ cup melted coconut oil

½ cup raw honey

2 teaspoons pure vanilla extract

2 large eggs, at room temperature

¾ cup plain Greek yogurt

2 lemons (see Notes)

1¾ cups whole-wheat pastry flour

2 teaspoons baking powder

½ teaspoon baking soda

2 tablespoons poppyseeds

½ teaspoon fine pink Himalayan salt

1½ cups fresh or frozen blueberries (see Notes)

3 tablespoons high-quality blueberry jam (I like Bonne Maman)

GLAZE

1 lemon

2 tablespoons raw honey

⅔ cup confectioners' sugar

1. Preheat the oven to 350°F. Line a 12-cup muffin tin with paper liners.

2. **MAKE THE MUFFINS.** In a large bowl, whisk together the coconut oil, honey, vanilla, eggs, yogurt, the zest of 1 lemon, and 4 tablespoons lemon juice until combined. Add the flour, baking powder, baking soda, poppyseeds, and salt. Stir until just combined. Gently fold in the blueberries and jam, being careful not to overmix; the batter should look like it has a swirl through it.

3. Divide the batter evenly among the muffin cups, filling each three-quarters of the way. Bake until a toothpick inserted into the center of a muffin comes out clean, 25 to 30 minutes.

4. **MEANWHILE, MAKE THE GLAZE.** Using a vegetable peeler, peel wide strips of zest from the lemon, then slice the zest into thin strips. (Alternatively, grate the zest off the lemon.) In a small bowl, whisk together 2 tablespoons of lemon juice, the honey, and the confectioners' sugar until smooth and thin enough to pour. Stir in 1 to 2 tablespoons of the lemon zest strips.

5. Drizzle the glaze over the muffins while they're warm and serve. Store the muffins in an airtight container at room temperature for 3 to 4 days, or in the freezer for up to 3 months.

NOTES

If you can get your hands on Meyer lemons, I recommend using them. They're less tart and sweeter than regular lemons—they make the best bakery treats! They're in season during the winter.

If you're using frozen blueberries, you don't need to wait for them to thaw. Just throw them in!

chocolate chip (and banana) pancakes

PREP 10 MINUTES

COOK 10 MINUTES

TOTAL 20 MINUTES, PLUS RESTING TIME

SERVES 4 TO 6

Chocolate chip–banana pancakes were the first thing I learned to cook. Our first year in Colorado, I was fourteen, and being the new kid in school and all, I ended up spending my afternoons with my mom. I was starting to fall in love with cooking, and I would come home and make these pancakes for my mom as our after-school snack, especially on cold, snowy days (which was . . . often). I loved making her banana pancakes—with lots of chocolate—and she, of course, loved eating them. It was definitely our thing, and even now she'll occasionally ask for a special mother-daughter pancake lunch. We love them with (extra) chocolate chips and bananas, but Asher, who's in on the tradition now, prefers them without banana, so feel free to leave it out. And don't get thrown off by the pumpkin. You can't taste it at all—seriously, the two of them would protest—but in addition to adding extra fiber, it makes the pancakes moist and fluffy.

PANCAKES

1¼ cups milk of your choice, plus more as needed

½ cup pumpkin or butternut squash puree

2 large eggs, at room temperature

2 tablespoons salted butter, melted

1 tablespoon pure maple syrup or raw honey, plus more for serving

2 teaspoons pure vanilla extract

1¼ cups whole-wheat pastry flour

¾ cup oat flour (see Note)

2 teaspoons baking powder

½ teaspoon baking soda

½ teaspoon ground cinnamon

½ teaspoon fine pink Himalayan salt

Butter or coconut oil, for the pan

1 cup semisweet or dark chocolate chips

1 to 2 bananas, sliced, plus more for serving (optional)

MAPLE BUTTER

4 tablespoons (½ stick) salted butter, at room temperature

3 tablespoons pure maple syrup

¼ teaspoon ground cinnamon

Fine pink Himalayan salt

1. MAKE THE PANCAKES. In a large bowl, whisk together the milk, pumpkin, eggs, melted butter, maple syrup, and vanilla. Add both flours, the baking powder, baking soda, cinnamon, and salt. Stir until just combined. It's okay if the batter is a little lumpy, but if you feel like it's too thick, add more milk, 1 tablespoon at a time. Let sit, uncovered, for 10 minutes at room temperature before proceeding. (Alternatively, you can cover and refrigerate it overnight.)

2. MEANWHILE, MAKE THE MAPLE BUTTER. In a small bowl, stir together the butter, maple syrup, cinnamon, and a pinch of salt.

3. Melt a bit of butter in a large skillet or griddle over medium-low heat. Scoop a few ¼-cup portions of the batter into the skillet and use a spatula to spread and smooth them into rounds (3 or 4 should fit comfortably). Sprinkle chocolate chips on top, then add a few banana slices (if using). Cook until bubbles appear on the surface, about 2 minutes, then use a spatula to gently flip each pancake. Cook on the second side until golden, about 1 minute more. Transfer the pancakes to a plate. Repeat with the remaining batter, adding more butter to the skillet if needed.

4. To serve, spread each pancake with a bit of maple butter, drizzle with maple syrup or honey, and top with banana slices (if using).

NOTE ————

If you don't have oat flour, you can use more whole-wheat pastry flour instead.

double apple dutch baby

PREP 10 MINUTES
COOK 15 MINUTES
TOTAL 25 MINUTES
SERVES 4 TO 6

If you know me, you know I love a Dutch baby. So impressive, but so easy. My nonnie, my mom's mom, always used to make them for me when we'd visit her in Florida every summer. She would top hers with whipped cream, strawberries, and plenty of processed, fake maple syrup. It wasn't the healthiest, but I loved every last bite. Ever since, I've made Dutch babies on my own, adapting them a bit for the seasons and making them healthier with some simple swaps. Enter this cozy version that is perfect to make if you have a lot of apples on hand; it uses both sliced apples and apple butter. You get a ton of flavor from the browned butter and the caramelized apples, and the batter is sweet without having to add any sugar. As soon as it hits the pan, your kitchen will smell like you've been baking apple cobblers all day. It's truly the most amazing smell. Nonnie would fully approve—she loved anything with apples! The Dutch baby will start to deflate as soon as it comes out of the oven, so bring the skillet straight to the table.

4 large eggs, at room temperature

⅔ cup milk of your choice, at room temperature

⅓ cup whole-wheat pastry flour

⅓ cup all-purpose flour

¾ teaspoon ground cinnamon, plus more for serving

½ teaspoon ground cardamom

½ teaspoon fine pink Himalayan salt

2 tablespoons Maple Apple Butter (page 20) or store-bought apple butter, plus more for serving

2 teaspoons pure vanilla extract

3 tablespoons salted butter

1 medium apple, preferably Honeycrisp, cored, halved, and thinly sliced

Whipped cream, for serving

Pure maple syrup, for serving

1. Preheat the oven to 450°F with a rack in the center position.

2. In a medium bowl, using an electric mixer, beat together the eggs, milk, both flours, cinnamon, cardamom, salt, apple butter, and vanilla until the batter is smooth, about 1 minute. Be sure no large clumps of flour remain.

3. Melt the butter in a medium cast-iron skillet over medium heat. Add the sliced apple and cook, stirring once or twice, until the butter is browning and the apple is just beginning to caramelize, about 5 minutes. Using tongs or a slotted spoon, transfer the apples to a plate, leaving the butter in the skillet.

4. Pour the batter into the hot skillet. Arrange half of the caramelized apples over the batter, reserving the remainder. Bake until the pancake is puffed up and browned on top, about 15 minutes. Do not open the oven during cooking—doing so might deflate the Dutch baby.

5. Top the Dutch baby with the remaining caramelized apples and the whipped cream, sprinkle with cinnamon, and drizzle with syrup. Serve immediately with more apple butter.

chai orchard doughnuts

PREP 15 MINUTES

COOK 40 MINUTES

TOTAL 55 MINUTES,
PLUS COOLING TIME

MAKES 12 DOUGHNUTS

For me, really nothing is better than an autumn weekend spent baking with the ingredients of the season. Like a lot of you, I am sure, my favorite fall activity is to head to an apple orchard and pick enough apples to fill my buckets all the way up to the top. I have to prepare for all the baking that's to come, you know? But let me tell you the real reason I love apple picking so much: the cinnamon-sugar-coated apple cider doughnuts that always, always follow . . . and the cup of hot chocolate that goes with them, too. But sometimes all that sugar on top of all that adventure leaves me feeling a little sluggish afterward. So I started making my own doughnuts at home to enjoy later. They're pretty, and they taste even better than they look. Think of your favorite apple cider doughnut. Okay, now lose the taste of the frying oil, and add a bit more apple flavor, plus a homemade mix of chai spices. THAT is these doughnuts. And don't forget a steaming mug of hot cocoa—or even a chai—for the full effect!

4 tablespoons (½ stick) salted butter, melted, plus more at room temperature for greasing

1½ cups apple cider

1 large egg, at room temperature

½ cup Maple Apple Butter (page 20) or store-bought apple butter

¼ cup pure maple syrup

1½ cups whole-wheat pastry flour

½ cup all-purpose flour

1 teaspoon baking powder

1 teaspoon baking soda

2 teaspoons ground cinnamon

½ teaspoon ground ginger

½ teaspoon ground allspice

½ teaspoon ground cardamom

¼ teaspoon freshly grated nutmeg

¼ teaspoon ground cloves

½ teaspoon fine pink Himalayan salt

⅛ teaspoon freshly ground pepper

½ cup granulated sugar

1. Preheat the oven to 350°F. Grease two 6-cup doughnut pans.

2. In a small saucepan over high heat, bring the apple cider to a boil. Reduce the heat to medium-low and simmer until reduced by two-thirds, about 20 minutes; you should have ½ cup. Remove the pan from the heat and let cool for 10 minutes.

3. Meanwhile, in a large bowl, beat the egg. Add 2 tablespoons of the melted butter, the apple butter, and the maple syrup. Whisk to incorporate. Add both flours, the baking powder, baking soda, 1 teaspoon of the cinnamon, and the ginger, allspice, cardamom, nutmeg, cloves, salt, and pepper. Add the reduced apple cider. Stir well until the batter is smooth and no lumps remain. Spoon the batter into the doughnut pans, filling each cavity two-thirds full.

4. Bake until the doughnuts are golden and springy when lightly pressed, 18 to 20 minutes. Remove from the oven and let cool in the pan for about 5 minutes. Then release the doughnuts from the pan.

5. In a shallow bowl, stir together the sugar and remaining 1 teaspoon cinnamon. Working with one doughnut at a time, brush the smooth top with the remaining melted butter. Dip the doughnut into the sugar, pressing to adhere, and transfer to a serving platter. Repeat with the remaining doughnuts. Store at room temperature in an airtight container for up to four days.

NOTE

If you don't have doughnut pans, you can use a muffin tin. The cook time is the same.

seeded whole-grain bread

PREP 30 MINUTES

COOK 40 MINUTES

TOTAL 1 HOUR 10 MINUTES, PLUS RISING AND COOLING TIME

MAKES 1 LOAF

 DF SF V

Bread is a big deal in my family, mostly because my mom loves bread of any kind. Since before I was even born, my mom has eaten the same breakfast every morning: toast and hot chocolate. When I was younger, she favored pumpernickel bagels, but somewhere along the way, she switched to whole-grain toast. After we moved to Colorado, she had a really hard time finding a good seeded bread. Over the years, I made attempts to create a new favorite for her, but none of my loaves quite measured up . . . until this guy. You've got to use a mix of seeds for the ultimate crunch on the outside. My favorites are pepitas, sunflower seeds, and sesame seeds, but mix and match depending on what you love most. The real secret to this bread, however, is in the baking method, in a super-hot Dutch oven. It's a must for getting a loaf that's crusty on the outside but soft on the inside. And the whole house will fill with the incredible smell.

2 cups warm water

2 teaspoons raw honey

2¼ teaspoons active dry yeast

1 cup old-fashioned rolled oats

2 cups whole-wheat pastry flour, plus more as needed

1 cup dark rye flour

½ cup all-purpose flour, plus more for kneading

¼ cup ground flaxseed

1½ teaspoons fine pink Himalayan salt

½ cup mixed seeds, such as pepitas, sunflower seeds, flaxseeds, and sesame seeds

1 large egg, beaten

1. In a stand mixer, combine 1 cup of the warm water, the honey, and the yeast. Let sit until the mixture is bubbly, 5 to 10 minutes.

2. In a medium bowl, combine the oats with the remaining 1 cup warm water. Let sit until softened, about 10 minutes.

3. Add the oat mixture to the yeast mixture. Add all the flours, the ground flaxseed, and the salt. Using the dough hook, knead on medium speed, adding more whole-wheat pastry flour, 2 tablespoons at a time, as needed, until the dough comes together and pulls away from the sides of the bowl, 1 to 2 minutes. Add ¼ cup of the seeds and mix to combine. Cover with a clean kitchen towel and let rise in a warm place until doubled in size, 1 to 2½ hours.

4. If time allows, to develop a stronger flavor, punch the dough down, cover, and refrigerate it overnight.

5. Preheat the oven to 475°F with a rack in the center position. Place a covered Dutch oven on the rack to preheat as well.

6. On a floured work surface, turn out the dough; it should be loose and sticky. Form the dough into a ball and place it on a sheet of parchment paper. Gently brush the dough with the beaten egg. Cover with an upside-down bowl and let sit for 10 minutes.

7. Carefully remove the heated pan from the oven and uncover it. Using the parchment paper, lift the ball of dough and place it, still on the parchment paper, in the pan. Sprinkle the remaining ¼ cup of seeds over the top. Using a sharp knife, cut a small slit down the center of the loaf.

8. Cover and bake until the bread has risen slightly and a crust begins to form, 20 to 25 minutes. Carefully remove the lid and continue baking until the bread is deep golden brown, 20 to 30 minutes more. Remove the pan from the oven. Using the parchment paper, carefully lift the bread out of the pan and place it on a rack to cool completely, about 2 hours. It will continue to cook as it cools.

cheddar-fried eggs
with bacon and herbs

PREP 15 MINUTES
COOK 5 MINUTES
TOTAL 20 MINUTES
SERVES 1

Fried eggs are the ultimate go-to meal. Sure, they're great for breakfast, but I'm all about that late-night situation enjoyed straight from the stove with crusty bread for scooping up the runny yolk. Not much tastes better—except THESE eggs, because a layer of crispy cheddar cheese will make pretty much anything better. If you don't have cheddar on hand, Parmesan, provolone, or Gruyère would all be delicious, too. I added a light and bright herb salad for a pop of freshness and color, but there's absolutely nothing fancy or complicated about these eggs, which only adds to their charm and appeal. Before you start cooking, throw some bacon in the oven so that by the time your perfect eggs are finished, you'll have it to enjoy alongside.

HERB SALAD

1 tablespoon extra-virgin olive oil

Juice of ½ lemon

1 teaspoon raw honey

½ small shallot, finely chopped or grated

Fine pink Himalayan salt and freshly ground black pepper

Crushed red pepper flakes

¼ cup roughly chopped fresh parsley

2 tablespoons roughly chopped fresh dill

2 tablespoons roughly chopped fresh basil leaves

2 tablespoons roughly chopped fresh oregano

1 tablespoon chopped fresh chives

½ avocado, cubed

EGGS

⅓ cup grated sharp cheddar cheese

2 large eggs

Fine pink Himalayan salt and freshly ground black pepper

Crispy bacon, for serving (see Note)

Crushed red pepper flakes or Aleppo pepper

1. **MAKE THE HERB SALAD.** In a medium bowl, whisk together the olive oil, lemon juice, honey, and shallot. Season with salt, pepper, and red pepper flakes. Add the parsley, dill, basil, oregano, chives, and avocado. Gently toss to combine.

2. **MAKE THE EGGS.** In a small skillet over medium heat, sprinkle the cheese in an even layer. When the cheese begins to melt and release a bit of oil, after about 1 minute, crack the eggs over the cheese, keeping the yolks intact. Season the eggs with salt and black pepper. Cook, undisturbed, until the whites are just set but the yolk is still runny, 2 to 3 minutes, or to your preference.

3. Slide the eggs onto a plate. Add the herb salad and crispy bacon. Sprinkle everything with red pepper flakes. Serve immediately.

NOTE

To get the crispiest possible bacon, I like to bake mine. Arrange however many slices you like on a baking sheet and pop them in the oven at 425°F until beginning to crisp, 10 to 15 minutes. When you take them out, let them sit for a few extra minutes to crisp up some more.

jerusalem-style egg and cheese bagel

with green zhug

PREP 10 MINUTES
COOK 10 MINUTES
TOTAL 20 MINUTES
SERVES 2

When it comes to a breakfast bagel, I don't mess around. I'm not opposed to the classic bacon, egg, and cheese combo, but this Jerusalem-inspired version is even better. So much better. What makes it so? The homemade zhug, za'atar-spiced eggs, and sesame bagel. Let's break this down piece by piece. First, zhug is a popular hot sauce throughout Israel. It can be red or green, but it's spicy either way. The green version is made with herbs, chiles, and spices—mine uses cumin and turmeric. It really adds a nice kick to your bagel. And then, the za'atar eggs. Za'atar is a spice blend popular throughout the Middle East. You can easily find it in most grocery stores or make your own, and it adds an herby, savory note to your otherwise predictable eggs. And finally, the bagels. Jerusalem-style bagels, called *ka'ak al-quds*, are soft, airy, and oval-shaped, with a subtle sweetness from honey-tossed sesame seeds. They're not easy to find everywhere, so the next best thing is a thin or flat sesame-seed bagel (sometimes called a "flagel"). Just make sure it's COVERED in sesame seeds.

4 large eggs

1 tablespoon za'atar (see Note)

Fine pink Himalayan salt and freshly ground pepper

3 tablespoons salted butter

1 cup baby spinach, roughly chopped

2 whole-wheat sesame seed bagels, halved

½ cup Green Zhug (recipe follows) or store-bought zhug

2 to 4 thin slices sharp white cheddar cheese

1. In a medium bowl, beat together the eggs, za'atar, and a pinch each of salt and pepper.

2. Melt 2 tablespoons of the butter in a medium skillet over medium heat. Pour in the egg mixture and cook, undisturbed, until beginning to set on the bottom, 1 to 2 minutes. Using a spatula, lift up the edges and let the uncooked egg run underneath. Scatter the spinach over the top. When the bottom is almost set, fold in the sides toward the middle so the eggs take on a rectangular, omelet-like shape and enclose the spinach to wilt it. Slide the omelet onto a cutting board and cut it in half.

3. On the bottom half of each bagel, spread a layer of the zhug, then top with an omelet half and cheese. Add the top halves of the bagels. In the same skillet, melt the remaining 1 tablespoon butter. Add the bagels, top-side down, and cook, pushing down to flatten them, until the cheese is melted and the sesame seeds are deeply golden brown, 3 to 5 minutes. Carefully flip the bagels and cook 3 to 5 minutes more.

4. Slice the bagels in half and serve immediately, with more zhug alongside if desired.

green zhug

MAKES 1 CUP

1 bunch fresh parsley

1 bunch fresh cilantro

1 large jalapeño, seeded if desired

1 garlic clove, finely chopped or grated

1 teaspoon ground cumin

½ teaspoon ground turmeric

⅓ cup extra-virgin olive oil

2 tablespoons fresh lemon juice

½ teaspoon fine pink Himalayan salt, plus more to taste

In a blender or food processor, combine the parsley, cilantro, jalapeño, garlic, cumin, turmeric, olive oil, lemon juice, and salt. Pulse until finely chopped. If the zhug is too thick, add water, 1 tablespoon at a time, to thin. Taste and add more salt as needed. Store refrigerated in an airtight container for up to 1 week.

NOTE

The spice blend za'atar is pretty widely available, but if you can't find it, you can make your own! Combine 3 tablespoons dried oregano, 2 tablespoons toasted sesame seeds, 1 tablespoon dried thyme, 1 tablespoon ground sumac (or 1 tablespoon lemon zest plus a pinch of black pepper), and 1 teaspoon salt. You'll have about ½ cup, and it'll keep at room temperature for up to a month!

garlic yogurt with poached eggs

and chile butter

PREP 10 MINUTES

COOK 6 MINUTES

TOTAL 16 MINUTES

SERVES 2

When it comes to my everyday breakfast, I strive for simplicity. Oftentimes I have all these ideas for breakfast dishes that require multiple steps: sautéing, roasting, then assembling. Everything sounds delicious, but I have to stop myself. No one can take an hour to make breakfast on a Monday morning! Sure, maybe for Sunday brunch, but when it comes to the daily grind, about 15 minutes is all I am spending on breakfast, TOPS. Instead of turning to frozen waffles on the regular (though they do have their time and place), I make this bowl. It's got a lot going on, but takes only minutes to put together. Garlicky yogurt, soft runny eggs, and spicy butter, all of which are inspired by a classic Turkish dish called *cilbir*. For color, I add a sprinkling of edible flowers if I have them on hand, then I toast up a thin bagel, and suddenly my weekday breakfast feels like something I'd order from one of my favorite New York City brunch spots. To make assembly even faster, mix up the yogurt in advance. It keeps perfectly in the fridge for about five days, developing even more flavor over time.

1 cup plain Greek yogurt

1 garlic clove, finely chopped or grated

Zest and juice of 1 lemon, plus ½ lemon, seeded and sliced into wedges

Fine pink Himalayan salt

4 large eggs, at room temperature

1 tablespoon sesame oil

4 tablespoons salted butter or ghee

2 tablespoons crushed red pepper flakes or Aleppo pepper

½ teaspoon paprika

1 tablespoon sesame seeds, plus more for serving

Fresh herbs, such as dill, parsley, basil, and/or mint, for serving

Toasted Seeded Whole-Grain Bread (page 32) or other bread, for serving (optional)

1. In a small bowl, stir together the yogurt, garlic, lemon zest and juice, and a pinch of salt.

2. Bring a large sauté pan filled with water to a gentle boil over medium-high heat. Crack one egg into a ramekin or small bowl. Lower the lip of the bowl to the surface of the water and gently slide the egg into the water. Repeat with the remaining eggs. Cook until the whites are set around the yolks, about 3 minutes. Using a slotted spoon, gently transfer the eggs to a plate.

3. In a small saucepan over medium heat, combine the sesame oil, butter, lemon wedges, red pepper flakes, paprika, and a pinch of salt. Cook, undisturbed, until the lemon is browned, 3 to 4 minutes. Remove the pan from the heat and discard the lemon wedges. Stir the sesame seeds into the sauce.

4. Spread the yogurt into the bottoms of serving bowls. Add the eggs, then spoon the sauce over both the eggs and the yogurt. Top with plenty of fresh herbs and more sesame seeds. Serve with the bread alongside, if desired.

prosciutto breakfast cups
with chive pesto

PREP 15 MINUTES
COOK 10 MINUTES
TOTAL 25 MINUTES
SERVES 6 TO 8

This is the brunch recipe you should make if you're looking to impress guests but want to put in zero effort . . . which probably describes every person who has ever hosted guests for breakfast. These require almost no prep work and come out of the oven looking gorgeous every time. I love prosciutto here because it's leaner than bacon and crisps up perfectly in the oven—it has just the right amount of crunch, and it goes so well with eggs. If you can't find Manchego cheese, try Parmesan or crumbled feta. The spoonful of fresh chive pesto adds nice color, too. This dish is delicious and beautiful, a perfect individual meal in a little cup. How else could you cook up a dozen eggs for guests without any stress?

Extra-virgin olive oil, for greasing

2 cups fresh basil leaves, finely chopped

2 tablespoons chopped fresh chives

2 teaspoons lemon zest

1 garlic clove, finely chopped or grated

Fine pink Himalayan salt and freshly ground black pepper

Crushed red pepper flakes

½ cup sun-dried tomatoes packed in olive oil, drained and oil reserved

1 cup baby spinach, chopped

12 thin slices prosciutto

½ cup grated Manchego cheese

12 large eggs

1. Preheat the oven to 425°F. Lightly grease a 12-cup muffin tin.

2. In a small bowl, combine the basil, chives, lemon zest, garlic, and a pinch each of salt and red pepper flakes. Add ¼ cup of the reserved sun-dried tomato oil. Stir the pesto to mix well.

3. In a medium bowl, combine the spinach, sun-dried tomatoes, and ¼ cup of the pesto. Toss to combine.

4. Drape one slice of prosciutto along the bottom and up the sides of each muffin cup. If needed, tear smaller pieces to fill in any bare spots. Sprinkle half of the cheese among the muffin cups, dividing evenly. Add a spoonful of the spinach mixture to each, then carefully crack 1 egg into each. Sprinkle evenly with the remaining cheese and season with salt and pepper.

5. Bake for 10 to 12 minutes for runny eggs, or 13 to 15 minutes for completely set eggs. Gently run a butter knife around the edges of each cup to release them from the pan. Serve warm with the remaining pesto spooned over the top.

naan breakfast sandwich

with soft scrambled eggs and honey

PREP 10 MINUTES
COOK 10 MINUTES
TOTAL 20 MINUTES
SERVES 2

My love for naan is no joke. It's without a doubt one of the best breads out there. Nothing beats homemade naan, fresh off the skillet in all its buttery glory. On the rare occasion I happen to have any leftovers lying around, I turn them into a grilled cheese. It's one of the best late-night dinners you can make. Well, this is the breakfast version, which honestly works whether it's 7 a.m. or 11 p.m. Lots of cheese, garlic, and sweet honey to seal the deal. I also snuck in a pinch of turmeric with my soft scrambled eggs. Turmeric is an anti-inflammatory and antioxidant, among other things. The honey (which, trust me, is essential here), acts as a prebiotic. Together these two ingredients will help prepare your gut for a whole day of challenges. We all know a healthy gut is the real secret to happiness. So you see what I did there? I turned our breakfast sandwich into a superfood. Some might call that a stretch, but go with me on this one . . . and enjoy that melty goodness.

- 4 tablespoons (½ stick) salted butter or ghee, at room temperature
- 1 garlic clove, finely chopped or grated
- 2 tablespoons chopped fresh tender herbs, such as parsley, chives, and/or dill
- 2 pieces naan (see Note)
- 1 cup shredded Gouda cheese
- 4 large eggs
- ½ teaspoon ground turmeric
- Fine pink Himalayan salt
- 1 cup chopped fresh spinach
- ¼ to ½ teaspoon crushed red pepper flakes, plus more for serving
- Raw honey, for serving
- 1 tablespoon toasted black or white sesame seeds, for serving (optional; see Note on page 53)

1. In a small bowl, stir together 3 tablespoons of the butter, the garlic, and the herbs. Spread one side of each piece of naan with the garlic butter. Flip over the naan and sprinkle the cheese along one half of the unbuttered sides.

2. In a medium bowl, beat the eggs with the turmeric and a pinch of salt. Melt the remaining 1 tablespoon butter in a medium skillet over medium heat. Add the eggs and sprinkle the spinach on top. Cook, undisturbed, until just set around the edges. Using a rubber spatula, gently push the eggs around the skillet, letting the uncooked egg run underneath, and cook until fluffy and just barely set, about 2 minutes. Remove the skillet from the heat and immediately transfer the eggs to the naan, layering them on top of the cheese and dividing evenly. Sprinkle the red pepper flakes on top.

3. Heat a 12-inch skillet over medium heat. Fold over each naan to create two sandwiches. Place the sandwiches in the skillet and cook, pressing down with a spatula, until the cheese is melted and the naan is toasted, about 2 minutes per side. Transfer to serving plates.

4. Top with honey, sesame seeds (if using), more red pepper flakes, and salt. Serve.

NOTE

If you've been following me for a while, you know I love to make my own naan. If you prefer store-bought, that's okay, too! Just pop it in the microwave for 20 to 30 seconds before you load it up so it's soft and pliable.

appetizers & sides

maple-sesame
smashed sweet potatoes

PREP 15 MINUTES
COOK 45 MINUTES
TOTAL 1 HOUR
SERVES 6

These potatoes are going to surprise you. In fact, the recipe might sound odd to you, but you just have to trust me on it. They're a super-fun way to totally reinvent the average sweet potato. Toss thick slices of baked sweet potato in a sweet, spicy maple mix, then give them a smash before broiling to create rounds that become crispy in some spots and soft and buttery in others. Just after the potatoes come out of the oven, top them with butter and watch it melt. Just try them—they're what I like to describe as roll-your-eyes-back delicious.

4 medium sweet potatoes, cut into ½-inch-thick rounds

2 tablespoons extra-virgin olive oil

Fine pink Himalayan salt

2 tablespoons pure maple syrup

½ teaspoon ground cinnamon

½ to 1 teaspoon ground cayenne pepper

4 tablespoons (½ stick) salted butter, at room temperature

2 tablespoons toasted sesame seeds (see Note on page 53)

Flaky sea salt

Fresh mint leaves, for serving (optional)

1. Preheat the oven to 425°F.

2. On a baking sheet, combine the sweet potatoes, olive oil, and a pinch of pink salt. Toss to coat. Arrange in an even layer. Bake for 20 minutes.

3. Meanwhile, in a small bowl, stir together the maple syrup, cinnamon, and cayenne. Remove the potatoes from the oven and drizzle the maple mixture over them. Return to the oven and bake until the potatoes are tender, 15 minutes more.

4. Remove the potatoes from the oven. Using a fork, flip them over, then gently press down to lightly smash the potatoes, keeping the rounds mostly intact. Set the oven to broil, return the potatoes once more, and cook until lightly charred, another 5 to 10 minutes.

5. Transfer the potatoes to a serving platter. Generously smear the butter on top of each potato slice. Sprinkle them with the sesame seeds, flaky salt, and mint (if using). Serve warm.

easy garlic knots

PREP 30 MINUTES
COOK 20 MINUTES
TOTAL 50 MINUTES, PLUS RISING TIME
MAKES 12 KNOTS

There's a restaurant in Rocky River, Ohio, called Danny Boy's. Everyone in town knows Danny Boy's, and everyone in town adores their garlic bread—the pieces are more like soft, buttery knots than loaves. They come warm, loaded with tons of garlic, Parmesan, butter, and parsley, and with their house marinara sauce on the side. I've eaten A LOT of their garlic bread—everyone has. It's the best. These knots? Well, they're similar, but a little lighter. I used double the amount of herbs (because I love an herb moment), and whole-wheat flour gives them more fiber and nutrients. But don't worry—I didn't skimp on the butter or Parmesan. Sometimes you really just need them. That time is now, with these knots. I also included a cinnamon-sugar variation because, trust me, you need that, too. Every good pizza spot can pull off both savory and sweet, but the truth? They're better when made at home.

1 cup warm water

1 teaspoon raw honey

1 packet (2¼ teaspoons) active dry yeast

1½ cups all-purpose flour

1 cup whole-wheat pastry flour, plus more as needed

1 teaspoon fine pink Himalayan salt

¼ cup plus 2 tablespoons grated Parmesan cheese

3 garlic cloves, finely chopped or grated

1 tablespoon dried parsley

1 tablespoon dried basil

2 teaspoons dried oregano

4 tablespoons (½ stick) salted butter, at room temperature

Marinara sauce, for serving

1. In a stand mixer, combine the warm water, honey, and yeast. Using a spatula, stir to combine, then let sit until the mixture is bubbly, 5 to 10 minutes.

2. Add both flours and the salt. Using the dough hook, mix on medium speed until the dough comes together, 1 to 2 minutes, adding more whole-wheat pastry flour, 1 tablespoon at a time, as needed, until the dough pulls away from the sides of the bowl and is smooth. Cover the dough with a clean kitchen towel and let rise in a warm place until doubled in size, 1 to 2 hours.

3. In a small bowl, combine the Parmesan, garlic, parsley, basil, and oregano. Set aside 2 tablespoons of the seasoning mix in a separate small bowl. Then add 3 tablespoons of the butter to the remaining seasoning mix and stir well to combine.

4. Preheat the oven to 375°F. Line a baking sheet with parchment paper.

5. On a floured work surface, roll out the dough into a 12 × 12-inch square about ¼ inch thick, adding more flour to the dough as needed if it's sticky. Spread the herby butter over the dough. Fold the dough in half and cut it into 12 even strips. Twist each strip and then tie the ends into a loose knot. Don't worry—they don't need to be perfect. Place the knots on the prepared baking sheet. Cover with a clean kitchen towel and let rise until puffed on top, 20 to 30 minutes.

6. Bake until golden brown on top, 15 to 20 minutes.

7. Melt the remaining 1 tablespoon butter. Brush the warm knots with the melted butter, then sprinkle the reserved seasoning mix over the top. Serve warm with marinara for dipping.

cinnamon sugar knots

To make cinnamon sugar knots, just change up the seasoning mix. Skip step 3 above, and in step 5, spread the dough with 3 tablespoons of salted butter. Follow the directions for shaping, rising, and baking. Then after you brush the knots with the melted butter, sprinkle on a mixture of 3 tablespoons sugar and 1 tablespoon ground cinnamon.

herb and mustard potato stacks

PREP 20 MINUTES
COOK 55 MINUTES
TOTAL 1 HOUR 15 MINUTES
SERVES 6

My family loves these—I mean, who doesn't love a crispy roasted potato? I usually make a version for our Christmas Eve dinner with lots more cheese, but these lightened-up stacks are great all year round. The secret is to slice the potatoes super thin before you layer them together to create the stacks. As they bake away, the edges crunch up while the middle turns soft and buttery. Hints of thyme and garlic creep into every bite. Warning: These are always the first dish to disappear from the table, so if you are feeding a crowd, you might want to double the recipe. I know from experience!

¼ cup extra-virgin olive oil, plus more for greasing

1 tablespoon apple cider or champagne vinegar

1 tablespoon Dijon or whole-grain mustard

¼ cup chopped fresh oregano, plus more for serving

2 tablespoons fresh thyme leaves

1 garlic clove, finely chopped or grated

¼ cup grated Parmesan cheese, plus more for serving

Fine pink Himalayan salt and freshly ground pepper

4 medium russet or Idaho potatoes, cut into ⅛-inch-thick rounds

1. Preheat the oven to 400°F. Lightly grease a 12-cup muffin tin.

2. In a large bowl, stir together the olive oil, vinegar, mustard, oregano, thyme, garlic, Parmesan, and a large pinch each of salt and pepper. Add the potatoes and toss to coat well.

3. Place the potatoes in the muffin cups, dividing evenly and stacking them up to the top. Cover the muffin tin loosely with foil and place it on a baking sheet. Bake for 30 minutes. Remove the foil and continue cooking until the potatoes are tender and golden, 20 to 25 minutes more.

4. Gently run a butter knife around the edges of each cup to release the stacks from the pan. Sprinkle with more Parmesan, oregano, and salt. Serve immediately.

summer melon

with cucumber and feta

PREP 20 MINUTES

TOTAL 20 MINUTES

SERVES 8

I've never been to Greece, but my brother Brendan took a trip there a few years ago. In addition to bringing home some really nice olive oil for me, he sent plenty of pictures of all the incredible Greek food he was enjoying, especially the simple cucumber and feta salads. They were his favorite! Since Bren loved them so much, I wanted to make my own version, and I couldn't help but add a colorful twist. Joining the cucumbers are chunks of sweet summer melon along with a simple minty vinaigrette, pistachios, and, of course, plenty of delicious feta cheese! I like to use Persian cucumbers since they're smaller and less watery than other varieties. This one may be easy, but I promise you: no boring salads. Ever!

4 cups cubed mixed melon

3 Persian cucumbers, thinly sliced

½ cup fresh basil, whole or sliced if leaves are large, plus more for serving

⅓ cup extra-virgin olive oil

Juice of 1 lemon or lime

2 tablespoons raw honey

2 tablespoons fresh mint leaves, chopped

2 tablespoons chopped fresh chives

¼ to ½ teaspoon crushed red pepper flakes

Pink Himalayan salt and freshly ground black pepper

8 ounces feta cheese, crumbled

¼ cup toasted pistachios, chopped (see Note)

1. In a large serving bowl, combine the melon, cucumbers, and basil. Gently toss to mix.

2. To make the vinaigrette, in a medium bowl, whisk together the olive oil, lemon juice, honey, mint, and chives. Season with red pepper flakes, salt, and pepper.

3. Drizzle half the vinaigrette over the salad, gently tossing to coat. Add the feta and pistachios, then drizzle the remaining vinaigrette over the top. Garnish the salad with more basil before serving.

NOTE

Toasting nuts and seeds is an extra step, but worth it—it emphasizes the warm flavors. Just place them in a dry skillet over medium-low heat and stir (constantly!) until they're fragrant and a shade or two darker, 3 to 5 minutes. Watch closely—they can go from perfectly toasted to black and very burned in a flash. I know from experience . . .

oven-fried
mozzarella bites

PREP 15 MINUTES

COOK 10 MINUTES

TOTAL 25 MINUTES, PLUS FREEZING TIME

MAKES 24 BITES

Mozzarella sticks are the perfect appetizer in almost any situation. Crispy breading on the outside and melty cheese on the inside is delicious no matter what. But I find that with fried foods, all you can taste is the oil they were cooked in. And let's be real, it can also be a mess and real "pull out your hair" process! Not only is this baked version less oily, but it's also easier and, most important, these sticks taste better than whatever you're used to ordering out. I couldn't decide between Buffalo (my family's favorite) and pizza (my personal favorite), so I'm sharing both!

2 tablespoons all-purpose flour

1 large egg, beaten

1 cup panko bread crumbs

2 teaspoons dried parsley

2 teaspoons dried chives

1 teaspoon dried dill

1 teaspoon garlic powder

1 teaspoon onion powder

12 mozzarella string cheese sticks, halved horizontally (I like Horizon Organic)

Extra-virgin olive oil, for brushing or misting

BUFFALO SAUCE

4 tablespoons (½ stick) salted butter, melted

½ cup hot sauce (I like Frank's RedHot)

¾ teaspoon seasoned salt

Pinch of freshly ground black pepper

1. **MAKE THE MOZZARELLA BITES.** Line a baking sheet with parchment paper.

2. Place the flour in a shallow bowl. Place the egg in a separate shallow bowl. Place the bread crumbs, parsley, chives, dill, garlic powder, and onion powder in a third shallow bowl and stir to combine. Working with a few pieces at a time, roll the mozzarella sticks in the flour to coat, then dip them into the egg to coat, allowing any excess to drip off. Then dredge them in the bread crumb mixture, pressing to adhere. Arrange the coated mozzarella bites on the prepared baking sheet. Freeze for at least 2 hours, or overnight.

3. Preheat the oven to 425°F with a rack positioned in the upper third of the oven.

4. **MAKE THE BUFFALO SAUCE.** In a small bowl, stir together the melted butter, hot sauce, salt, and pepper.

5. Brush or mist the frozen mozzarella bites all over with olive oil. Bake for 3 to 5 minutes. Flip the bites and bake until the coating is crisp and lightly browned and the cheese is just beginning to ooze, 3 to 5 minutes more.

6. Arrange the mozzarella bites on a serving platter and drizzle the Buffalo sauce over the top. Serve warm, with more sauce alongside for dipping.

spicy pizza mozzarella bites

To make spicy pizza mozzarella bites, just change up the seasoning mix. In step 2, combine the 1 cup panko bread crumbs with 2 teaspoons dried basil, 2 teaspoons dried oregano, 1 teaspoon garlic powder, 1 teaspoon crushed fennel seeds, and 1 teaspoon crushed red pepper flakes. Follow the directions for baking in step 5, but skip the Buffalo sauce and serve with store-bought marinara instead!

giant spinach and artichoke soft pretzel

PREP 30 MINUTES

COOK 30 MINUTES

TOTAL 1 HOUR, PLUS RISING TIME

SERVES 10 TO 12

Spinach and artichoke dip is an absolute classic—so how do you make everyone's favorite dip new and exciting? You stuff it into a giant pretzel. Definitely new, exciting, and, yes, so delicious. It's a fun appetizer to serve any time of year. Whether at the holidays or a summer party, it's always a hit. I mean, it's soft pretzel dough stuffed with cheese . . . that's hard to beat. To make this giant pretzel a little bit more wholesome, I made the dough with whole-wheat flour, which also adds extra depth to the flavor. For the dip, I used Greek yogurt in place of the usual cream cheese, and I doubled up on the spinach and artichokes for more flavor—and for more vegetables. It's not fancy by any means, but this one is a real showstopper, and it's easier to make than it looks. And the added bonus? The leftovers are delicious the next day with a big pile of greens on top. I eat it calzone-style with a fork and knife.

PRETZEL

1½ cups warm water, plus more as needed

2 teaspoons raw honey

2¼ teaspoons active dry yeast

4 tablespoons (½ stick) salted butter, melted

2½ cups all-purpose flour

1¾ cups whole-wheat pastry flour

1½ teaspoons fine pink Himalayan salt

1 tablespoon baking soda

¼ cup hot water

1 large egg, beaten

Coarse sea salt or pretzel salt

FILLING

½ cup plain Greek yogurt

¾ cup shredded low-moisture whole-milk mozzarella cheese

¼ cup grated Parmesan cheese

1 garlic clove, finely chopped or grated

½ teaspoon crushed red pepper flakes

½ teaspoon fine pink Himalayan salt

½ cup thawed and squeezed dry frozen chopped spinach

1 (6-ounce) jar marinated artichokes, drained and chopped

1. **MAKE THE PRETZEL.** In a stand mixer, combine the warm water, honey, and yeast. Using a spatula, stir to combine, then let sit until the yeast is foamy, 5 to 10 minutes.

2. Add the melted butter, both flours, and the salt. Using the dough hook, mix on low speed until combined, 2 to 3 minutes. Increase the speed to medium and continue mixing until the dough is smooth and begins to pull away from the sides of the bowl, 3 to 4 minutes. If the dough feels dry, add more water, ¼ cup at a time. Cover the bowl with a clean kitchen towel and place in a warm spot until the dough has doubled in size, 1½ to 2 hours.

3. **MEANWHILE, MAKE THE FILLING.** In a medium bowl, stir together the yogurt, mozzarella, Parmesan, garlic, red pepper flakes, and salt. Add the spinach and artichokes and stir to combine.

4. Preheat the oven to 425°F. Line a baking sheet with parchment paper.

5. On a lightly floured work surface, roll the dough out into a very long strip, about 40 inches long and 4 inches wide. Spread the filling along the length of the strip on one side. Beginning from the side with the filling, roll the dough up into a log, enclosing the filling. Pinch the seams together, then very gently roll the dough with your hands to form an even cylinder and completely enclose the filling.

6. Transfer the dough to the prepared baking sheet. Shape the rope into a pretzel: Pull the two ends away from you to form a U shape, then bring the ends down toward you, twisting the ropes together twice to form the center of the pretzel. Bring the ends down to meet the bottom of the U shape, and press each down to create a pretzel shape, pinching to seal.

7. In a small bowl, stir the baking soda into the hot water. Lightly brush the pretzel with the mixture. Then brush the pretzel with the beaten egg. Season the pretzel liberally with sea salt.

8. Bake until the pretzel is a deep golden brown, 25 to 30 minutes. Remove the pretzel from the oven and let cool for about 5 minutes. Serve warm.

cheddar ranch snack crackers

PREP 15 MINUTES

COOK 15 MINUTES

TOTAL 30 MINUTES, PLUS COOLING TIME

MAKES 5 TO 6 CUPS

If you ask me, Cheez-Its are one of the greatest little snacks ever. When I was in grade school, my mom would pack them for me almost every day—they were cheaper than Goldfish crackers and still had that perfect salty-cheesy thing going on. Pretty sure they're one of those nostalgic foods for everyone . . . Who could not love them?! I wanted to make a cracker with real cheese and whole-wheat flour that everyone can feel a little better about snacking on. These are an adult version of my childhood favorite. This recipe is perfect for getting kids into the kitchen with you because they know there will be something fun on the other side of baking. The crackers will change from chewy to crispy as they cool. And don't worry, you'll still end up with flavor-dust on your fingertips, even without any of the fake powdered stuff. That's the best part!

2 tablespoons dried parsley

2 tablespoons dried chives

2 teaspoons dried dill

2 teaspoons garlic powder

2 teaspoons onion powder

2 teaspoons paprika

¼ teaspoon fine pink Himalayan salt

3 cups shredded sharp cheddar cheese

1 cup whole-wheat pastry flour

4 tablespoons (½ stick) salted butter, at room temperature

2 tablespoons cold water

1. Preheat the oven to 350°F. Line two baking sheets with parchment paper.

2. In a small bowl, stir together the parsley, chives, dill, garlic powder, onion powder, paprika, and salt.

3. In a food processor, combine the cheese, flour, and half of the spice mixture. Process until combined, about 30 seconds. Add the butter and pulse until just combined, 2 to 3 pulses. With the motor running, add the water, 1 tablespoon at a time, until the dough comes together and forms a ball.

4. Turn the dough out onto a floured work surface and shape the dough into a ball using your hands. Divide the dough in half. Working with one piece, roll out the dough to about an ⅛-inch thickness. Cut into ½-inch squares. Repeat with the remaining dough.

5. Transfer the squares to the prepared baking sheets, spacing them ¼ inch apart. Using the end of a skewer, poke a small hole in the center of each square.

6. Bake until the crackers are lightly golden, 10 to 15 minutes. Remove the pan from the oven and let cool for 5 minutes. Transfer the crackers to a large bowl. Add the remaining spice mixture and toss to coat. Let cool completely. Store at room temperature in an airtight container for up to 1 week. Enjoy . . . by the handful.

NOTE

You can make these crackers even without a food processor. Combine the cheese with the flour and half of the spice mixture in a large bowl, then stir in the butter. Slowly add the cold water as directed.

candied blt

with brown butter aioli

PREP 10 MINUTES
COOK 10 MINUTES
TOTAL 20 MINUTES
SERVES 4

I have always had this thing with BLTs and sharing a BLT "recipe." Do you really need a recipe to tell you how to layer three things onto a piece of bread? No. But . . . this version? It is elevated yet still true to the classic. Bacon is always a good thing, but candied bacon takes the sandwich to a whole new level, as it's both sweet and savory— and, if you want, spicy too. (Around here, you know we say the spicier, the better.) Then the thick, creamy brown butter aioli—it's extra special and beyond delicious. Beyond. Heirloom tomatoes are ideal when they're in season, but when my tomatoes aren't great, adding flaky salt perks them right up. In the dead of winter, sometimes I'll use cherry tomatoes for more flavor. Honestly, even if your tomatoes leave a lot to be desired, the bacon and aioli more than make up for them.

NOTE ⸻

If your aioli seems thin or greasy or if the oil and butter appear to be separated out, it might be broken. To fix it, place an egg yolk in a clean bowl and, drop by drop, whisk in your broken aioli until the yolk is incorporated and the aioli is smooth.

8 slices thick-cut bacon

2 tablespoons chopped fresh rosemary

½ to 1 teaspoon ground cayenne pepper (optional)

2 teaspoons pure maple syrup

8 slices sourdough bread, lightly toasted

Brown Butter Aioli (recipe follows) or store-bought aioli

2 small tomatoes, preferably heirloom, thickly sliced

Flaky sea salt and freshly ground black pepper

1 small head of romaine lettuce, separated into leaves

1. Preheat the oven to 400°F. Line a baking sheet with foil.

2. Arrange the bacon on the prepared baking sheet and rub it with the rosemary and cayenne (if using). Drizzle the maple syrup over the slices. Bake for 5 minutes. Use tongs to flip the bacon and bake until crispy, 3 to 5 minutes more.

3. Spread one side of each bread slice with aioli. Season the tomato with salt and pepper. Layer the lettuce, tomato, and bacon onto half of the slices, dividing evenly, then top the sandwiches with the remaining slices, aioli-side down.

brown butter aioli

MAKES 1 CUP

½ cup (1 stick) salted butter

2 egg yolks, at room temperature

1 teaspoon Dijon mustard

2 teaspoons fresh lemon juice

½ cup extra-virgin olive oil

Ground cayenne pepper

Fine pink Himalayan salt

1. Heat the butter in a large skillet over medium heat. Cook, stirring often, until it begins to brown, 3 to 4 minutes. Transfer the butter to a medium bowl and let cool to room temperature, 10 to 15 minutes.

2. On a work surface, create a loose circle with a clean kitchen towel, and nestle a large bowl in the center to hold it in place. Put the egg yolks, mustard, and lemon juice in the bowl, and whisk to combine. Add a few drops of the olive oil, whisking vigorously to combine completely. Add a few drops more, whisking again. Continue in this manner until all of the olive oil is incorporated, about 2 minutes total. Repeat the process with the brown butter, slowly increasing the additions and whisking vigorously for 1 to 2 minutes, until the ingredients are completely combined and the mixture has thickened. Season with cayenne and salt to taste. Store refrigerated in an airtight container for up to 1 week. Let the aioli come to room temperature on the counter (do not warm it) before using.

apple and brie crostini

with prosciutto crumbs

PREP 15 MINUTES
COOK 35 MINUTES
TOTAL 50 MINUTES
SERVES 6 TO 8

Baked Brie with apples on top is always a crowd pleaser. These crostini were inspired by that classic appetizer, with crispy sourdough toasts standing in for the more decadent puff pastry. Sweet fruit and buttery, savory cheese—yes, please! I also added salty, crispy prosciutto because, well, everything is better with prosciutto. You won't be able to eat just one of these.

2 apples, preferably Honeycrisp, cored and sliced

2 tablespoons extra-virgin olive oil, plus more for brushing

2 tablespoons pure maple syrup

4 sprigs of fresh thyme, plus more leaves for serving

3 ounces thinly sliced prosciutto, torn

¼ cup raw pepitas

1 sourdough loaf or baguette, cut into ⅓-inch-thick slices

2 tablespoons Maple Apple Butter (page 20) or store-bought apple butter

8 ounces Brie cheese, thinly sliced

Flaky sea salt

1. Preheat the oven to 425°F with one rack in the center position and another in the lower third of the oven. Line a baking sheet with parchment paper.

2. In a 9 × 13-inch baking dish, combine the apples, olive oil, and maple syrup and toss to coat. Nestle in the sprigs of thyme. Bake on the center rack until the apples have softened and the liquid has thickened, 25 to 30 minutes.

3. Meanwhile, arrange the torn prosciutto on the prepared baking sheet. Sprinkle the pepitas around the prosciutto. Bake on the lower rack until the prosciutto is crisp and the pepitas are toasted, about 8 minutes. Leave the oven on. Let cool slightly, then transfer the prosciutto and pepitas to a food processor and pulse into coarse crumbs.

4. Brush both sides of the bread with olive oil and arrange the slices on the same baking sheet you used for the prosciutto and pepitas. Toast in the oven for about 5 minutes. Remove the baking sheet from the oven, flip over the bread, spread the top of each slice with apple butter, and add a piece of Brie. Return the bread to the oven and bake until the Brie is melted, about 5 minutes more.

5. Spoon the roasted apples over each slice of bread, letting them sink into the melting Brie a bit. Top with the prosciutto crumbs, flaky salt, and thyme leaves. Serve warm.

garlic butter brussels sprouts

with shortcut lemon aioli

PREP 10 MINUTES
COOK 30 MINUTES
TOTAL 40 MINUTES
SERVES 4

GF **SF**

A lot of people associate Brussels sprouts with Thanksgiving, but the truth is, they're great any day of the year. I make these to go with chicken, steak, and seafood, and they're a nice switch-up from the usual broccoli. If you think you don't like Brussel sprouts, try this recipe—it will change your mind. Roasting them brings out a hint of sweetness, and the salty flavor from the bacon is just the right amount. Of course, if you prefer to omit the bacon, you can add a splash of soy sauce instead for that salty umami flavor. Also, this shortcut aioli is a great back-pocket trick, and you can change up the seasoning however you like! I love to spread the aioli onto a platter, then spoon the crispy sprouts on top so everybody gets a little bit of both when they take a scoop. You could also serve these as an appetizer with toothpicks or little forks with the aioli alongside for dipping. You really can't go wrong either way.

BRUSSELS SPROUTS

1 pound Brussels sprouts, trimmed and halved

3 tablespoons extra-virgin olive oil

2 tablespoons fresh thyme leaves or 1 teaspoon dried, plus a few fresh thyme sprigs for serving

Pinch of crushed red pepper flakes

4 slices thick-cut bacon, chopped

2 tablespoons salted butter, melted

2 garlic cloves, finely chopped or grated

Lemon wedges, for serving

AIOLI

½ cup mayonnaise

2 tablespoons lemon juice

1 garlic clove, finely chopped or grated

½ to 1 teaspoon ground cayenne pepper

½ teaspoon smoked paprika

Fine pink Himalayan salt

1. Preheat the oven to 425°F with a rack positioned in the lower third of the oven.

2. **MAKE THE BRUSSELS SPROUTS.** On a rimmed baking sheet, toss together the Brussels sprouts, olive oil, thyme, and red pepper flakes. Arrange the Brussels sprouts cut-side down on the baking sheet. Sprinkle the bacon around the sprouts. Roast until the sprouts are deeply browned and the bacon is crisp, 20 to 25 minutes.

3. In a small bowl, stir together the melted butter and the garlic. Remove the sprouts from the oven and pour the butter mixture over them. Toss to coat. Return the sprouts to the oven and roast until crispy, 10 minutes more.

4. **MEANWHILE, MAKE THE AIOLI.** In a small bowl, stir together the mayonnaise, lemon juice, garlic, cayenne, and paprika. Taste and add salt as needed.

5. Pile the Brussels sprouts onto a serving plate, sprinkle with the remaining fresh thyme sprigs, and squeeze a couple lemon wedges over top. Nestle the bowl of aioli into the sprouts for dipping.

honey roasted carrots
with herb oil

PREP 10 MINUTES
COOK 25 MINUTES
TOTAL 35 MINUTES
SERVES 4

I love a roasted carrot, but I usually never do anything out of the ordinary with them—I just season them and pop them in the oven. It's funny, now that I think about it, you have never seen a carrot recipe from me! It feels fitting that my first carrot recipe, in addition to being so tasty, is good for you, too. Carrots are naturally sweet, and roasting them brings that out even more, while the honey creates a nice glaze. Then the herb oil helps balance all that sweetness and is a nice complement to the dish. I love using goat cheese here, which is easy to digest, but you could also swap in feta if that's more your thing. And those pomegranate seeds? They are sweet and tart and loaded with antioxidants . . . so healthy and sooo delicious.

12 medium carrots (about 2 pounds), scrubbed (see Note)

⅓ cup plus 2 tablespoons extra-virgin olive oil

1 tablespoon raw honey

Fine pink Himalayan salt and freshly ground black pepper

1 garlic clove, finely chopped or grated

¼ cup chopped fresh parsley

¼ cup chopped fresh dill

2 tablespoons fresh thyme leaves

Pinch of crushed red pepper flakes

4 ounces goat cheese

¼ cup pomegranate seeds

1. Preheat the oven to 450°F.

2. On a rimmed baking sheet, toss together the carrots, 2 tablespoons of the olive oil, the honey, and a pinch each of salt and pepper. Roast until the carrots are lightly charred, 20 to 25 minutes.

3. Meanwhile, in a small bowl, combine the remaining ⅓ cup oil, the garlic, parsley, dill, and thyme. Taste and season with salt and red pepper flakes, as desired.

4. Arrange the carrots on a serving platter. Crumble the goat cheese over the top, then drizzle the herb oil all over them. Sprinkle with the pomegranate seeds. Serve warm.

NOTE
I never peel my carrots . . . or any other vegetables or fruits with edible skin, really, since the skin holds most of the fiber and vitamins. Just give them a good scrub before using.

crispy sour cream and onion potatoes

PREP 15 MINUTES

COOK SEE SPECIFIC DEVICE METHOD

SERVES 6

When I was kid—before we were living in Colorado—we went on a ski trip to Utah with another family. They had a daughter about my age, and I remember her being absolutely obsessed with sour cream and onion potato chips. She would dip them in ketchup, which I thought was pretty much the grossest thing I'd ever seen. I didn't really eat potato chips of any kind, and especially not sour cream and onion (I know, I know). Of course, now I understand the obsession—though I still don't get the ketchup part, but to each their own. Sour cream and onion is a classic, delicious combination. Chips are great and all, but these hot, crispy smashed potatoes are even better. I plate them over a bed of seasoned Greek yogurt, but if you feel like going for it, by all means, use real-deal sour cream. The herby mixture on top will remind you of the powder that coats the chips . . . in a good way! You're going to be addicted to these, even more than you are to the chips.

½ cup extra-virgin olive oil, plus more for greasing

2 pounds baby Yukon gold potatoes

1 tablespoon kosher salt, plus more to taste

2 cups plain Greek yogurt or sour cream

2 tablespoons chopped fresh chives, plus more for serving

2 teaspoons onion powder

1 teaspoon garlic powder

1 teaspoon dried parsley

1 teaspoon dried dill

2 tablespoons grated Parmesan cheese

Freshly ground pepper

Fresh herbs, such as parsley or dill, for serving

Flaky sea salt

OVEN

COOK 50 MINUTES

1.   Preheat the oven to 450°F. Grease a baking sheet.

2.   Place the potatoes and the kosher salt in a large pot. Add enough water to cover the potatoes by two inches. Bring to a boil over high heat, then reduce the heat to medium. Cook until the potatoes are fork-tender, about 15 minutes. Drain the potatoes and transfer to the prepared baking sheet. Let cool slightly.

3.   Place another baking sheet on top of the potatoes, then push down firmly to smash the potatoes. (Alternatively, you can use the bottom of a mug or drinking glass to smash each potato individually.) Roast the potatoes until crispy and golden brown, 20 to 30 minutes.

4.   Meanwhile, in a small bowl, stir the yogurt and chives together. Season with kosher salt.

5.   In a separate small bowl, whisk together the ½ cup olive oil, onion powder, garlic powder, parsley, dill, Parmesan, and a pinch each of kosher salt and pepper. Pour the oil mixture over the roasted potatoes and toss to coat, gently breaking up the potatoes.

6.   Spread the seasoned yogurt onto a serving plate and then add the potatoes on top. Sprinkle with chives, additional herbs, and flaky salt.

PRESSURE COOKER

COOK 6 MINUTES, PLUS ADDITIONAL TIME TO COME TO PRESSURE

1.   Preheat the oven to 450°F. Grease a baking sheet.

2.   In the pressure cooker pot, combine the potatoes, 2 cups of water, and the kosher salt. Lock the lid in place and cook on high pressure for 6 minutes. Quick or natural release and open when the pressure subsides. Drain the potatoes and transfer to the prepared baking sheet. Let cool slightly.

3.   Finish as directed for the oven starting from step 3.

strawberry basil margarita

MAKES 1 DRINK

Who doesn't love a good margarita? They're fun to drink and easy to mix up. But I DON'T love overly sweet margs that leave you with what my family calls a "sugar hangover." It doesn't feel good the next day. That's why homemade margaritas are so great. I make mine with very little sugar, using raw honey to sweeten them up ever so slightly. While I switch up the flavors depending on the season, this version is on repeat on Friday nights in my kitchen. It's a touch sweet and a little bit spicy, and that ginger beer adds a fizzy kick. My best piece of advice is to quadruple the ingredients and make a giant pitcher. Trust me, everyone will want a re-up.

LIME SALT

2 tablespoons fine pink Himalayan salt

1 teaspoon lime zest, plus 1 lime wedge

Pinch of sugar (optional)

MARGARITA

4 cucumber slices

4 to 6 fresh strawberries, hulled and chopped, plus more for serving

6 fresh basil leaves, plus more for garnish

2 teaspoons freshly grated ginger

Juice from ½ lime

2 ounces (¼ cup) silver tequila (I like Clase Azul)

½ ounce (1 tablespoon) orange liqueur

2 teaspoons raw honey

Ginger beer, for topping (optional)

1. **MAKE THE LIME SALT.** On a shallow plate, combine the salt, lime zest, and sugar (if using).

2. Run the lime wedge around the rim of a rocks glass, then press the rim into the lime salt to adhere. Fill the glass with ice.

3. **MAKE THE MARGARITA.** In a cocktail shaker or glass jar with a lid, muddle together the cucumber, strawberries, basil, ginger, and lime juice. Add the tequila, orange liqueur, and honey and shake until combined. Add ice, then shake for another 30 seconds.

4. Strain the margarita into the prepared glass. Top with ginger beer, if desired. Garnish with fresh basil.

lemon chai bourbon smash

MAKES 1 DRINK

Throughout the winter months, if my family or friends are in town, come 5 p.m., they walk through the studio doors looking for a cocktail after being out in the snow all day. Bourbon is always popular, but if this drink screams anyone's name in particular, it's the brother just older than me in the lineup, Brendan. He's not one to turn down a drink—ever—but he does have favorites, and this is one of them. The spiced lemon syrup is what makes it work. It's delicious, and you'll have enough from one recipe to mix up a few drinks. My ideal winter night is to have this cozy, warming cocktail in hand with a fire crackling in the background. It's Bren's, too—and soon it will be yours.

½ lemon, quartered

4 fresh mint leaves or 1 to 2 teaspoons fresh rosemary leaves

2 ounces (¼ cup) bourbon (I like Off Hours)

1 to 2 ounces (2 to 4 tablespoons) Chai Simple Syrup (recipe follows)

Dash of orange bitters

Sparkling water, for topping

Orange slices or zest, cinnamon stick, and star anise, for garnish (optional)

1. In a cocktail shaker or glass jar with a lid, muddle together the lemon wedges and mint. Add the bourbon, chai syrup, and bitters. Fill the shaker with ice and shake to combine for 15 to 30 seconds.

2. Strain into a rocks glass filled with ice. Top off with sparkling water. Garnish with the orange slices, cinnamon stick, and star anise, if desired.

chai simple syrup

MAKES ¼ CUP

4 chai tea bags

⅓ cup pure maple syrup

In a medium saucepan, bring 1 cup of water to a boil over high heat. Remove the pan from the heat, add the tea bags, cover, and steep for 10 to 15 minutes; the longer it steeps, the more flavor the tea bags will impart. Discard the tea bags and stir in the maple syrup. Return to a boil over high heat. Cook until reduced by nearly half, about 5 minutes. Remove the pan from the heat. Let the syrup cool completely before using. Store refrigerated in an airtight container for up to 2 weeks.

double-the-ginger
frozen cranberry moscow mule

MAKES 4 DRINKS

 30 **DF** **GF** **V**

As you might've guessed, the Gerard fam loves a good drink. We've got bourbon drinkers, tequila drinkers, and then the vodka fans who love a Moscow Mule more than anything. It's the ginger beer that really locks everyone in, if you ask me. Spicy flavor, subtle sweetness, and fizz make any drink better. I've had a lot of versions of the classic Moscow mule, and you know something? This frozen version is better than them all, and it's pretty fun, too. I love a slushy moment, but when you add vodka . . . it's GOOD. I do these up with a double dose of ginger and keep things colorful with cranberries. This drink is on the festive side, so it's great for the holidays, but if cranberries aren't your thing, use pomegranate juice, pineapple juice, or just go heavy on the fresh grapefruit juice.

8 ounces (1 cup) vodka (I like Tito's)

1¼ cups no-sugar-added cranberry or pomegranate juice (I like R.W. Knudsen or POM Wonderful)

Juice of 1 small grapefruit (about ½ cup)

Juice of 2 limes (about ½ cup)

¾ cup fresh or frozen cranberries (optional)

¼ to ½ cup raw honey

1 (1-inch) piece of fresh ginger, peeled and grated

2 (12-ounce) cans ginger beer

Fresh mint leaves, for garnish

Sugared Cranberries, for garnish (recipe follows)

1.   In a blender, combine 2 to 3 cups of ice, the vodka, cranberry juice, grapefruit juice, lime juice, cranberries (if using), honey, and ginger. Blend until the honey is incorporated, 30 seconds to 1 minute.

2.   Pour a splash of ginger beer into each of four copper mugs or highball glasses. Add the vodka mixture, dividing evenly. Top each drink with more ginger beer as desired.

3.   Garnish with mint and sugared cranberries.

sugared cranberries
MAKES 2 CUPS

2 cups fresh cranberries

½ cup pure maple syrup

1½ cups granulated sugar

In a medium bowl, combine the cranberries and syrup. Stir to coat. Let sit for 10 to 15 minutes. Strain the cranberries (reserve the syrup for another use; try using it instead of the honey in the cocktail recipe) and then transfer them to a parchment-lined baking sheet. Add the sugar and toss to coat well. Spread into an even layer. Let the cranberries dry for at least 1 hour before serving. To store, let dry completely overnight, then transfer to an airtight container and keep at room temperature for up to 3 days.

spiced blackberry whisky sour

MAKES 1 DRINK

I really like to keep my cocktails simple. Sure, I'll have fun with a flavored syrup, but that's usually as far as I'll go. That is, until I came across the classic whisky sour, which is traditionally made with egg white to create foam at the top of the drink. Many omit the egg white, but I had a quick talk with my brother Kai, who loves to order this drink. He said, "Tieg, if you're going to do a whisky sour, DO a whisky sour. Use good whisky, add blackberries if you want, but you have to do the egg white. It's what makes the drink." Well, he was right. This drink is fancyyy, but also so easy to make. If you're opposed to the egg, I get it. I encourage you to give it a try, but if you just can't, of course leave it out. With this spiced syrup and these garnishes, I promise your drink will be delicious either way.

¼ cup fresh blackberries, plus more for garnish

1 ounce (2 tablespoons) fresh lemon juice

2 ounces (¼ cup) whisky (I like Pendleton)

1 to 2 ounces (2 to 4 tablespoons) Spiced Syrup (recipe follows)

Dash of orange bitters

1 egg white (optional)

Rosemary sprigs, for garnish

Star anise, for garnish

1. In a cocktail shaker or glass jar with a lid, muddle together the blackberries and lemon juice. Add the whisky, spiced syrup, bitters, and egg white (if using). Shake for 30 seconds. Add ice and shake well, 15 to 30 seconds more.

2. Strain into a rocks glass filled with ice. If desired, lightly burn the rosemary by briefly lighting it on fire for a smoky effect. Garnish the drink with the burnt rosemary, fresh blackberries, and star anise.

spiced syrup

MAKES ¾ CUP

⅓ cup pure maple syrup

2 star anise

½ cinnamon stick

1 (2½-inch) strip orange zest

In a medium saucepan, combine ½ cup of water, the maple syrup, star anise, cinnamon stick, and orange zest. Bring to a boil over high heat. Cook until reduced slightly and very fragrant, about 3 minutes. Remove the pan from the heat and strain the syrup into a lidded container. Discard the solids and let the syrup cool completely before using. Store refrigerated in an airtight container for up to 2 weeks.

soup & salad

zuppa toscana
with gnocchi

PREP 15 MINUTES
COOK 20 MINUTES
TOTAL 35 MINUTES
SERVES 6

If you've ever been to an Olive Garden, you've probably had Zuppa Toscana. Everybody loves it, and understandably so. Normally, this soup is thick and heavy thanks to cream, pork sausage, potatoes, and lots of cheese. This copycat version is lightened up a bit with coconut milk (I promise you'll only taste its creaminess), chicken sausage, cauliflower gnocchi, and, well, still lots of cheese. It's every bit as delicious and leaves you feeling happy and satisfied. This recipe calls for tons of fresh herbs, garlic, and a little fennel, so your kitchen will smell like an Italian grandmother's! Hearty and filling, with a slice of crusty bread alongside (like the loaf on page 32), it's the perfect dinner.

4 slices thick-cut bacon, chopped

½ pound spicy Italian chicken sausage (see Note)

1 small yellow onion, chopped

4 garlic cloves, finely chopped or grated

2 celery stalks, chopped

6 cups low-sodium chicken broth

1 tablespoon dried basil

1 tablespoon dried oregano

Pinch of crushed red pepper flakes

Fine pink Himalayan salt and freshly ground black pepper

4 to 6 cups stemmed and chopped Tuscan kale

¾ cup full-fat coconut milk

⅓ cup grated Parmesan cheese, plus more for serving

24 ounces Cauliflower Gnocchi (page 119) or store-bought gnocchi of your choice

Fresh thyme leaves, for serving (optional)

1. Place the bacon in a large Dutch oven over medium heat. Cook, stirring occasionally, until the bacon is crispy and the fat has rendered, about 5 minutes. Using a slotted spoon, transfer the bacon to a plate or cutting board. Discard all but 1 tablespoon of fat from the pot, and return the pot to medium heat (see Note on page 186).

2. Add the chicken sausage and onion to the pot. Cook, breaking up the sausage with a wooden spoon, until the sausage is browned and the onion is soft and translucent, 5 to 8 minutes. Add the garlic and celery and cook, stirring occasionally, until the celery is soft, about 2 minutes. Stir in the broth, basil, oregano, and red pepper flakes. Season with salt and pepper. Increase the heat to high and bring to a boil. Cook until the flavors have melded, about 5 minutes. Stir in the kale to wilt. Reduce the heat to medium and add the coconut milk, Parmesan, and gnocchi. Simmer until the gnocchi is cooked, 3 to 5 minutes.

3. Divide the soup among bowls. Before serving, top with the reserved bacon, additional Parmesan, and fresh thyme, if desired.

NOTE ———

I buy spicy Italian chicken sausage at Whole Foods. If you can't find it, you can use spicy Italian pork sausage, or you can make your own by adding the following spice mix to one pound of ground chicken: 1 tablespoon each of fennel seeds (I like to toast them first), dried thyme, dried basil, dried oregano, salt, and pepper; 2 teaspoons each of ground cayenne (or less, if you don't want it too spicy), paprika, and garlic powder; and 1 teaspoon each of smoked paprika and crushed red pepper flakes. This spice mix is great on grilled meat and vegetables, too! It'll keep in your pantry in an airtight container for a few months.

roasted beets and burrata

with warm cider dressing

PREP 15 MINUTES
COOK 50 MINUTES
TOTAL 1 HOUR 5 MINUTES
SERVES 4 TO 6

Beets are one of those vegetables people think they don't like, but this is the perfect recipe to change their minds—just ask my dad! He had only ever had bland canned beets, but these sold him. I swear, it's because of this dressing. Roasting the beets really brings out their natural sweetness, but when you hit them with this savory apple cider vinegar dressing, they take on a little shine. It's the perfect flavor combination. Plus, you can make it as spicy as you want with the crushed red pepper flakes. And has burrata ever not made something better? Your beets can be any color—I think a mix is prettiest—and you can slide the skins off if you like, but I prefer to keep them on (see Note on page 66).

6 small beets (about 1 pound), trimmed and scrubbed (see Note on page 66)

⅓ cup plus 2 tablespoons extra-virgin olive oil

2 tablespoons raw honey

½ teaspoon fine pink Himalayan salt, plus more as needed

1 medium shallot, thinly sliced

2 tablespoons apple cider vinegar

1 tablespoon fig preserves (I like Dalmatia)

1 tablespoon fresh thyme leaves, plus more for serving

1 teaspoon orange zest

Pinch of crushed red pepper flakes

Freshly ground black pepper

8 ounces burrata cheese, at room temperature

¼ cup pomegranate seeds

A few fresh basil leaves, for serving

1.   Preheat the oven to 400°F.

2.   On a rimmed baking sheet, toss together the beets, 2 tablespoons of the olive oil, the honey, the salt, and 2 tablespoons of water. Cover the sheet tightly with foil. Roast the beets until they are knife-tender, about 35 minutes. Remove the foil, increase the oven temperature to 450°F, and roast until most of the liquid has evaporated from the baking sheet and the beet skins have dried out, 10 to 15 minutes more. Let the beets cool for 5 to 10 minutes, until you can handle them, and then cut them into quarters.

3.   Meanwhile, heat the remaining ⅓ cup olive oil in a medium skillet over medium heat. When the oil shimmers, add the shallots and cook, stirring occasionally, until fragrant, 2 to 3 minutes. Remove the skillet from the heat and let the shallots cool slightly. Stir in the vinegar, preserves, thyme, and orange zest. Season with the red pepper flakes, and with salt and pepper to taste.

4.   Arrange the balls of burrata on a serving platter and break them open. Scatter the beets around the burrata, then drizzle the warm dressing over everything. Top with the pomegranate seeds and fresh thyme and basil leaves before serving.

salmon cobb salad

with nutty green ranch

PREP 15 MINUTES
COOK 20 MINUTES
TOTAL 35 MINUTES
SERVES 4

Every summer, starting when I was in third grade through my freshman year of high school, my nonnie and I would head to Florida for part of the summer, just the two of us. Her favorite way to spend the day was with a little shopping spree in the morning and lunch at a restaurant. One day I decided to order the same thing as Nonnie—a Cobb salad. At this restaurant, it was made with grilled chicken, double bacon, and a creamy blue cheese dressing. It was DELICIOUS. And ever since then, Cobb salad always reminds me of Nonnie! In this version, I swapped in omega-3-rich salmon and whipped up an herby ranch dressing with cashew butter, which is a little bit different but still crazy creamy. The ranch keeps in the fridge for a week, and if you cook the bacon and salmon on a meal prep day (grill the fish in the summer!), you can just throw the salad together when you're busy throughout the week.

SALAD

2 tablespoons extra-virgin olive oil

¼ cup fresh dill, roughly chopped

2 teaspoons smoked paprika

1 tablespoon lemon zest

Fine pink Himalayan salt and freshly ground pepper

4 (5-ounce) salmon fillets

1 tablespoon fresh lemon juice

4 slices thick-cut bacon

6 cups mixed greens, such as romaine, kale, and baby arugula

1 cup cherry tomatoes, halved if large

2 avocados, diced

4 hard-boiled eggs, sliced

¼ cup crumbled feta cheese

DRESSING

¼ cup cashew butter

¼ cup fresh lemon juice

1 teaspoon Dijon mustard

¼ cup fresh parsley or basil, roughly chopped

2 tablespoons fresh dill, roughly chopped

2 tablespoons chopped fresh chives

1 garlic clove, finely chopped or grated

¼ teaspoon ground cayenne pepper

Fine pink Himalayan salt and freshly ground black pepper

1. Preheat the oven to 425°F.

2. **MAKE THE SALAD.** In a small bowl, stir together the olive oil, dill, paprika, lemon zest, and a pinch each of salt and pepper. Spoon the mixture onto the salmon fillets, dividing evenly, and rub it in well. Pour the lemon juice over the salmon.

3. Arrange the bacon on one side of a baking sheet and place the salmon on the other. Bake together until the salmon reaches your desired doneness and the bacon is crispy, 10 to 12 minutes. Let cool slightly, then crumble the bacon.

4. **MEANWHILE, MAKE THE DRESSING.** In a blender or food processor, combine the cashew butter, lemon juice, mustard, parsley, dill, chives, garlic, cayenne, and a pinch each of salt and pepper. Add ¼ cup of water and blend until smooth, adding more water 1 tablespoon at a time, as needed, to thin. Taste and add more salt as needed.

5. Put the greens in a large serving bowl. Top the salad with the cherry tomatoes, avocado, salmon fillets, crumbled bacon, and eggs. Sprinkle the feta over the top, and drizzle on the ranch.

spiced lentil soup

with curried acorn squash

PREP 15 MINUTES
COOK SEE SPECIFIC DEVICE METHOD
SERVES 6

Sure, I have enjoyed some incredible meals as an adult, but for me, my most treasured food memories come from childhood. And more often than not, they involve my mom. Acorn squash was one of the ingredients she mastered, and she sure did make it well—and so simply. She's much more of a baker than a cook, so it won't shock you that her squash was always on the sweet side. She'd roast it up with butter, brown sugar, and cinnamon. Honestly, if it weren't a vegetable, I'd call it dessert for dinner! But I wanted to reinvent this favorite fall dish in a healthy way that REALLY qualifies as a well-balanced and delicious dinner. This soup is a number of steps removed from my mom's squash, but what's similar about it is that it's a recipe the family has come to love. It's creamy from coconut milk and spiced similarly to an Indian butter chicken with garam masala, turmeric, and a bit of cayenne. The lentils keep the dish filling and hearty without meat, and then the roasted squash on top is an extra-special topping that makes this simple soup a bit more exciting than your average bowl. It's a perfect dinner for cold nights, and the leftovers are great, too.

SQUASH

1 medium acorn squash, seeded and cubed (1¾ to 2 pounds)

2 tablespoons extra-virgin olive oil

1 teaspoon raw honey

2 teaspoons garam masala

Fine pink Himalayan salt and freshly ground black pepper

SOUP

2 tablespoons extra-virgin olive oil

1 medium yellow onion, chopped

2 tablespoons salted butter

1 (1-inch) piece of fresh ginger, peeled and grated

2 garlic cloves, finely chopped or grated

1 tablespoon garam masala

2 teaspoons ground turmeric

1 teaspoon ground cumin

½ to 1 teaspoon ground cayenne pepper

Fine pink Himalayan salt and freshly ground black pepper

4 cups low-sodium vegetable broth

¾ cup dried red lentils

1 (15-ounce) can full-fat coconut milk

2 cups baby spinach

⅓ cup fresh cilantro, chopped

FOR SERVING

2 cups cooked white or brown basmati rice

Mixed tender herbs, such as basil, cilantro, dill, and parsley

Plain Greek yogurt

Fresh naan or pita (optional)

STOVETOP

COOK 25 MINUTES

1. Preheat the oven to 450°F.

2. **MAKE THE SQUASH.** On a baking sheet, toss together the squash, olive oil, honey, garam masala, and a pinch each of salt and pepper. Roast until the squash is tender, 25 to 30 minutes, tossing halfway through.

3. **MEANWHILE, MAKE THE SOUP.** Heat the olive oil in a large Dutch oven over medium heat. When the oil shimmers, add the onion and cook, stirring, until soft, about 5 minutes. Add the butter, ginger, garlic, garam masala, turmeric, cumin, cayenne, and a pinch each of salt and pepper. Cook, stirring, until the butter is melted and the mixture is fragrant, about 2 minutes.

4. Add the broth and lentils. Season generously with salt. Increase the heat to high, bring to a boil, and then reduce the heat to low. Cover and cook until the lentils are soft, 15 to 20 minutes. Stir in the coconut milk and spinach and cook until the spinach is wilted, about 5 minutes. Remove the pan from the heat and stir in the cilantro.

5. To serve, divide the rice among bowls and ladle the soup over the top. Spoon the squash into the soup and top with the herbs and a dollop of yogurt. Serve with naan alongside, if desired.

PRESSURE COOKER

COOK 25 MINUTES, PLUS ADDITIONAL TIME TO COME TO PRESSURE

1.   Roast the squash as directed for the stovetop.

2.   Meanwhile, using the sauté function, heat the olive oil in the pressure cooker pot. Add the onion and cook, stirring, until soft, about 5 minutes. Add the butter, ginger, garlic, garam masala, turmeric, cumin, cayenne, and a pinch each of salt and pepper. Cook, stirring, until the butter is melted and mixture is fragrant, about 2 minutes.

3.   Add the broth and lentils. Season generously with salt. Lock the lid in place and cook on high pressure for 10 minutes. Quick or natural release, then open when the pressure subsides.

4.   Turn on the sauté function. Stir in the coconut milk and spinach, and cook until the spinach is wilted, 5 minutes. Turn off the pressure cooker. Stir in the cilantro.

5.   Serve the soup as directed for the stovetop.

SLOW COOKER

COOK 4 TO 8 HOURS

1.   **MAKE THE SOUP.** In the slow cooker pot, combine the olive oil, onion, butter, ginger, garlic, garam masala, turmeric, cumin, cayenne, broth, and lentils. Season with salt and pepper. Cover and cook on low for 6 to 8 hours or on high for 4 to 6 hours.

2.   During the last 15 minutes of cooking, stir in the coconut milk, spinach, and cilantro.

3.   Meanwhile, roast the squash as directed for the stovetop.

4.   Serve the soup as directed for the stovetop.

herby sun-dried tomato salad

with chickpeas and lemon vinaigrette

PREP 30 MINUTES
COOK 15 MINUTES
TOTAL 45 MINUTES
SERVES 4 TO 6

I made this salad for Christmas Eve dinner one year, and I've kept it on repeat ever since. If you've enjoyed any of my salad recipes before, you might have noticed I love to add fruit to them. But not here—this one is super savory. The crunchy seeds and the herbs are the shining stars, so do not skimp on either. Also, the chickpeas. I'm not the biggest chickpea fan, but these are completely addicting. The secret is pan-frying them in a little bit of butter. They crisp on the outside but stay soft on the inside. Add a touch of salt and move them right from the skillet to the salad. The heat from the chickpeas helps to break down the kale and really helps everything meld. The leftovers are equally great since the flavors have even more time to come together and almost marinate all those greens. It's great for packing up and taking with you, too!

SALAD

⅓ cup mixed seeds, such as pepitas, sunflower seeds, sesame seeds, and pine nuts

1 tablespoon salted butter

1 (15-ounce) can chickpeas, drained, rinsed, and patted dry

1 tablespoon chopped fresh oregano

Fine pink Himalayan salt and freshly ground black pepper

1 bunch Tuscan kale, stemmed and shredded

4 cups baby arugula

2 Persian cucumbers, thinly sliced

1 (8-ounce) jar sun-dried tomatoes packed in olive oil, oil drained and reserved, tomatoes chopped

¼ cup fresh dill, roughly chopped

¼ cup fresh basil leaves, roughly chopped

2 tablespoons chopped fresh chives

6 ounces goat cheese, crumbled

1 or 2 avocados, sliced

VINAIGRETTE

2 tablespoons fresh lemon juice

2 tablespoons apple cider vinegar

1 teaspoon raw honey

Crushed red pepper flakes

Fine pink Himalayan salt and freshly ground black pepper

1. **MAKE THE SALAD.** Heat a large skillet over medium heat. Add the seeds and cook, stirring occasionally, until lightly golden and toasted, 2 to 3 minutes. Transfer the seeds to a plate.

2. To the same skillet, add the butter, chickpeas, oregano, and a pinch each of salt and pepper. Cook, stirring occasionally, until the chickpeas are crisped all over, 8 to 10 minutes.

3. Meanwhile, in a large serving bowl, combine the kale, arugula, cucumbers, sun-dried tomatoes, dill, basil, and chives. Add the crispy chickpeas and toss to combine well.

4. **MAKE THE VINAIGRETTE.** In a medium bowl, whisk ⅓ cup of the reserved sun-dried tomato oil with the lemon juice, vinegar, and honey. Season with red pepper flakes, salt, and pepper.

5. Pour the vinaigrette over the salad. Toss to coat. Top the salad with the toasted seeds, goat cheese, and avocado. Serve.

chipotle cheddar corn chowder

PREP 10 MINUTES

COOK 25 MINUTES

TOTAL 35 MINUTES

SERVES 4

Corn chowder never really sounded appealing to me. The words *corn* and *chowder*—they just don't do it for me, not together. But a few summers back, in very late August, my mom asked me to make some. Of all the foods she loves, corn and soup are way up there. I was going to politely ignore her request, but after an overzealous grocery haul left me with too many ears of sweet late-summer corn, I figured I'd indulge her. Besides, surely I could find a way to make it delicious. Since I most often think of corn prepared in Mexican and southwestern dishes, I decided to put a spicy, smoky, cheesy spin on the soup by using chipotle peppers and lots of cheddar—my personal favorite combination. I serve the chowder with a mix of fresh toppings to brighten up the soup, like diced avocado and lots of cilantro. It's creamy-tasting without feeling heavy, and sooo good. Just ask my mom.

4 slices thick-cut bacon, chopped

1 medium yellow onion, chopped

4 cups fresh or frozen corn kernels (from about 4 ears)

1 russet potato, peeled and cut into 1-inch cubes

1 poblano pepper, seeded and chopped

2 canned chipotle peppers in adobo, chopped

2 garlic cloves, finely chopped or grated

Fine pink Himalayan salt and freshly ground black pepper

4 cups low-sodium chicken broth

1 cup milk of your choice

1 cup shredded sharp cheddar cheese

½ cup shredded pepper Jack cheese

⅓ cup fresh cilantro, chopped

FOR SERVING

Diced avocado

Plain Greek yogurt (optional)

Crumbled cotija or feta cheese

Chopped fresh cilantro

1. Place the bacon in a large Dutch oven. Cook, stirring, over medium-high heat until the bacon is crispy and the fat has rendered, about 5 minutes. Using a slotted spoon, transfer the bacon to a paper towel–lined plate. Drain off all but 1 tablespoon of bacon fat (see Note on page 186).

2. Add the onion to the pot and cook, stirring, until soft, about 5 minutes. Add the corn, potato, poblano, chipotles, and garlic. Season with salt and pepper and stir to combine. Pour in the broth. Bring to a boil, then reduce the heat to medium-low and simmer until the potato is soft, 10 to 15 minutes.

3. Transfer half of the chowder to a blender and pulse a few times; you want to keep it a bit chunky rather than puree it. Return the chowder to the pot. (Alternatively, use an immersion blender to blend lightly directly in the pot.) Stir in the milk, cheddar, and pepper Jack. Cook, stirring, until the cheeses have melted and the chowder thickens slightly, about 5 minutes. Stir in the cilantro and remove the pot from the heat.

4. Ladle the chowder into bowls. Top with the reserved bacon, avocado, yogurt (if using), cotija, and cilantro. Serve immediately.

rosemary chicken avocado salad

with bacon shallot vinaigrette

PREP 15 MINUTES
COOK 25 MINUTES
TOTAL 40 MINUTES
SERVES 6

When I do salads, I really DO salads, meaning I don't mess around with mere bowls of lettuce. Instead, I make them dinner-worthy—salads you actually look forward to eating. I enjoy this one all year round, though I love it most in the winter and early spring, when the days are cold, because of the heartier ingredients. The chicken is roasted with a mix of lemon, rosemary, and Dijon mustard, until it's tender and super flavorful. If you're making it in the summer, throw the chicken on the grill instead! But the vinaigrette is what makes this salad over-the-top good. The bacon adds a salty, crunchy element to every bite, and the sautéed shallots bring a slight sweetness and tanginess that complements the chicken. When you add creamy burrata and avocado, you have a real-deal salad worthy of your dinner plate. This one is delicious the next day, too—warm or cold!

SALAD

3 tablespoons extra-virgin olive oil

2 tablespoons Dijon mustard

Zest and juice of 1 lemon

4 garlic cloves, finely chopped or grated

1 medium shallot, finely chopped

2 tablespoons chopped fresh rosemary or 1 tablespoon dried

1 teaspoon smoked paprika

Fine pink Himalayan salt and freshly ground black pepper

1 pound boneless, skinless chicken tenders

6 cups mixed greens, such as romaine and baby arugula

1 cup cherry tomatoes, halved

1 or 2 nectarines or peaches, sliced

1 to 2 balls burrata cheese, at room temperature

2 avocados, sliced

VINAIGRETTE

4 slices thick-cut bacon, chopped

¼ cup extra-virgin olive oil

2 medium shallots, thinly sliced

3 tablespoons champagne vinegar

⅓ cup chopped fresh tender herbs, such as oregano, basil, and dill

Crushed red pepper flakes

Fine pink Himalayan salt and freshly ground black pepper

1. Preheat the oven to 425°F.

2. **MAKE THE SALAD.** In a medium bowl, stir together the olive oil, mustard, lemon zest and juice, garlic, shallot, rosemary, paprika, and a pinch each of salt and pepper. Add the chicken and turn to coat. Transfer the chicken to a baking sheet. Roast until the chicken is cooked through, 20 to 25 minutes. Remove the baking sheet from the oven and cut it into bite-size pieces.

3. **MEANWHILE, MAKE THE VINAIGRETTE.** Place the bacon in a large skillet over medium heat and cook, stirring, until the bacon is crispy and the fat has rendered, about 5 minutes. Transfer the bacon to a plate. Drain off the fat.

4. To the same skillet over medium heat, add the olive oil and shallots. Cook, stirring occasionally, until the shallots are soft and fragrant, 2 to 3 minutes. Remove the skillet from the heat and let cool slightly. Whisk in the vinegar and herbs. Season with red pepper flakes, salt, and pepper. Stir the cooked bacon into the vinaigrette.

5. In a large serving bowl, combine the greens, cherry tomatoes, and nectarines. Add ½ cup of the vinaigrette and toss to coat. Break the burrata over the salad. Add the chicken and avocado. Drizzle the remaining vinaigrette over the top.

shredded brussels sprout salad

with brown butter walnuts

PREP 15 MINUTES
COOK 5 MINUTES
TOTAL 20 MINUTES
SERVES 6

Brussels sprouts are a food some people love and other people love to hate. When someone hates them, nine times out of ten, that person hasn't tried them the right way. But once you try a GOOD Brussels sprout recipe, you will be hooked. This is that recipe. I love them roasted year-round, but come fall and winter, this salad is a go-to for me. There are two secrets here: first, a touch of orange in the vinaigrette, and second, the brown butter walnuts. The vinaigrette provides the salad with a sweet tanginess that complements the sprouts, while the walnuts add a savory, rich flavor that offsets the sweetness. It doesn't sound like it should work, but it really does. The best part is that you can prep this salad a few hours ahead of time. Just hold off on adding the walnuts, pomegranate seeds, and cheese until right before serving, so they don't lose their texture.

1/3 cup extra-virgin olive oil

1 medium shallot, finely chopped

2 tablespoons apple cider vinegar

1 teaspoon orange zest

2 tablespoons fresh orange juice

2 teaspoons raw honey

Crushed red pepper flakes

Fine pink Himalayan salt and freshly ground black pepper

6 cups shredded Brussels sprouts (about 12 ounces)

2 tablespoons salted butter

1 cup raw walnuts, roughly chopped

1 tablespoon fresh thyme leaves

Flaky sea salt

1 apple, cored and thinly sliced (I like Honeycrisp)

1½ cups pomegranate seeds or dried cranberries

1 cup crumbled blue cheese or feta cheese

1. In a large serving bowl, whisk together the olive oil, shallot, vinegar, orange zest and juice, honey, and a pinch each of red pepper flakes, pink salt, and pepper. Add the Brussels sprouts and toss to coat.

2. Heat the butter and walnuts together in a medium skillet over medium heat. Cook, stirring occasionally, until the butter is foamy and the walnuts are toasted, about 5 minutes. Remove the skillet from the heat. Stir in the thyme and a pinch of flaky salt.

3. Add the walnuts and any butter left in the pan to the bowl with the Brussels sprouts. Toss to combine. Top with the apple, pomegranate seeds, and blue cheese.

4. Serve the salad at room temperature.

pale ale cauliflower soup

with rosemary bacon

PREP 15 MINUTES
COOK 35 MINUTES
TOTAL 50 MINUTES
SERVES 4

My family moved to Colorado full-time when I was in ninth grade, but I spent my childhood in a suburb of Cleveland, Ohio, and I still think of it as home. Cleveland is known for a few things: brutal winters, great local beer, and probably most notably, LeBron James. But let's focus on that beer because it's the heart of this cheesy (in a good way) soup. Great Lakes Brewing Company ships beer worldwide, and their brewpub—yes, in Cleveland—is a super-fun spot for lunch. When it's cold out, I always order the gold lager cheddar soup. It is made with their Dortmunder Gold lager and Stilton and cheddar cheeses. It's as decadent as it sounds and a real treat on any dreary fall or winter day. I was inspired to make a version every bit as delicious, but that I can have—yes, in Colorado—whenever the craving hits. I added some cauliflower to keep the soup extra creamy without using flour or cream. And that crispy rosemary bacon on top? Well, it really seals the deal, as I love to say.

4 slices thick-cut bacon, chopped

1 tablespoon chopped fresh rosemary

1½ teaspoons smoked paprika

¼ to ½ teaspoon ground cayenne pepper

1 medium yellow onion, chopped

3 celery stalks, chopped

2 cups low-sodium vegetable broth

1 head of cauliflower, cored and separated into florets (about 6 cups)

2 garlic cloves, finely chopped or grated

2 tablespoons fresh thyme leaves or 2 teaspoons dried, plus more fresh thyme leaves for serving

Crushed red pepper flakes

Fine pink Himalayan salt and freshly ground black pepper

1 (12-ounce) can pale ale or golden lager (I like Great Lakes Brewing Company)

½ cup milk of your choice

2 tablespoons salted butter (optional)

½ cup shredded cheddar cheese

Fresh thyme leaves or sliced green onions, for serving

1. Cook the bacon in a large Dutch oven over medium heat until the fat is rendered and the bacon is crispy, about 5 minutes. Using a slotted spoon, transfer the bacon to a small bowl, reserving the bacon fat in the pot. Add the rosemary, ½ teaspoon of the paprika, and the cayenne to the bacon. Toss to coat.

2. Add the onion and celery to the pot. Cook, stirring occasionally, until soft, about 5 minutes. Add ½ cup of the broth and cook, scraping up any browned bits from the bottom of the pot. Add the cauliflower, garlic, thyme, remaining 1 teaspoon paprika, and a pinch each of red pepper flakes, salt, and black pepper. Toss to coat the florets. Add the remaining 1½ cups broth and the beer. Increase the heat to high and bring to a boil, then reduce the heat to medium-low. Cook until the cauliflower is fork-tender, 15 to 20 minutes.

3. Using an immersion blender, blend the soup until creamy, about 2 minutes. (Alternatively, transfer the soup to a blender, process until smooth, and return it to the pot.) Stir in the milk and butter (if using). Cook, stirring occasionally, over medium-low heat until warmed through, about 5 minutes.

4. Ladle the soup into bowls. Sprinkle with the rosemary bacon, cheddar, and fresh thyme leaves and serve.

kale caesar

with house dressing and sourdough croutons

PREP 20 MINUTES
COOK 10 MINUTES
TOTAL 30 MINUTES
SERVES 6

I usually go all out with my salads, but sometimes you just need something simple that you can throw together to serve as a side to your dinner. This salad is exactly that, and it's hands down my favorite everyday version. Greens, avocado, and then things start to get exciting with some sourdough croutons. But the secret sauce here, literally, is the dressing. It's reminiscent of a Caesar dressing, but it's not traditional. I don't use raw eggs or anchovies, but I promise, it is so creamy and has ALL the flavor you need. I like to use the good fats of tahini to keep it creamy, but if you prefer a more classic flavor, try your favorite mayo. Seriously, make a double—maybe triple—batch of this dressing. It's a salad you'll be excited to have at every meal.

CROUTONS

3 tablespoons extra-virgin olive oil

2 cups cubed day-old sourdough bread

Fine pink Himalayan salt

DRESSING

⅓ cup extra-virgin olive oil

3 tablespoons tahini, avocado oil mayonnaise, or vegan mayonnaise

2 tablespoons fresh lemon juice

2 tablespoons Dijon mustard

1 tablespoon champagne vinegar

2 teaspoons low-sodium tamari or fish sauce

2 teaspoons raw honey

⅓ cup grated Parmesan cheese or nutritional yeast, plus more shaved Parmesan or nutritional yeast for serving

2 garlic cloves, roughly chopped

Fine pink Himalayan salt and freshly ground pepper

SALAD

1 large bunch Tuscan kale, stemmed and thinly sliced

1 medium head of romaine lettuce, thinly sliced

2 avocados, diced

1. Preheat the oven to 425°F.

2. **MAKE THE CROUTONS.** On a baking sheet, toss together the olive oil and bread. Bake until crisp and golden, 10 to 15 minutes. Season with salt and let cool.

3. **MEANWHILE, MAKE THE DRESSING.** In a blender or food processor, combine the olive oil, tahini, lemon juice, mustard, vinegar, tamari, honey, Parmesan, garlic, and a generous pinch each of salt and pepper. Blend until smooth, about 1 minute. Add water, 1 tablespoon at a time, until your desired consistency is reached. Taste and add salt and pepper as needed.

4. **MAKE THE SALAD.** In a large serving bowl, combine the kale and romaine. Toss the croutons in with the salad. Add the dressing and toss to combine and coat well. Top the salad with avocado and additional Parmesan before serving.

easier italian wedding soup

PREP 10 MINUTES
COOK 25 MINUTES
TOTAL 35 MINUTES
SERVES 6 TO 8

Despite what you may think, Italian wedding soup isn't served at weddings. Rather, the name comes from the fact that the flavors in it—broth, meat, and green vegetables—*marry* so well together. But like most good marriages, this soup traditionally takes a lo-o-ong time to make, with homemade stock and a million tiny meatballs. My version has a bit of a shortcut. I season ground chicken with lots of herbs and spices and then brown it. You get all the same flavors and textures as the meatballs without as much work (and without the bread crumbs), and the soup is still made silky and rich by eggs stirred in at the end that cook into yummy wisps. Some marriages happen fast!

¼ cup extra-virgin olive oil

1 pound ground chicken or turkey

1 medium yellow onion, chopped

¼ cup fresh parsley, chopped

1 tablespoon dried basil

1 tablespoon dried oregano

2 teaspoons smoked paprika

1 teaspoon fennel seeds

½ cup grated Parmesan cheese, plus more shaved Parmesan for serving

Crushed red pepper flakes

Fine pink Himalayan salt and freshly ground black pepper

6 medium carrots, chopped

4 celery stalks, chopped

4 garlic cloves, finely chopped or grated

8 cups low-sodium chicken broth

6 cups baby spinach

10 ounces fresh cheese tortellini

Juice of 2 lemons

2 large eggs

Fresh parsley or basil leaves, for serving

1.   In a large Dutch oven, combine the olive oil, chicken, onion, parsley, basil, oregano, paprika, fennel seeds, ¼ cup of the Parmesan, and a pinch each of red pepper flakes, salt, and pepper. Place the pot over medium-high heat and cook, breaking up the meat with a wooden spoon, until the meat is browned and the onion is soft and translucent, 5 to 8 minutes.

2.   Add the carrots, celery, and garlic. Cook, stirring occasionally, until slightly softened, 5 minutes. Add the broth and season with salt and pepper. Bring to a simmer over medium heat and cook until the flavors are married, 10 to 15 minutes. Stir in the spinach, tortellini, and lemon juice. Cook until the spinach is wilted and the tortellini is al dente, 5 minutes more.

3.   In a small bowl, whisk together the eggs and the remaining ¼ cup Parmesan. Slowly drizzle the egg mixture into the broth, stirring the soup constantly and gently to form thin strands of cooked egg, about 30 seconds. Taste the soup and adjust the seasoning as needed.

4.   Ladle the soup into bowls and serve immediately, topped with shaved Parmesan and fresh parsley or basil leaves.

spiced chopped chicken salad

with pita crisps and tahini vinaigrette

PREP 30 MINUTES
COOK 15 MINUTES
TOTAL 45 MINUTES
SERVES 4

Shawarma is one of the most popular Middle Eastern foods. Traditionally, it is made with spiced, marinated meat that is roasted on a vertical spit before being sliced into super thin pieces. It's usually served inside a pita or on a plate with hummus, but I was inspired to use the flavors from this favorite street food in a giant chopped salad, complete with all the usual shawarma toppings and go-withs. Pan-seared spiced chicken tossed together with greens, tomatoes, cucumbers, herbs, and the most addicting creamy, lemony tahini vinaigrette. It's all the things. Yes, this recipe has many ingredients, and you can subtract as you like, but they all add layers of flavor and texture. It comes together relatively quickly and nothing is the least bit difficult. This is one you will be truly excited to eat—it's my dream salad!

CHICKEN

1 pound boneless, skinless chicken breasts or thighs, cut into bite-size pieces

5 tablespoons extra-virgin olive oil

3 garlic cloves, finely chopped or grated

2 teaspoons smoked or sweet paprika

2 teaspoons ground cumin

½ teaspoon ground turmeric

⅛ teaspoon ground cinnamon

¼ to ½ teaspoon crushed red pepper flakes

Fine pink Himalayan salt and freshly ground black pepper

TAHINI VINAIGRETTE

¼ cup extra-virgin olive oil

Juice of 1 lemon

2 tablespoons red wine vinegar

2 tablespoons tahini

2 teaspoons raw honey

1 garlic clove, finely chopped or grated

Fine pink Himalayan salt and freshly ground black pepper

SALAD

6 cups shredded romaine lettuce

1 cup cherry tomatoes, halved

2 Persian cucumbers, chopped

½ cup roughly chopped fresh parsley

½ cup roughly chopped fresh dill

1 large avocado, sliced

½ cup crumbled feta cheese

1½ cups pita chips

Quick-Pickled Red Onions (page 221) or store-bought pickled onions, for serving

1. **MAKE THE CHICKEN.** In a medium bowl, combine the chicken, 3 tablespoons of the olive oil, the garlic, paprika, cumin, turmeric, cinnamon, red pepper flakes, and a large pinch each of salt and black pepper. Let marinate for 15 minutes at room temperature or overnight in the refrigerator.

2. **MEANWHILE, MAKE THE VINAIGRETTE.** In a glass jar or measuring cup, combine the olive oil, lemon juice, vinegar, tahini, honey, garlic, and a pinch each of salt and pepper. Shake or whisk vigorously until mixed well and smooth. Taste and add more salt and pepper as needed.

3. In a small skillet over medium heat, heat the remaining 2 tablespoons olive oil. When it shimmers, add the chicken in a single layer and cook, stirring once or twice, until the chicken is opaque and cooked through, 5 to 10 minutes.

4. **MAKE THE SALAD.** Put the romaine in a large serving bowl. Top with the tomatoes, cucumber, parsley, dill, avocado, and feta. Add the chicken, pita chips, and pickled red onion. Drizzle with the vinaigrette and serve immediately.

pasta &
pizza

garlicky greens pizza

PREP 10 MINUTES
COOK 20 MINUTES
TOTAL 30 MINUTES, PLUS PREHEATING TIME
SERVES 4

I love pretty much every pizza recipe, but of them all, I think I make this one the most. I usually have the ingredients on hand, and putting it together is pretty quick. It's simple, but it's one of those pizzas everyone really loves. Caramelizing the garlic cloves in a little olive oil before smashing them into a prepared pesto to spread over the base of the pizza is KEY. It gives you a nice sweet flavor but doesn't overpower everything else. It's just perfect. If you want to switch things up a bit, try swapping the spinach for kale or shredded Brussels sprouts. I've done both—all variations are equally great!

- 2 tablespoons extra-virgin olive oil, plus more for greasing and drizzling
- 5 garlic cloves, peeled
- ⅓ cup pesto
- 2 teaspoons lemon zest, plus lemon wedges
- ½ pound pizza dough, homemade (recipe follows) or store-bought, at room temperature
- 4 ounces crumbled goat cheese
- 1 teaspoon fennel seeds
- Crushed red pepper flakes
- Fine pink Himalayan salt and freshly ground black pepper
- 4 cups baby spinach
- 4 ounces low-moisture whole-milk mozzarella cheese, torn
- Fresh basil leaves, for serving

1. At least 30 minutes and preferably 1 to 2 hours before baking, preheat the oven to 500°F with a rack positioned in the upper third of the oven. If you have a baking stone, preheat it at the same time.

2. Heat the olive oil and garlic cloves in a small skillet over medium heat. Cook, stirring until the garlic is golden, 5 to 7 minutes. Transfer the garlic to a bowl and mash with a fork. Stir in the pesto and lemon zest.

3. On a lightly floured work surface, roll out the pizza dough to a ¼-inch thickness. Carefully transfer the dough to a piece of parchment paper.

4. Spread the pesto mixture all over the dough, leaving a 1-inch border. Top with the goat cheese, then sprinkle on the fennel, red pepper flakes, and a pinch each of salt and pepper. Layer on the spinach and scatter the mozzarella on top. Drizzle a bit of olive oil all over the pizza. Carefully transfer the parchment paper to the preheated baking stone or a baking sheet.

5. Bake until the crust is golden and the cheese has melted, 15 to 20 minutes. Top with fresh basil, a squeeze of lemon juice, and more red pepper flakes, if desired. Serve immediately.

pizza dough

MAKES 3 (½-POUND) BALLS

- 1 cup plus 2 tablespoons warm water
- 2 teaspoons active dry yeast
- 1½ cups all-purpose flour, plus more for dusting
- 1½ cups bread flour
- 2 teaspoons fine pink Himalayan salt
- Extra-virgin olive oil, for brushing

1. In a stand mixer, combine the water and yeast. Let sit until the mixture is bubbly, 5 to 10 minutes. Add both flours and the salt. Using the dough hook, mix until a dough comes together but is still sticky, 5 to 10 minutes. (Alternatively, you can mix the dough in a large bowl with a wooden spoon.)

2. On a floured work surface, turn out the dough and form it into a ball. Knead the dough until smooth and elastic, about 5 minutes. Rub the bowl used to mix the dough with olive oil, and then place the dough in the bowl, turning to coat it in oil. Cover with plastic wrap and let rest in a warm place until doubled in size, 1 to 2 hours.

3. The dough is ready to use now, but I find it has better flavor after a second rise: Punch it down and return it to the bowl. Cover again and place in the refrigerator overnight or for up to 3 days. Remove the dough from the refrigerator 3 to 4 hours before baking. The dough can be stored in an airtight container in the freezer for up to 3 months; thaw overnight in the refrigerator or for 3 to 4 hours on the counter before using.

wild mushroom pappardelle

PREP 15 MINUTES
COOK 20 MINUTES
TOTAL 35 MINUTES
SERVES 6

This is the pasta you'll want to make on the coldest nights of the year. I like to think of it as "cozy cabin pasta," because it gives off all those rustic, warm vibes I always crave. The mushrooms add heartiness and depth of flavor to this light yet still-rich dish. But it's the crunch of hazelnuts and the little bit of butter that really make this pasta stand out. The hazelnuts slowly toast as the butter browns, resulting in a rich, extra-nutty sauce that pairs wonderfully with the earthy mushrooms. The crispy kale adds welcome texture. My dad has officially said this is one of his favorite pastas, though he might be a bit biased because he loves mushrooms in everything. I strongly suggest you pull up a chair by the fire and enjoy.

1 large bunch Tuscan or curly kale, stemmed and torn

4 tablespoons extra-virgin olive oil

2 tablespoons grated Parmesan cheese

Fine pink Himalayan salt and freshly ground black pepper

¾ pound pappardelle or other long-cut pasta

12 ounces mixed wild mushrooms, roughly torn or sliced

2 tablespoons salted butter

¼ cup roughly chopped raw hazelnuts (optional)

2 garlic cloves, finely chopped or grated

2 tablespoons fresh thyme leaves, plus more for serving

2 tablespoons chopped fresh sage

Pinch of crushed red pepper flakes

¾ cup dry white wine, such as pinot grigio or Sauvignon Blanc

2 tablespoons crumbled goat cheese

1. Preheat the oven to 400°F.

2. On a rimmed baking sheet, massage the kale with 2 tablespoons of the olive oil until slightly softened, about 1 minute. Sprinkle the Parmesan over the kale and season with salt. Bake, tossing halfway through, until the kale is crispy, 15 to 20 minutes.

3. Meanwhile, bring a large pot of salted water to a boil over high heat. Cook the pasta until al dente according to the package directions. Reserve ½ cup of the pasta cooking water, then drain the pasta.

4. Heat the remaining 2 tablespoons olive oil in a large skillet over high heat. When the oil shimmers, add the mushrooms and season with salt and pepper. Cook, stirring occasionally, until golden brown, 6 to 8 minutes. Reduce the heat to medium and add the butter and hazelnuts (if using). Season with salt and pepper. Cook, stirring, until the butter is golden brown, 2 to 3 minutes more. Add the garlic, thyme, sage, and a pinch each of salt, pepper, and red pepper flakes. Cook, stirring, until fragrant, 1 to 2 minutes.

5. Pour the wine into the skillet. Cook, scraping up the browned bits from the bottom of the pan with a wooden spoon, until the liquid has reduced slightly, 2 to 3 minutes. Add the drained pasta and goat cheese. Toss until the pasta is coated and the sauce is creamy, adding the reserved pasta cooking water, 1 tablespoon at a time, as needed to thin the sauce.

6. Remove the skillet from the heat and season with salt and pepper to taste. Add the crispy kale and toss to combine. Serve the pasta immediately, topped with more thyme.

nutty, herby spring pasta

PREP 15 MINUTES

COOK 35 MINUTES

TOTAL 50 MINUTES

SERVES 6

All winter long, I am super into warm, cheesy pasta bakes straight from the oven. And when spring finally arrives . . . Guess what? It's still snowy and pretty cold here in Colorado. Of course, we have gorgeous days filled with sun, but our spring is short and sweet. That means I still want to eat something cozy, but I want it to have a lighter feel. Asparagus, leeks, and dry white wine—especially all together— make me think "spring." You basically need only one pot for this recipe, and if you don't feel like taking out your food processor, you could even just chop everything finely by hand. My favorite pasta shapes to use are ditalini, elbow macaroni, and orzo. I like to eat this dish fresh off the stove, but it makes for great leftovers, too. Pack it up and serve it at room temperature at your first picnic of the season!

½ pound baby potatoes, halved or quartered if large

1 pound short-cut pasta of your choice

¼ cup plus 2 tablespoons extra-virgin olive oil

2 tablespoons apple cider vinegar

Zest and juice of 1 lemon

1 cup fresh basil leaves, chopped, plus more for serving

2 tablespoons chopped fresh chives

¼ cup raw mixed nuts and seeds, such as pine nuts, pepitas, pistachios, and walnuts

Fine pink Himalayan salt and freshly ground pepper

2 leeks, white and light green parts only, halved vertically and sliced into half-moons

1 bunch asparagus, ends trimmed, cut into ¼-inch pieces

3 garlic cloves, finely chopped or grated

Crushed red pepper flakes

¼ cup dry white wine, such as pinot grigio or Sauvignon Blanc

¾ cup grated Manchego cheese (about 3 ounces), plus more for serving

1. Bring a large pot of salted water to a boil over high heat. Add the potatoes and cook for about 10 minutes. Add the pasta and cook until the pasta is al dente according to the package directions and the potatoes are tender. Drain the potatoes and the pasta.

2. Meanwhile, in a food processor, pulse together ¼ cup of the olive oil, the vinegar, lemon zest and juice, basil, chives, and nuts and seeds until finely chopped. Season with salt and pepper and pulse a few more times to combine.

3. In the pot used for cooking the pasta, heat the remaining 2 tablespoons olive oil over medium-high heat. When the oil shimmers, add the leeks and cook, stirring, until caramelized and fragrant, 5 to 8 minutes. Add the asparagus, garlic, red pepper flakes, and a pinch each of salt and pepper. Cook, stirring occasionally, until the asparagus is tender, about 5 minutes more. Pour in the wine and cook, scraping up any browned bits from the bottom of the pan with a wooden spoon, until the liquid has reduced slightly, 2 to 3 minutes.

4. Add the potatoes, pasta, and Manchego to the pot, tossing well to coat. Add the herby olive oil mixture and toss to combine. Divide among bowls and serve immediately topped with additional basil and Manchego.

garlic parmesan bread pizza
with salad

PREP 10 MINUTES

COOK 15 MINUTES

TOTAL 25 MINUTES, PLUS PREHEATING TIME

SERVES 4

When I was growing up, my dad would make dinner for the family every single night. He'd prepare one dish for my mom, brothers, and me, and then he'd make a salad for himself. You see, my dad loves good food, but when we kids were younger, we pretty much only ate "kid food." You know, chicken and rice, tacos, chicken fingers, and, especially, pizza. His salads were mostly giant piles of chopped romaine with dressing—usually ranch dressing. He'd eat his bowl of heavily dressed lettuce and then finish his meal by clearing off whatever was left on our plates. This memory got me thinking, what if I combined all the parts of his piecemeal dinner into one dish everyone would enjoy? This pizza puts together his ranchy salad with our cheesy pizza. Then, for good measure, I turned the crust into garlicky Parmesan bread, because everyone loves that. It's unusual for sure, but in the best way possible. You will love every bite.

PIZZA

½ pound pizza dough, homemade (page 107) or store-bought, at room temperature

2 tablespoons salted butter

2 tablespoons extra-virgin olive oil

4 garlic cloves, finely chopped or grated

2 tablespoons chopped fresh tender herbs, such as parsley, oregano, and/or basil

¼ teaspoon crushed red pepper flakes

½ cup grated Parmesan cheese

2 tablespoons Quick Greek Yogurt Ranch (recipe opposite) or store-bought ranch dressing, plus more for serving

1½ cups shredded low-moisture whole-milk mozzarella

⅓ cup shredded cheddar cheese

SALAD

¼ cup extra-virgin olive oil

Juice of 1 lemon

2 tablespoons Dijon mustard

1 tablespoon raw honey

1 tablespoon red wine vinegar

Fine pink Himalayan salt and freshly ground black pepper

1 small shallot, thinly sliced or chopped

3 cups mixed greens

¼ cup fresh tender herbs, such as parsley, oregano, and/or basil

¼ cup freshly shaved Parmesan cheese

1. At least 30 minutes and preferably 1 to 2 hours before baking, preheat the oven to 500°F with a rack positioned in the upper third of the oven. If you have a baking stone, preheat it at the same time.

2. **MAKE THE PIZZA.** On a lightly floured work surface, roll out the pizza dough to a ¼-inch thickness. Carefully transfer the dough to a piece of parchment paper.

3. In a small skillet over low heat, combine the butter, olive oil, and garlic. Cook, stirring occasionally, until the butter is melted and the garlic is fragrant, 2 to 3 minutes. Remove the skillet from the heat and stir in the herbs and red pepper flakes. Brush the garlic-herb butter over the dough, all the way to the edges. Sprinkle ¼ cup of the grated Parmesan all over. Drizzle on the ranch dressing, leaving a 1-inch border. Evenly layer the mozzarella and cheddar over the ranch. Sprinkle the remaining ¼ cup grated Parmesan on the crust. Carefully transfer the parchment paper to the preheated baking stone or a baking sheet.

4. Bake the pizza for 10 minutes, then rotate and continue baking until the crust is golden and the cheese has melted, 3 to 5 minutes more.

5. **MEANWHILE, MAKE THE SALAD.** In a large bowl, whisk together the olive oil, lemon juice, Dijon, honey, vinegar, and a pinch each of salt and pepper. Add the shallot and let sit for 5 minutes. Add the greens, herbs, and shaved Parmesan. Toss to coat well.

6. Top the pizza with the salad. Slice and serve with more ranch dressing alongside for drizzling and dipping.

quick greek yogurt ranch

MAKES ¼ CUP

½ cup plain Greek yogurt

2 tablespoons buttermilk

2 tablespoons chopped fresh chives

1 teaspoon dried parsley

1 teaspoon dried dill

½ teaspoon garlic powder

½ teaspoon onion powder

Fine pink Himalayan salt and freshly ground pepper

In a small bowl or glass jar, combine the yogurt, buttermilk, chives, parsley, dill, garlic powder, onion powder, and a pinch each of salt and pepper. Stir until smooth. Taste and adjust the seasoning as needed. Store refrigerated in an airtight container for up to 2 weeks.

roasted red pepper bolognese

PREP 20 MINUTES
COOK SEE SPECIFIC DEVICE METHOD
SERVES 8

When I was a kid, bell peppers were one of my main food groups. My dad would pile them high atop his Friday Night Pasta Bake, and they'd slow-roast in the oven until they turned sweet. I swear, they were candy-like—and so addicting. I riffed on Dad's idea a bit and cooked up this dish, which not only has a creamy roasted red pepper sauce but also thinly sliced bell peppers. This Bolognese still feels like your grandma's—a classic is a classic for a reason—but with additional flavor from the extra veggies. After you toss the sauce up with rigatoni, you finish the dish with burrata for another layer of creaminess. Add a sprinkle of basil, and everyone at the dinner table will be mumbling "yummm" between mouthfuls. To complete the meal, I love to serve this dish with the sun-dried tomato salad on page 89, which adds a pretty pop of color to the table, too!

- 2 tablespoons extra-virgin olive oil
- 3 medium shallots, chopped
- 2 red bell peppers, seeded and thinly sliced
- 6 garlic cloves, finely chopped or grated
- 1 pound lean ground beef, lamb, or chicken
- ¾ pound ground spicy Italian chicken sausage (see Note on page 80)
- 2 tablespoons dried oregano
- 2 tablespoons dried basil
- Fine pink Himalayan salt and freshly ground black pepper
- Crushed red pepper flakes
- 1 (16-ounce) jar roasted red peppers, drained
- 1 (6-ounce) can or (4.5-ounce) tube tomato paste
- 2 sprigs of fresh thyme
- ⅓ cup grated Parmesan cheese
- 1 pound rigatoni, or pasta of your choice
- 8 ounces burrata cheese, at room temperature
- Fresh basil leaves, for serving

STOVETOP

COOK 3 HOURS 15 MINUTES TO 3 HOURS 45 MINUTES

1. Heat the olive oil in a large Dutch oven over medium-high heat. When the oil shimmers, add the shallots and bell peppers. Cook, stirring occasionally, until the shallots are soft and fragrant, about 5 minutes. Add the garlic, beef, sausage, oregano, and dried basil, and season with salt, pepper, and red pepper flakes. Cook, breaking up the meat with a wooden spoon, until browned, about 10 minutes.

2. Meanwhile, in a food processor or blender, combine the roasted red peppers and tomato paste. Puree until smooth, about 30 seconds.

3. Add the red pepper puree and 2 cups of water to the pot. Add the thyme and season with salt and black pepper. Stir to combine well. Cover, reduce the heat to medium-low, and cook, stirring occasionally, until the flavors are melded, about 3 hours.

4. Discard the thyme. Stir in the Parmesan. If the sauce is too thin, cook over medium heat, uncovered, until thickened, 20 to 30 minutes more.

5. Meanwhile, bring a large pot of salted water to a boil over high heat. Add the pasta and cook until al dente according to the package directions. Drain.

6. Put the pasta in the sauce and toss well. Divide the pasta among bowls, top with the burrata and fresh basil, and serve.

RECIPE CONTINUES

SLOW COOKER

COOK 4 HOURS 10 MINUTES TO 8 HOURS 30 MINUTES

1. Follow steps 1 and 2 of the stovetop method.

2. Transfer the meat mixture to the slow cooker pot. Add the red pepper puree and 1¼ cups of water. Add the thyme and season with salt and pepper. Stir to combine well. Cover and cook on low for 6 to 8 hours or on high for 4 to 6 hours.

3. Remove the lid and discard the thyme. Stir in the Parmesan. If the sauce is too thin, cook on high, uncovered, until thickened, 20 to 30 minutes.

4. Finish as directed for the stovetop.

PRESSURE COOKER

COOK 40 MINUTES, PLUS ADDITIONAL TIME TO COME TO PRESSURE

1. Heat the olive oil in the pressure cooker pot using the sauté function. When the oil shimmers, add the shallots and bell peppers. Cook, stirring occasionally, until the shallots are soft and fragrant, about 5 minutes. Add the garlic, beef, sausage, oregano, and dried basil, and season with salt, pepper, and red pepper flakes. Cook, breaking up the meat with a wooden spoon, until browned, 10 to 15 minutes. Turn off the pressure cooker.

2. Meanwhile, in a food processor or blender, combine the roasted red peppers and tomato paste. Puree until smooth, about 30 seconds.

3. Add the red pepper puree and 1¼ cups of water to the pot. Add the thyme and season with salt and pepper. Stir to combine. Lock the lid in place and cook on high pressure for 20 minutes. Quick or natural release, and open when the pressure subsides.

4. With the pressure cooker on sauté mode, bring the sauce to a boil. Cook until the liquid reduces slightly, 5 to 10 minutes. Turn off the pressure cooker. Discard the thyme and stir in the Parmesan.

5. Finish as directed for the stovetop.

brussels sprouts and gnocchi

in rosemary butter sauce

PREP 20 MINUTES
COOK 20 MINUTES
TOTAL 40 MINUTES
SERVES 4 TO 6

I love a little Brussels sprout–bacon action . . . but I mean, most people do. Something about the pairing just works. This combination is one of my favorites in the fall and winter months, when all I want is a cozy, hearty dish. Nothing is better than tossing the sprouts with gnocchi. First, I sear the sprouts in a little bacon fat to get them nice and crispy. Then I make a quick brown butter sauce with fresh rosemary and a splash of wine. It's simple, but the outcome is delish. And when you add in gnocchi? Well, the buttery sauce clings to them and makes every bite beyond perfect. What's special about this gnocchi is that it's made with cauliflower instead of potato. It feels a little lighter and works better in recipes that incorporate more ingredients since it doesn't "steal the show." It's a great way to get in more nonstarchy vegetables, too. Sometimes I'll buy it from Trader Joe's when I am in a time crunch, but I love to make it and keep it on hand in my freezer. All of that said, you can use potato gnocchi instead—whatever you love most! Either way, the sprouts and sauce are going to taste GOOD.

3 slices thick-cut bacon, chopped (optional)

1 pound Brussels sprouts, trimmed and quartered, or trimmed and halved if small

Fine pink Himalayan salt and freshly ground black pepper

1 tablespoon extra-virgin olive oil

4 tablespoons (½ stick) salted butter

3 garlic cloves, finely chopped or grated

1 tablespoon chopped fresh rosemary

Pinch of crushed red pepper flakes

1 cup low-sodium vegetable or chicken broth

½ cup dry white wine, such as pinot grigio or Sauvignon Blanc

24 ounces cooked Cauliflower Gnocchi (page 119) or store-bought gnocchi of your choice

1. Cook the bacon (if using). Place the bacon in a large skillet over medium heat and cook, stirring occasionally, until the bacon is crispy and the fat has rendered, about 5 minutes. Using a slotted spoon, transfer the bacon to a plate, leaving the fat behind in the pan. (If you're not using the bacon, heat 2 tablespoons of olive oil until it shimmers.)

2. Add the Brussels sprouts to the skillet over medium heat, cut-side down, and season with salt and pepper. Cook, undisturbed, until the sprouts begin crisping on the edges, 3 to 4 minutes. Toss the sprouts, add the olive oil, and cook, stirring occasionally, until crisp all over, 2 to 3 minutes more. Transfer the Brussels sprouts to the plate with the bacon.

3. To the same skillet over medium heat, add the butter, garlic, rosemary, and red pepper flakes. Cook, stirring occasionally, until the butter is lightly browned and the sauce is fragrant, 4 to 5 minutes. Pour in the broth and wine, scraping up any browned bits from the bottom of the skillet. Increase the heat to high and bring to a boil. Season with salt and pepper. Cook until the sauce has reduced slightly, about 5 minutes. Drop the cooked gnocchi into the sauce and toss gently to combine.

4. Divide the gnocchi and sauce among plates. Add the Brussels sprouts and bacon. Serve.

RECIPE CONTINUES

cauliflower gnocchi

MAKES ABOUT 24 OUNCES

Pink Himalayan salt

4 to 5 cups cauliflower florets (about 1 pound)

¾ cup grated Parmesan cheese

¾ to 1 cup all-purpose flour or gluten-free all-purpose flour, plus more as needed

1.   Bring a large pot of salted water to a boil over high heat. Add the cauliflower florets and cook until tender, about 10 minutes. Drain well. Lay the cauliflower on a clean kitchen towel and squeeze out excess liquid.

2.   Transfer the cauliflower to a food processor and process until smooth (or simply mash well with a fork in a bowl). Add the Parmesan and 1 teaspoon of salt and pulse to combine. Transfer the mixture to a medium bowl. Add ¾ cup of the flour and stir to combine. If the the dough seems wet, add more flour, 1 tablespoon at a time, until it forms a ball. The dough should be sticky.

3.   Dust a baking sheet with flour. Generously flour a clean work surface and scrape the dough out onto it. Cut the dough into four equal sections. Working with one section at a time, roll the dough into a rope about 1 inch thick and cut the rope into bite-size gnocchi pieces. Transfer the gnocchi to the prepared baking sheet. Repeat with the remaining dough.

4.   At this point, you can cook the gnocchi by boiling them until they float to the surface, 2 to 3 minutes. Or you can store them refrigerated in an airtight container for up to 1 day, boiling them just before eating. You can also freeze the gnocchi: arrange them on two parchment-lined baking sheets, freeze for 1 hour, and then transfer them to a plastic zip-top bag or airtight container and freeze for up to 3 months. To cook frozen gnocchi, add 1 to 2 minutes to the boiling time.

mushroom pizza
with miso butter shallots

PREP 10 MINUTES

COOK 55 MINUTES

TOTAL 1 HOUR 5 MINUTES, PLUS PREHEATING TIME

SERVES 4

My cousin Abby LOVES a mushroom pizza. She's an adventurous eater and is down to try pretty much anything at least once, so I really appreciate her for that. When she was in town for an extended stay over the holidays, I wanted to turn out a pizza for her that felt just a smidge more special than all the rest. Here is the thing, though: I literally had only mushrooms and cheese on hand, and since it was the busy ski season, I really did not want to brave the overcrowded grocery store. So I made do with what I had, and, well, I got a little creative with the last remaining shallots stashed in the back of the pantry, baking them with miso and butter. And you know what happened? The pizza turned out to be SO GOOD. Those last-ditch-effort shallots really steal the show. They are sweet, salty, and just a little bit buttery. Best of all, they are totally unexpected on a mushroom pizza, but a perfect addition with their hit of umami, which I find extra delicious combined with the savoriness of a cheese pizza.

MISO BUTTER SHALLOTS

6 small shallots

6 tablespoons unsalted butter, melted

3 tablespoons white miso paste

1½ cups warm water

2 sprigs of thyme

PIZZA

½ pound pizza dough, homemade (page 107) or store-bought, at room temperature

1 cup stemmed and shredded Tuscan kale

1½ cups sliced cremini mushrooms

2 tablespoons extra-virgin olive oil, plus more for greasing

2 garlic cloves, finely chopped or grated

Crushed red pepper flakes

Fine pink Himalayan salt

1 cup shaved fontina cheese

⅓ cup grated Parmesan cheese

Fresh basil leaves

1. At least 30 minutes and preferably 1 to 2 hours before baking, preheat the oven to 500°F with one rack positioned in the center and another rack positioned in the upper third of the oven. If you have a baking stone, preheat it on the upper rack at the same time.

2. **MAKE THE SHALLOTS.** Halve the shallots lengthwise, keeping the roots intact but discarding the papery skin. (If your shallots are large, quarter them.) Place the shallots cut-side down in an 8 × 8-inch baking dish, being sure not to crowd the dish.

3. In a medium bowl, whisk together the melted butter, miso, and warm water. Pour the miso butter over the shallots. Place the thyme sprigs on top. Cover the baking dish tightly with foil.

4. Bake on the center rack for 25 minutes. Remove the baking dish from the oven. Remove the foil, flip the shallots over, and spoon the sauce in the dish over the shallots. Return the dish to the oven, uncovered, and bake until the shallots are browned and the sauce is gravy-like, 20 minutes more. Leave the oven on.

5. **MAKE THE PIZZA.** On a lightly floured work surface, roll out the pizza dough to a ¼-inch thickness. Carefully transfer the dough to a piece of parchment paper.

6. In a medium bowl, toss the kale and mushrooms with the olive oil, garlic, and a pinch each of red pepper flakes and salt. Scatter the mixture all over the dough, leaving a 1-inch border. Top with the fontina and Parmesan, then spoon the shallots and sauce evenly over the cheese. Carefully transfer the parchment paper to the preheated baking stone or a baking sheet.

7. Bake for 5 minutes. Rotate the pizza and bake until the crust is golden, 5 to 8 minutes more. Scatter the basil leaves over the top. Serve immediately.

zucchini sauce pasta

PREP 10 MINUTES
COOK 20 MINUTES
TOTAL 30 MINUTES
SERVES 6

This recipe was inspired by Meghan Markle. Yes, the same one who married Prince Harry. I don't really follow the British royal family, but I once stumbled across an article that mentioned Meghan loves cooking. The article said she loves to make zucchini pasta—it didn't include a recipe, but it did note she doesn't use any cream, just the vegetable. That sounded pretty interesting, so I took that little bit of info and did up my own version. When zucchini is cooked down, it becomes buttery. And it naturally releases a lot of liquid, so it sort of automatically creates its own sauce. Add a little butter and Parmesan, and it's totally silky and perfect for tossing pasta in—and you'd get a similar effect using ghee or vegan butter and nutritional yeast, respectively. You can use any cut of pasta, but I love using something short with ridges to really help the sauce cling to the noodles. Since the dish is so simple, plenty of basil and fresh lemon juice add that extra hit of flavor at the end.

1 pound pasta

3 tablespoons extra-virgin olive oil

2 to 3 medium zucchini and/or yellow summer squash (about 1 pound), sliced

Kosher salt and black pepper

2 tablespoons salted butter

4 garlic cloves, finely chopped or grated

2 teaspoons dried oregano

Crushed red pepper flakes

½ cup basil pesto

⅔ cup freshly grated Parmesan cheese

1 cup loosely packed fresh basil, roughly chopped, plus more for garnish

Fresh lemon juice, for serving (optional)

1. Bring a large pot of salted water to a boil over high heat. Cook the pasta until al dente, according to the package directions. Reserve 1 cup of the pasta cooking water, then drain the pasta and add it back to the hot pot.

2. Meanwhile, heat the olive oil in a large skillet over medium heat. When the oil shimmers, add the zucchini and season with salt and black pepper. Cook, stirring occasionally, until the zucchini is soft and lightly golden brown, 5 to 8 minutes. Stir in the butter, garlic, oregano, and a pinch of red pepper flakes. Cook until the butter is melted and the herbs are fragrant, 1 to 2 minutes. Remove from the heat and dump the zucchini into the pot full of pasta.

3. Add the basil pesto and Parmesan, and toss to melt the cheese, about 2 minutes. Add pasta cooking water, 2 tablespoons at a time, as needed to thin the sauce.

4. Stir in the basil to wilt. Serve immediately, topped with lemon juice, if desired, and more basil.

NOTE

If you prefer a smoother sauce, you can give your zucchini a blast in the food processor or hit it with an immersion blender.

saucy garlic peanut noodles

with sesame sweet potatoes

PREP 15 MINUTES

COOK 30 MINUTES

TOTAL 45 MINUTES

SERVES 6

It is probably pretty obvious, but we really love peanut butter over here—I use it in countless recipes. This dish was inspired first by Chinese-style cold sesame noodles, which became a Chinese American staple in the United States in the 1970s, when they were often made with peanut butter because sesame paste was harder to come by. Here, I toss still-warm noodles in a spicy, slightly salty, creamy peanut sauce, but they're just as good cold the next day. The ginger and garlic are KEY and add all the flavor here, so don't be shy with either. And then, as the sweet potatoes roast, the honey caramelizes on the edges, creating the perfect crisp on the outside while the inside gets soft. Want the truth? The sweet potatoes alone are reason enough to make this recipe. My best piece of advice is to double them. They're like candy—you won't be able to stop eating them.

2 small sweet potatoes, cut into ¼-inch-thick rounds

2 tablespoons extra-virgin olive oil

3 tablespoons raw honey

Fine pink Himalayan salt

2 tablespoons sesame seeds

Crushed red pepper flakes

3 cups shredded kale or napa cabbage

½ cup peanut butter

⅓ cup low-sodium soy sauce or tamari

3 tablespoons rice vinegar

2 tablespoons toasted sesame oil

1 tablespoon sambal oelek

1 (1-inch) piece of fresh ginger, peeled and grated

2 garlic cloves, finely chopped or grated

1 pound Chinese egg noodles or thick-cut rice noodles

Peanuts, for serving

Sliced green onions, for serving (optional)

1.   Preheat the oven to 425°F.

2.   On a rimmed baking sheet, combine the sweet potatoes, 1 tablespoon of the olive oil, 1 tablespoon of the honey, and a pinch of salt. Arrange the potatoes in an even layer. Roast, flipping halfway through, until the potatoes are softened and sticky, 20 to 25 minutes. Remove the potatoes from the oven, add the sesame seeds and a pinch of red pepper flakes, and toss to coat.

3.   In a medium bowl, toss the kale with the remaining 1 tablespoon olive oil and a pinch each of salt and pepper. Add the kale to the baking sheet with the potatoes. Return to the oven and roast until the kale is wilted, 5 minutes more.

4.   Meanwhile, in a blender or food processor, combine the peanut butter, soy sauce, vinegar, sesame oil, sambal oelek, ginger, garlic, and the remaining 2 tablespoons honey. Blend until smooth, adding water, 1 tablespoon at a time, as needed to thin the sauce.

5.   Bring a large pot of salted water to a boil over high heat. Add the noodles and cook according to the package directions. Drain, then return the noodles to the pot. Pour the sauce over the hot noodles and toss to coat.

6.   To serve, divide the noodles among bowls. Top with the sweet potatoes and kale. Sprinkle on the peanuts and green onions (if using), and more red pepper flakes, if desired.

pizza alla diavola

with nutty roasted red pepper sauce

PREP 10 MINUTES

COOK 15 MINUTES

TOTAL 25 MINUTES, PLUS
PREHEATING TIME

SERVES 4

*P*izza alla diavola literally means "the devil's pizza" in Italian. So can you guess what's happening? SPICE. "The spicier the better" is the saying around here. But don't be afraid—you can adjust the spice level to your liking (you know I go heavy on those chiles). The unique element to my version of this pizza is the romesco sauce, which is made with walnuts (heart-healthy!) and roasted red peppers. It's nutty, spicy, smoky, and tangy all at the same time. It's the heart and soul of this dish—it brings all the flavor, so don't be shy about layering it on. This sauce is actually so good that I'd go as far as to recommend doubling it. You can use it as a dip, toss it with pasta, and even spread it on sandwiches. The final component here might sound odd, but you NEED to drizzle on some honey just as the pizza comes out of the oven. The sweetness balances out the spice and creates an addicting slice.

½ pound pizza dough, homemade (page 107) or store-bought, at room temperature

½ cup Nutty Roasted Red Pepper Sauce (recipe follows) or store-bought romesco

2 tablespoons chopped pickled hot peppers

4 ounces low-moisture whole-milk mozzarella cheese, torn

⅓ cup grated Parmesan cheese

1 ounce thinly sliced spicy salami

1 shallot, quartered

2 teaspoons extra-virgin olive oil

Fine pink Himalayan salt

Fresh basil leaves, torn, for serving

Raw honey, for drizzling

1. At least 30 minutes and preferably 1 to 2 hours before baking, preheat the oven to 500°F with a rack positioned in the upper third of the oven. If you have a baking stone, preheat it at the same time.

2. On a lightly floured work surface, roll out the pizza dough to a ¼-inch thickness. Carefully transfer the dough to a piece of parchment paper.

3. Spread the red pepper sauce evenly over the dough, leaving a 1-inch border. Layer on the pickled peppers, mozzarella, and Parmesan. Arrange the salami on top.

4. Separate the layers of the shallot quarters into single "leaves" and place in a small bowl. Add the olive oil and a pinch of salt and toss to coat. Arrange the shallots all over the pizza. Carefully transfer the parchment paper to the preheated baking stone or a baking sheet.

5. Bake for 10 minutes, then rotate the pizza and bake until the crust is golden and the shallots are charred, 3 to 5 minutes more. Top with fresh basil and drizzle with honey. Slice and serve.

nutty roasted red pepper sauce

MAKES 2 CUPS

1 (12-ounce) jar roasted red peppers, drained

½ cup toasted walnuts (see Note on page 53)

¼ cup tomato paste

2 garlic cloves, finely chopped or grated

2 tablespoons fresh parsley

½ cup extra-virgin olive oil

2 tablespoons sherry vinegar

2 teaspoons raw honey

1 teaspoon smoked paprika

½ teaspoon ground cayenne pepper

Fine pink Himalayan salt

In a blender or food processor, combine the red peppers, walnuts, tomato paste, garlic, parsley, olive oil, vinegar, honey, paprika, cayenne, and a generous pinch of salt. Blend until smooth, about 1 minute. Store refrigerated in an airtight container for up to 1 week.

easy ricotta ravioli
with lemon herb corn

PREP 30 MINUTES
COOK 15 MINUTES
TOTAL 45 MINUTES
SERVES 6 TO 8

One of the questions I am asked over and over is what my favorite store-bought items are. I will be the first to say the grocery store has incredible options these days, so I am all in on certain items that make everyday cooking easier. Some can make healthy eating at home easier, too, so don't ever feel bad about incorporating them into your recipes. I love Rao's marinara sauce, always keep a few jars of Siete salsa on hand, and am a sucker for every single Primal Kitchen bottled dressing. Now, that said, there are other foods I think really are worth taking the time to make at home. Ravioli is at the top of that list. Sometimes I spend a whole weekend day making it from scratch, and other times, I use my favorite shortcut: store-bought wonton wrappers in place of fresh pasta. I love switching around the fillings and sauces depending on what's in season. This version is for late summer or early fall. It highlights all that corn and those bright garden herbs but feels warming and cozy at the same time. So, you might say these are half-store-bought and half-homemade. I think it's a good compromise!

RAVIOLI

½ cup whole-milk ricotta cheese

½ cup shredded fontina cheese

¼ cup grated Parmesan cheese

5 ounces frozen chopped spinach, thawed and squeezed dry

Fine pink Himalayan salt and freshly ground black pepper

40 to 50 round or square wonton wrappers

SAUCE

2 tablespoons extra-virgin olive oil

3 cups fresh or frozen corn kernels (from 3 to 4 ears, if fresh)

2 tablespoons salted butter

2 garlic cloves, finely chopped or grated

1 tablespoon fresh thyme leaves, plus more for serving

2 teaspoons chopped fresh rosemary

½ teaspoon crushed red pepper flakes, plus more as desired

Fine pink Himalayan salt and freshly ground black pepper

½ cup dry white wine, such as pinot grigio or Sauvignon Blanc

¼ cup fresh lemon juice

½ cup fresh basil leaves, chopped, plus more for serving

1. **MAKE THE RAVIOLI.** In a medium bowl, stir together the ricotta, fontina, Parmesan, spinach, and a pinch each of salt and pepper.

2. Working in small batches, lay out a few wonton wrappers on a clean, dry work surface. Spoon about 1 tablespoon of the filling into the center of each wrapper. Brush the edges with water. Lay a second wrapper on top. Press down on the edges to seal, pressing out any air as you go. Crimp the edges with a fork. Cover the ravioli with a damp kitchen towel to prevent them from drying out.

3. Bring a large pot of salted water to a boil over high heat. Working in batches, add the ravioli and cook until they float on the surface of the water, 1 to 2 minutes. Drain the ravioli.

4. **MEANWHILE, MAKE THE SAUCE.** Heat the olive oil in a large skillet over medium heat. When the oil shimmers, add the corn and cook, stirring, until the kernels are golden, about 5 minutes. Add the butter, garlic, thyme, and rosemary. Cook until the butter begins to brown and the corn smells sweet, 3 to 4 minutes more. Season with red pepper flakes, salt, and pepper. Reduce the heat to low. Pour in the wine and lemon juice and cook, scraping up any browned bits on the bottom of the pan with a wooden spoon, until the sauce has reduced slightly, 3 to 5 minutes.

5. Drop the cooked ravioli into the sauce, gently tossing to combine. Remove the skillet from the heat and stir in the basil to wilt. Divide the ravioli among plates, and top with more basil and thyme.

lasagna alla vodka

PREP 20 MINUTES

COOK 1 HOUR

TOTAL 1 HOUR 20 MINUTES

SERVES 6

One of the questions I receive most often is what I serve when I'm entertaining. My answer is always the same: Lasagna! I mean, sure, I switch up the exact recipe depending on who's coming over, but when I've got a group of people coming, I turn to lasagna. This version has become my favorite for a couple of reasons. First of all, it's delicious. Instead of the usual marinara sauce, I swap in my vodka sauce, which adds flavor, depth, and richness. People always want a second serving. And then, I love how adaptable the recipe is. You can use brown rice noodles to make it gluten-free, or vegan ricotta, nutritional yeast, and vegan cheese to make it dairy-free. Most of the time, I make it vegetarian, but when my brothers are in town, I brown up some spicy Italian chicken sausage and stir it into the vodka sauce . . . and with that simple addition, it becomes one of their favorite dinners. But what I love most about entertaining with lasagna is that I can assemble the entire dish way ahead of time and then bake it off just before dinner. The kitchen smells amazing, and everyone gets excited when they walk in. I serve up a big salad on the side (the one on page 98 is my go-to) and a nice crusty bread. Perfect dinner, every time.

1 pound lasagna noodles of your choice

¼ cup extra-virgin olive oil

2 shallots, finely chopped

8 garlic cloves, finely chopped or grated

2 teaspoons dried oregano

1 cup tomato paste

1 to 2 teaspoons crushed red pepper flakes

½ cup vodka (I like Tito's)

1 cup full-fat coconut milk or heavy cream

¾ cup pesto

Fine pink Himalayan salt and freshly ground black pepper

2 tablespoons salted butter or ghee

⅓ cup grated Parmesan cheese, plus more for serving

¼ cup fresh basil leaves, roughly chopped, plus more for serving

2 cups whole-milk ricotta cheese

2 (10-ounce) packages frozen spinach, thawed and squeezed dry

1 cup shredded provolone cheese

1. Preheat the oven to 350°F.

2. Bring a large pot of salted water to a boil over high heat. Add the pasta and cook to al dente according to the package directions. Reserve 1½ cups of the pasta cooking water, then drain the pasta.

3. Meanwhile, heat the olive oil in a large skillet over medium-low heat. When the oil shimmers, add the shallots, garlic, and oregano. Cook, stirring occasionally, until the shallots begin to soften, 3 to 5 minutes. Reduce the heat to low, add the tomato paste and red pepper flakes, and cook, stirring, until the paste is incorporated and turns dark red, 1 to 2 minutes more. Stir in the vodka and cook for another 2 minutes. Stir in the coconut milk and pesto to incorporate. Season with salt and pepper. Add the butter, stirring to melt. If your sauce seems too thick, add the reserved pasta cooking water, 1 tablespoon at a time, as needed. Simmer until the flavors are melded, about 5 minutes. Add the Parmesan and basil. Remove the pan from the heat.

4. Spread a quarter of the sauce in the bottom of a 9 × 13-inch baking dish. Top with lasagna noodles, overlapping as needed to create an even layer. Dollop on half of the ricotta, half of the spinach, and then another quarter of the sauce. Repeat the lasagna, ricotta, and spinach layers, and then add another quarter of the sauce. Top with the lasagna noodles to cover, and then finish with the remaining sauce. Sprinkle the provolone over the top.

5. Cover with foil and bake for 20 minutes. Discard the foil and bake until the provolone is bubbling and lightly golden, 15 to 20 minutes more. Let stand for 10 minutes. Top with Parmesan and fresh basil and serve.

pizza pasta

with pepperoni bread crumbs

PREP 10 MINUTES

COOK 20 MINUTES

TOTAL 30 MINUTES

SERVES 6

A classic pepperoni pizza will forever and always be my favorite. Don't get me wrong, I love switching up my pizza toppings and trying out new combinations, but I always come back to classic pepperoni. Truth is, I love pepperoni. It might not be the healthiest pizza topping out there, but most everything is okay every now and again. This dish is my very favorite pizza, but in pasta form. It's a little less cheesy than your average pizza, but the sauce and bread crumbs make up for it. The sauce is simple, but SO GOOD. The secret is all in the garlic, herbs, and spices, so don't skimp on any of them. And then those pepperoni bread crumbs? They are the superstars. Crispy, spicy, and even a little cheesy . . . they taste just like pizza, I swear! They would make for a pretty darn delicious salad topping. Just an idea if you want to double the crumbs and save some for lunch during the week!

1 pound pasta of your choice

4 tablespoons extra-virgin olive oil

4 garlic cloves, finely chopped or grated

1 tablespoon dried basil

3 teaspoons dried oregano

2 teaspoons dried thyme

1 teaspoon fennel seeds

1 to 2 teaspoons crushed red pepper flakes

1 (28-ounce) can crushed tomatoes

2 teaspoons fig preserves (I like Dalmatia) or raw honey

Fine pink Himalayan salt and freshly ground black pepper

¾ cup panko bread crumbs

3 ounces pepperoni, thinly sliced

¾ cup grated Parmesan cheese, plus more for serving

½ cup fresh basil leaves, chopped, plus more for serving

1. Bring a large pot of salted water to a boil. Add the pasta and cook until al dente according to the package directions. Reserve ½ cup of the pasta cooking water, then drain the pasta.

2. Meanwhile, heat 2 tablespoons of the olive oil in a large skillet or Dutch oven over medium heat. When the oil shimmers, add the garlic, dried basil, 2 teaspoons of the oregano, the thyme, fennel seeds, and red pepper flakes. Cook, stirring occasionally, until fragrant, 3 to 5 minutes. Add the tomatoes, fig preserves, and a pinch each of salt and pepper. Increase the heat to medium-high and simmer until thickened slightly, 5 to 10 minutes.

3. Heat a medium skillet over medium heat. Add the remaining 2 tablespoons oil, the bread crumbs, the remaining 1 teaspoon oregano, and the pepperoni. Cook, stirring occasionally, until the bread crumbs are toasted, about 3 minutes. Stir in ¼ cup of the Parmesan and cook until golden and clinging to the bread crumbs, about 2 minutes. Transfer the bread crumbs to a plate. Season with salt.

4. Add the cooked pasta to the sauce. Add the remaining ½ cup Parmesan and the fresh basil. Toss to combine well. Add the reserved pasta cooking water, 1 tablespoon at a time, as needed to thin the sauce.

5. Divide the pasta among plates. Top with the pepperoni bread crumbs and additional Parmesan and fresh basil.

roasted cauliflower and lemon pesto pizza

PREP 15 MINUTES

COOK 40 MINUTES

TOTAL 55 MINUTES

SERVES 4

I have a lot of love for this pizza. Three elements absolutely MAKE it. First up, the cauliflower. It's spiced and roasted in the oven, where it gets crispy with just the right amount of char and so much flavor. Next, the pesto. This version is above average thanks to a little kick from jalapeño—it has just the right amount of heat. Finally, those thin lemon slices. As the pizza cooks, they roast, losing their bitterness and becoming sweet, and they bring a perfect acidity overall. (If they're in season, try using those extra-special Meyer lemons.) These three elements are great on their own, but when you combine them atop a pizza? It's a truly wonderful, delightful combination.

1 small head of cauliflower, cored and separated into florets (2 to 3 cups)

½ cup plus 2 tablespoons extra-virgin olive oil

1 teaspoon smoked paprika

Crushed red pepper flakes

Fine pink Himalayan salt and freshly ground black pepper

2 garlic cloves, finely chopped or grated

1½ cups fresh basil leaves, plus more for serving

2 cups baby spinach, baby arugula, or a mix

1 jalapeño, seeded if desired

¼ cup toasted nuts, such as pine nuts, walnuts, or pistachios (see Note on page 53)

⅓ cup grated Parmesan cheese or nutritional yeast

1 tablespoon fresh lemon juice, plus 1 lemon, thinly sliced

½ pound pizza dough, homemade (page 107) or store-bought, at room temperature

4 ounces burrata cheese, at room temperature

2 tablespoons roughly chopped fresh dill

1 tablespoon toasted sesame seeds (see Note on page 53)

1. Preheat the oven to 425°F with one rack positioned in the center and another rack positioned in the upper third of the oven. If you have a baking stone, preheat it on the upper rack at the same time.

2. On a baking sheet, combine the cauliflower, 1 tablespoon of the olive oil, the paprika, red pepper flakes, and a pinch each of salt and pepper. Toss to coat. Roast on the center rack until tender, 20 minutes. Add half of the garlic and toss to combine. Roast until fragrant, 5 minutes more.

3. Meanwhile, in a blender or food processor, combine the remaining garlic, the basil, 1 cup of the spinach, the jalapeño, nuts, Parmesan, and lemon juice. Pulse until smooth and combined, about 30 seconds. Add ½ cup of the olive oil and pulse again until just combined. Taste and add salt as needed.

4. Remove the cauliflower from the oven and increase the temperature to 500°F.

5. On a floured work surface, roll out the pizza dough to a ¼-inch thickness. Carefully transfer the dough to a piece of parchment paper.

6. Spread the pesto over the dough, leaving a 1-inch border. Arrange the lemon slices in an even layer. Top evenly with the roasted cauliflower. Carefully transfer the parchment paper to the preheated baking stone or a baking sheet.

7. Bake the pizza for 10 minutes, then rotate and continue baking until the crust is golden, 3 to 5 minutes more. Remove from the oven and immediately break the burrata over the pizza. Let sit for 5 minutes to warm.

8. Meanwhile, in a large bowl, combine the remaining 1 tablespoon olive oil, the remaining 1 cup spinach, the dill, the sesame seeds, and a pinch each of salt and pepper. Toss to combine well. Top the pizza with the spinach mixture and fresh basil leaves. Serve immediately.

sweet potato pierogi

in sage butter sauce

PREP 1 HOUR

COOK 1 HOUR 15 MINUTES

TOTAL 2 HOURS 15 MINUTES

SERVES 8 (MAKES ABOUT 30 PIEROGI)

I love pierogi so much. I grew up eating them and turned my childhood best friend onto them, too. They were always, always Mrs. T's, our favorite grocery store brand of frozen pierogi. One summer, I swear, we ate them every single day after lacrosse camp . . . we were much better at the snack than the sport. We'd eat pierogi with melted cheddar on top, followed by my mom's chocolate chip cookies. In the winter, my mom and I would repeat this perfect combination after school, chowing down while we cozied up by the fire. While those memories will forever live on, these days I take the time to make my own pierogi. This sweet potato version is both less expected and more nutritious than traditional white potato pierogi, but they're just as melt-in-your-mouth delicious. With the addition of Parmesan cheese, the filling is that perfect sweet-and-savory combination. These only need a simple sauce—nutty brown butter and lots of sage do the trick.

NOTE

You can easily freeze the pierogi to cook later. After you assemble the pierogi, give them a 30-minute freeze on a parchment-paper-lined baking sheet. Then transfer them to an airtight container and store in the freezer for up to 3 months. When you're ready to cook them, just boil them for a few extra minutes.

FILLING

2 pounds sweet potatoes
(2 to 3 medium sweet potatoes)

½ cup grated Parmesan or Manchego cheese

Fine pink Himalayan salt and freshly ground pepper

DOUGH

1¼ cups whole-wheat pastry flour, plus more as needed

¾ cup all-purpose flour

1 teaspoon fine pink Himalayan sea salt, plus more as needed

2 tablespoons extra-virgin olive oil

1 cup plain Greek yogurt, plus more for serving

1 large egg

SAUCE

6 tablespoons salted butter

8 fresh sage leaves, chopped

¼ teaspoon freshly grated nutmeg

Fine pink Himalayan salt and freshly ground pepper

1. Preheat the oven to 425°F.

2. **MAKE THE FILLING.** Prick the sweet potatoes all over with a fork. Bake directly on the oven rack until tender, 50 to 60 minutes.

3. **MEANWHILE, MAKE THE DOUGH.** In a medium bowl, stir together both flours with the salt, oil, yogurt, and egg to combine. The dough will be sticky. Cover with a clean kitchen towel and let sit for about 30 minutes.

4. Remove the sweet potatoes from the oven and let cool a bit, until you can handle them. Use your hands to peel off the potato skins; they should slip off easily. Place the potatoes in a medium bowl, and using a potato masher or fork, mash well. Stir in the cheese and season with a pinch each of salt and pepper.

5. Turn the dough out onto a floured work surface and, using a floured rolling pin, roll it to a ⅛-inch thickness. If your dough is too sticky, sprinkle some flour on it as well. Using a 3-inch biscuit cutter, cut out circles. Reroll the remaining dough and cut out more circles. You should have about 30 circles. Cover them with a damp kitchen towel.

6. Spoon 2 teaspoons of the filling into the center of each dough circle. Brush the edges with water and fold half the dough over the filling to enclose it. Press down on the edges to seal, pressing out the air as you go. Be sure to keep the dough covered with a damp kitchen towel as you work to prevent it from drying out.

7. Bring a large pot of salted water to a boil over high heat.

8. **MEANWHILE, MAKE THE SAUCE.** Heat the butter and sage together in a large skillet over medium heat. Cook, stirring frequently, until the butter begins to brown, 3 to 4 minutes. Stir in the nutmeg and season with salt and pepper. Remove the skillet from the heat.

9. Working in batches, add the pierogi to the boiling water and cook until they float on the surface of the water, 2 to 3 minutes. Drain the pierogi, transfer them to the skillet of sauce, and toss to coat.

10. To serve, divide the pierogi among plates, spooning the remaining sauce over the top. Serve with a dollop of Greek yogurt.

burrata margherita pizza

PREP 10 MINUTES

COOK 15 MINUTES

TOTAL 25 MINUTES, PLUS PREHEATING TIME

SERVES 4

I love pizza. The pizza oven in our studio space makes that pretty obvious, but before that oven was even a thought, I've always loved a slice. As a kid, I'd add more basil than any pizza really needed because it was the only fresh herb I knew, but like most kids, I was most excited about the chewy, stretchy cheese. Since then, I've also fallen for burrata, mozzarella's creamy twin that steals the show every single time. If you've never had burrata, it's just like fresh mozzarella on the outside, but when you break into it, a thickened cream oozes out. Add that to a classic margherita pizza? It's magical. Maybe I'm being dramatic, but it's true. The trick here is pulling the pizza out of the oven just before it is done, adding the burrata, and then letting the cheese warm through while the pizza cooks for a few more minutes. It's just the right consistency, melty and creamy. And again, magical. The basil crumbs on top were inspired by one of my favorite pizza spots in Los Angeles, Pizzana. Their Neo Margherita has basil crumbs, and it's the best, most genius topping. They add a subtle crunch to every bite. If you make one pizza from this book, let it be this pizza (but . . . I mean, you *should* make them all, eventually).

1 cup fresh basil leaves, chopped, plus more for serving

1 teaspoon ground fennel seeds

½ to 1 teaspoon crushed red pepper flakes

3 garlic cloves, finely chopped or grated

Fine pink Himalayan salt and freshly ground black pepper

½ pound pizza dough, homemade (page 107) or store-bought, at room temperature

½ cup crushed San Marzano tomatoes

½ cup grated Manchego or Parmesan cheese

1 ounce mini pepperoni slices (optional)

4 ounces burrata cheese, at room temperature

1 tablespoon extra-virgin olive oil

½ cup panko bread crumbs

1. At least 30 minutes and preferably 1 to 2 hours before baking, preheat the oven to 500°F with a rack positioned in the upper third of the oven. If you have a baking stone, preheat it at the same time.

2. In a small bowl, combine ½ cup of the basil with the ground fennel seeds, red pepper flakes, garlic, and a pinch each of salt and pepper.

3. On a lightly floured work surface, roll out the pizza dough to a ¼-inch thickness. Carefully transfer the dough to a piece of parchment paper.

4. Spread the tomatoes onto the dough, leaving a 1-inch border. Sprinkle the basil mixture over the top. Add the Manchego, then layer on the pepperoni (if using). Carefully transfer the parchment paper to the preheated baking stone or a baking sheet.

5. Bake the pizza for 10 minutes. Remove from the oven and break the burrata evenly over the pizza. Rotate the pizza, return it to the oven, and bake until the crust is golden and the burrata is melted, 3 to 5 minutes more.

6. Meanwhile, heat the olive oil in a medium skillet over medium heat. When the oil shimmers, add the bread crumbs and the remaining ½ cup basil. Cook, stirring occasionally, until the bread crumbs are toasted, about 3 minutes. Transfer to a plate and season with salt.

7. Scatter the basil bread crumbs all over the pizza. Top with additional fresh basil and serve.

vegetarian

sunday sauce

PREP 15 MINUTES
COOK SEE SPECIFIC DEVICE METHOD
SERVES 6

I have a love/hate relationship with Sundays. As a kid, I hated school, so the end of the weekend brought on a lot of anxiety. But something about Sunday family dinner always calmed my nerves, and even though we didn't always sit down together (well, we did, but it was . . . chaotic), my mom or dad would make something a little more special that day. Nothing fancy—maybe a roast chicken or pot roast—but it was a nice way to finish out the weekend. These days, Sundays look and feel very different for me, but I still love a good Sunday dinner, and Sunday sauce is one of my go-tos. I usually make a meaty, short rib–based version, but I absolutely love this hearty vegetarian take too. Even the meat-eaters in my family have come to really enjoy it! The key is using a mix of vegetables and cooking them allllll the way down to get the most flavor and best texture. I serve this sauce over pasta and, to be honest, it's great any day you want to serve it up!

2 tablespoons extra-virgin olive oil

2 pounds mixed mushrooms, such as cremini, shiitake, and porcini, finely chopped

2 tablespoons salted butter

Fine pink Himalayan salt and freshly ground black pepper

1 medium yellow onion, chopped

2 medium carrots, finely chopped

4 garlic cloves, finely chopped or grated

2 tablespoons fresh thyme leaves

1 tablespoon dried basil

1 tablespoon dried oregano

1 tablespoon chopped fresh sage or 2 teaspoons dried

2 teaspoons smoked paprika

2 teaspoons fennel seeds

1 teaspoon crushed red pepper flakes

¾ cups dry red wine, such as Sangiovese

2 cups low-sodium vegetable broth

1 (28-ounce) can crushed tomatoes

⅓ cup tomato paste

1 pound pappardelle or tagliatelle of your choice

Grated Parmesan cheese, for serving

Fresh basil leaves, for serving

STOVETOP

COOK 45 MINUTES

1.   Heat the olive oil in a Dutch oven over medium-high heat. When the oil shimmers, add the mushrooms and cook, stirring occasionally, until the mushrooms are softened and have cooked down, about 5 minutes. Stir in the butter to melt and season with salt and pepper. Cook until the mushrooms are caramelized, another 5 minutes. Add the onion, carrots, garlic, thyme, dried basil, oregano, sage, paprika, fennel, red pepper flakes, and a pinch each of salt and pepper. Cook, stirring occasionally, until the vegetables have softened, about 5 minutes more.

2.   Pour in the wine, increase the heat to high, and bring to a boil. Cook until the wine has reduced slightly, 2 to 3 minutes.

3.   Add the broth, tomatoes, and tomato paste, stirring to combine. Simmer the sauce over medium heat until thick and chunky, 25 to 30 minutes.

4.   Meanwhile, bring a large pot of salted water to a boil over high heat. Cook the pasta to al dente according to the package directions. Drain.

5.   Divide the pasta among plates, add the sauce, and toss well. Top each plate with Parmesan and fresh basil and serve.

SLOW COOKER

COOK 3 HOURS TO 6 HOURS 20 MINUTES

1.   Follow the directions for the stovetop through step 2.

2.   Transfer the mushroom mixture to the slow cooker pot. Add the broth, tomatoes, and tomato paste, stirring to combine. Cover and cook on low for 4 to 5 hours or on high for 2 hours. Remove the lid and continue to cook, stirring occasionally, until thickened, 30 minutes to 1 hour more.

3.   Finish as directed for the stovetop.

olive oil–braised beans

PREP 15 MINUTES
COOK 30 MINUTES
TOTAL 45 MINUTES
SERVES 4

Alternate recipe title? Lyndsie's Beans, because this recipe was 100 percent inspired by her. Lynds is my sister-in-law, and she's also a trusted recipe adviser, always telling me to make this or that, to try a cuisine I'm not familiar with. Most important, she tells me whether something sounds delicious . . . or just crazy. One of her most recent requests was for a cold-weather recipe in which beans are the star of the show. I'm not going to lie, I was really skeptical about a dish of beans and beans only, but as I got cooking, I got excited. These beans slowly simmer down in olive oil with fresh herbs until they become creamy, but they stay brothy at the same time. I love to finish them with a shaving of Parmesan cheese and a squeeze of lemon juice, which adds a hit of fresh flavor amid a whole lot of richness. Here is what is key, however: you MUST serve these beans with crusty, toasty sourdough bread. The bread works as your "spoon" for scooping up these guys. Trust me, it's delicious and will satisfy all of your cravings. And if you don't trust me—at least trust Lyndsie.

⅓ cup plus 2 tablespoons extra-virgin olive oil

1 sprig of fresh rosemary

Pinch of crushed red pepper flakes

4 to 6 garlic cloves, peeled

½ cup full-fat coconut milk

1 (15-ounce) can chickpeas

1 (15.5-ounce) can cannellini beans

6 to 8 fresh sage leaves

Pinch of freshly grated nutmeg

Fine pink Himalayan salt and freshly ground black pepper

FOR SERVING

Shaved Parmesan or Manchego cheese (optional)

Fresh lemon juice

4 slices crusty sourdough or Seeded Whole-Grain Bread (page 32), toasted

1.   In a Dutch oven, heat ⅓ cup of the olive oil with the rosemary and red pepper flakes over medium heat. Cook, stirring occasionally, until the rosemary is crisp, 3 to 4 minutes. Carefully transfer the oil to a small heatproof bowl. Pick out the rosemary. Remove the leaves from the stem, roughly chop the leaves, then add them back to the oil. Season the oil with salt.

2.   Return the Dutch oven to medium heat. Add the garlic and the remaining 2 tablespoons olive oil. Cook, stirring occasionally, until the garlic is light golden brown, about 5 minutes. Pour in the coconut milk, chickpeas, and cannellini beans, including the liquid from both cans of beans. Add the sage and nutmeg. Season with salt and pepper.

3.   Reduce the heat to low and simmer, stirring occasionally, until the liquid has reduced slightly, about 10 minutes. Using a wooden spoon, mash some of the beans against the side of the pot to release their starches. Continue to simmer until creamy, 5 to 10 minutes more. Taste and add more salt and pepper as needed. Using a slotted spoon or tongs, pick out the garlic cloves, mash them with a fork, and stir them back into the beans.

4.   Spoon the beans into bowls and drizzle the rosemary oil on top. Sprinkle with the Parmesan, stir in the lemon juice, and then serve with crusty bread alongside.

spinach and pesto–stuffed butternut squash

PREP 20 MINUTES

COOK 40 MINUTES

TOTAL 1 HOUR

SERVES 4 AS A MAIN OR 6 TO 8 AS A SIDE DISH

GF SF V

One of my favorite autumn vegetables is butternut squash. A lot of the time you'll see it pureed into soup, but my favorite way to enjoy it is to roast it. Most of the time, I will cube it and toss it with a little cinnamon and chili powder. But when I want to make it into more of a meal, I make this version: stuffed and cheesy; it's super filling and satisfying. I view it as a more veg-centric take on white spinach lasagna. The spinach mixture is similar, but roasted squash takes the place of noodles. You can serve this as a main dish with a side salad, or as a side dish along with pretty much anything. Either way, I think everyone at your table will love it!

2 small butternut or honeynut squash

¾ cup milk of choice or heavy cream

¼ cup basil pesto

1 teaspoon dried sage

1 teaspoon dried thyme

8 ounces frozen chopped spinach, thawed and squeezed dried

4 garlic cloves, finely chopped or grated

¼ cup whole-milk ricotta cheese

¼ to ½ teaspoon crushed red pepper flakes

Fine pink Himalayan salt and freshly ground black pepper

1 cup shredded fontina cheese

Fresh thyme, for serving

Flaky sea salt, for serving

1. Preheat the oven to 425°F.

2. Using the tines of a fork, prick the squash skin all over. Microwave the squash for 2 to 3 minutes to soften slightly. Let cool slightly, then cut in half lengthwise and scoop out and discard the seeds.

3. Meanwhile, in a medium bowl, stir together the milk, pesto, sage, thyme, spinach, garlic, ricotta, and red pepper flakes. Season with salt and pepper. Stir in ¼ cup of the fontina cheese.

4. Place the squash in a baking dish and season the cut sides with salt and pepper. Scoop the spinach mixture into the squash cavities, dividing evenly. Sprinkle the remaining ¾ cup fontina cheese over the top.

5. Cover the dish with foil and bake for 20 minutes. Remove the foil and continue baking until the squash is tender and the cheese on top is golden, 15 to 20 minutes more. (The filling will seem a little soupy; this is okay.)

6. Let the squash sit for about 5 minutes, then top with fresh thyme and sprinkle with flaky salt before serving.

reuben melt

PREP 10 MINUTES
COOK 20 MINUTES
TOTAL 30 MINUTES
MAKES 2 SANDWICHES

A classic Reuben is probably my brother Creighton's favorite sandwich, and the best ones are all about slow-cooked corned beef, Russian dressing, and lots and lots of melty cheese between griddled rye bread. (He also says the best ones are in Cleveland.) Well, I wanted a version without the meat—controversial, I know, and Creigh is 100 percent looking at me in disgust. But hear me out. I cooked down cabbage with all the spices and flavorings usually used to make corned beef. After that, the dressing is really the key. You've had Russian dressing and you've had Thousand Island dressing (they're fraternal twins), but you haven't had Billion Island. It's healthier than both, and if you ask me, that much more special, too. The second layer of cabbage—sauerkraut—provides probiotics and vitamin K_2, both known to help strengthen the immune system and improve digestion. And cheese, well, that just makes everything taste good. However you like to Reuben, I know you'll enjoy every last bite of this classic with a spin.

3 tablespoons extra-virgin olive oil

4 cups finely shredded red cabbage or Tuscan kale

2 garlic cloves, finely chopped or grated

1 teaspoon mustard seeds

2 tablespoons low-sodium soy sauce or tamari

Freshly ground pepper

½ cup sauerkraut, drained

1 tablespoon salted butter, at room temperature

4 slices rye or Seeded Whole-Grain Bread (page 32)

Billion Island Dressing (recipe follows) or store-bought Thousand Island dressing

4 slices Swiss cheese

1. Heat 2 tablespoons of the olive oil in a large skillet over medium-high heat. When the oil shimmers, add the cabbage. Cook, stirring occasionally, until wilted, 3 to 5 minutes. Add the garlic and mustard seeds and cook until fragrant, about 1 minute. Stir in the soy sauce and season with pepper. Continue cooking until the water has evaporated and the cabbage is completely wilted, 8 to 10 minutes more. Transfer the cabbage to a small bowl and stir in the sauerkraut.

2. Spread one side of each slice of bread with butter. Spread the other side of each slice with the dressing, then layer 1 slice of cheese on each and top with the cabbage mixture, dividing evenly. Layer another slice of cheese over the cabbage. Top with the remaining slices of bread, buttered-side up.

3. Wipe out the skillet from the cabbage and add the remaining 1 tablespoon olive oil over medium-low heat. Add the sandwiches to the skillet and cook until the bread is golden and the cheese is a bit melty, 3 to 5 minutes per side.

4. Transfer the sandwiches to a cutting board, halve, and serve warm.

billion island dressing

MAKES ¼ CUP

½ cup avocado oil mayonnaise

1 tablespoon ketchup (I like Primal Kitchen)

Juice of ½ lemon

1 teaspoon hot sauce, plus more to taste (I like Frank's RedHot)

1 tablespoon chopped pickles, plus 1 tablespoon pickle juice

½ teaspoon paprika

½ teaspoon garlic powder

½ teaspoon onion powder

Fine pink Himalayan salt and freshly ground pepper

In a small bowl, stir together the mayonnaise, ketchup, lemon juice, hot sauce, pickles and pickle juice, paprika, garlic powder, and onion powder to combine. Taste and season with salt and pepper. Add more hot sauce to taste. Store refrigerated in an airtight container for up to 2 weeks.

sweet and spicy ginger soy noodles

(inspired by dan dan noodles)

PREP 20 MINUTES
COOK 20 MINUTES
TOTAL 40 MINUTES
SERVES 6

Dan dan noodles are a spicy Chinese dish made with a dark sauce usually comprised of preserved vegetables, chili oil, minced pork, and green onions. The pork is caramelized and crisped, and then placed over sauced wheat noodles. The noodles are served as is or in a spicy broth. I've enjoyed them both ways, but my favorite is the latter. This dish is warming and just beyond good. Plus—you know how I feel about a good saucy moment: the more, the better. I was inspired to create a vegetarian dish with flavors similar to the classic. This sauce is a simple mix of soy sauce, honey, rice vinegar, and peanut butter. I like to add balsamic vinegar for some more complexity. And since I can't get my hands on traditional thin wheat noodles in my local grocery stores either, I often use egg noodles instead. Take the noodles for a dip in the broth, then spoon on the sautéed mushrooms. I top each bowl with chili oil and add fresh green onions.

8 ounces Chinese-style egg noodles or rice noodles

½ cup plus 2 tablespoons low-sodium soy sauce or tamari

¼ cup raw honey

2 tablespoons rice vinegar

1 tablespoon balsamic vinegar

3 tablespoons creamy peanut butter

1 (2-inch) piece of ginger, grated

3 garlic cloves, grated

2½ cups low-sodium vegetable broth

2 cups chopped Tuscan kale

2 tablespoons sesame oil

4 cups shiitake or cremini mushrooms, finely chopped

2 shallots, chopped

⅓ cup roughly chopped raw peanuts

½ to 1 teaspoon crushed red pepper

Freshly ground black pepper

4 green onions, sliced, for serving

Chili Garlic Oil (recipe follows) or store-bought chili crisp, for serving

1. Bring a large pot of salted water to a boil over high heat. Cook the noodles according to the package directions. Drain.

2. In a medium bowl, combine ½ cup of the soy sauce with the honey, rice vinegar, balsamic vinegar, peanut butter, 1 tablespoon of the ginger, ½ teaspoon of the garlic, and ⅓ cup of water. Whisk well.

3. In the pot used to cook the noodles, combine the broth and half of the soy sauce mixture. Bring to a simmer over high heat, then stir in the kale to wilt, 2 minutes. Keep warm.

4. Heat the oil in a large skillet over medium-high heat. Add the mushrooms. Cook, stirring, until the mushrooms are light golden, 5 minutes. Add the shallots, the remaining ginger, and the remaining garlic. Cook, stirring, until the shallots are softened, 4 to 5 minutes. Add the remaining 2 tablespoons soy sauce, the peanuts, the red pepper flakes, and a large pinch of black pepper. Cook, stirring occasionally, until the mushrooms are glossy, 2 to 3 minutes. Transfer the mixture to a plate.

5. In the same skillet over medium heat, bring the remaining soy sauce mixture to a simmer. Add the noodles and toss until warmed, 2 minutes.

6. Ladle the broth into bowls. Add the noodles and spoon the mushroom mixture over the top. Garnish with the green onions and chili garlic oil.

chili garlic oil

MAKES ABOUT ½ CUP

½ cup sesame oil

6 garlic cloves, thinly sliced or smashed

2 tablespoons sesame seeds

1 to 2 tablespoons crushed red pepper

Fine pink Himalayan salt

Combine the sesame oil and garlic in a small saucepan over medium-low heat. Cook, stirring occasionally, until the garlic is lightly browned, about 5 minutes. Remove the pan from the heat. Add the sesame seeds. Stir in the red pepper flakes and salt to taste. Let cool. Store at room temperature in an airtight container for up to 2 weeks.

crispy feta cauliflower bowls

with goddess sauce

PREP 30 MINUTES

COOK 30 MINUTES

TOTAL 1 HOUR

SERVES 6

Greek cuisine provides some of my favorite inspiration for cooking at home. The fresh flavors and use of lemon, olive oil, and herbs are right up my alley . . . and I am a sucker for anything with feta cheese. When I'm craving the flavors of a gyro, often I'll riff on it and marinate chicken with traditional spices to serve with homemade pita. But sometimes I make these bowls instead, using roasted cauliflower and crispy feta in place of the meat. It's just as filling and I love the crunch you get from the charred pieces. The goddess sauce on top adds a vibrant, creamy element, but that fried feta . . . it is reason enough to mix up this bowl. It gets crispy on the outside and stays soft inside—totally delicious and addicting. If I were you, I'd double up on the recipe and save the leftovers for lunch tomorrow.

BOWLS

1 large head of cauliflower, cored and separated into florets (3 to 4 cups)

1 small red onion, chopped

2 garlic cloves, finely chopped

5 tablespoons extra-virgin olive oil

1 tablespoon balsamic vinegar

1 teaspoon smoked paprika

1 tablespoon chopped fresh oregano or 2 teaspoons dried

¼ to ½ teaspoon crushed red pepper

Fine pink Himalayan salt and freshly ground pepper

1 (15-ounce) can chickpeas, drained, rinsed, and patted dry

1 large egg

½ cup panko bread crumbs

1 (8-ounce) block feta cheese, patted dry and cut into ¼-inch slices

Goddess Sauce (recipe follows) or store-bought dressing

FOR SERVING

Shredded romaine lettuce or arugula

Sliced Persian cucumbers

Cherry tomatoes

1 tablespoon lemon zest

Pita chips or pita bread

1. Preheat the oven to 425°F.

2. On a rimmed baking sheet, combine the cauliflower, onion, garlic, 3 tablespoons of the olive oil, the vinegar, paprika, oregano, red pepper flakes, and a pinch each of salt and pepper. Toss well to coat evenly. Roast for 15 minutes. Add the chickpeas to the baking sheet and toss to combine. Continue roasting until the cauliflower is tender and lightly charred and the chickpeas are warmed through, about 5 minutes more.

3. Meanwhile, beat the egg in a shallow bowl. Place the bread crumbs in a separate shallow bowl. Dip the feta slices in the egg, turning to coat and allowing any excess to drip off. Dredge the feta through the bread crumbs, turning to coat and pressing gently to adhere.

4. Heat the remaining 2 tablespoons of olive oil in a large, high-sided skillet over medium heat. When the oil shimmers, add the feta in a single layer and cook until golden, 1 minute per side. Transfer to a plate.

5. To serve, put the lettuce into bowls. Top with the cauliflower and chickpea mixture, cucumbers, and tomatoes. Add the feta and sprinkle with the lemon zest. Drizzle on the goddess sauce. Serve with pita alongside.

goddess sauce

MAKES ABOUT 1¼ CUPS

1 avocado, halved and pitted

1 jalapeño, halved and seeded (optional)

¼ cup plain Greek yogurt

Juice of 1 lemon

1 cup fresh cilantro

½ cup fresh basil leaves

1 teaspoon ground cumin

Fine pink Himalayan salt

In a blender or food processor, combine the avocado, jalapeño (if using), yogurt, lemon juice, cilantro, basil, cumin, a pinch of salt, and 1 tablespoon of water. Blend until smooth and creamy, adding water 1 tablespoon at a time, as needed, to thin the sauce. Taste and add more salt as needed. Store refrigerated in an airtight container for up to 1 week.

oven-fried eggplant parm

PREP 30 MINUTES

COOK 1 HOUR 15 MINUTES

TOTAL 1 HOUR 45 MINUTES

SERVES 8

I will be the first to tell you eggplant has never excited me. That may or may not be why I don't cook it a whole lot. But like with most ingredients, what I've discovered is that when prepared properly, eggplant is indeed delicious. Case in point: this eggplant Parm. The cheese and bread crumbs are KEY here (though they'd make pretty much anything delicious, if we're being honest). While the eggplant is traditionally pan-fried in oil, I like to do mine in the oven—it's hands-off, less messy, and I personally think the taste comes through better. In fact, I think of this dish as a kind of lasagna bake, minus the noodles, plus pesto and insanely delicious cheesy oregano bread crumbs. The one thing to note is that it's important to salt the eggplant before cooking to draw out excess moisture, so be sure not to skip this step. And feel free to prep the dish in advance, all the way up to the final bake. You can keep it in the fridge for a day or two, then fire it off and add the bread crumbs before you serve it. This is eggplant to get excited about. Trust me.

4 pounds eggplant, cut lengthwise into ¼-inch-thick planks

Fine pink Himalayan salt and freshly ground black pepper

2 tablespoons extra-virgin olive oil, plus more for greasing and drizzling

¾ cup panko bread crumbs

½ cup grated Parmesan cheese, plus more for serving

2 tablespoons fresh oregano leaves

1 cup whole-milk ricotta cheese

¾ cup pesto

Crushed red pepper flakes

1 (24-ounce) jar marinara sauce (I like Rao's)

1 cup shredded low-moisture whole-milk mozzarella cheese

Fresh basil leaves, for serving

1. Preheat the oven to 400°F. Grease two baking sheets.

2. Place the eggplant on a clean kitchen towel and heavily salt each side. Let drain for 15 minutes.

3. Meanwhile, in a small bowl, stir together the olive oil, bread crumbs, ¼ cup of the Parmesan, and the oregano. Season with salt.

4. In a separate small bowl, stir together the ricotta, pesto, and a pinch of red pepper flakes.

5. Pat the eggplant dry. Drizzle both sides with olive oil and season with pepper. Arrange on the prepared baking sheets (it's okay if the slices overlap). Roast, rotating the pans halfway through, until the eggplant is soft and beginning to brown slightly, 25 to 30 minutes.

6. Spread ½ cup of the marinara sauce on the bottom of a 9 × 13-inch baking dish. Arrange a quarter of the eggplant over the sauce, overlapping as needed to create an even layer. Dollop with about ½ cup of the ricotta mixture and spread it out evenly. Spread on another ½ cup marinara sauce. Repeat the layers twice more. Add the remaining eggplant, the remaining marinara, the mozzarella, and top with the remaining ¼ cup Parmesan.

7. Cover with foil and bake until the mozzarella is melted and bubbly, about 30 minutes. Remove the foil, sprinkle the bread crumb mixture over the top, and continue baking until the topping is lightly golden and crisp, about 15 minutes more. Let stand for about 10 minutes.

8. Top with fresh basil leaves and serve.

balsamic stuffed mushrooms

with basil and orzo

PREP 25 MINUTES
COOK 22 MINUTES
TOTAL 50 MINUTES
SERVES 6

I first started making stuffed mushrooms when I'd cook the appetizers for my family's New Year's Eve gatherings. All of my cousins love mushrooms, and that serving platter was always one of the first ones cleared off. They were little baby bella mushrooms—sooo addictive. Then, even after the holiday, I started stuffing larger portabella mushrooms to have for dinner on busy nights. I figured why not make the holiday last a little longer, right? Now they're one of my favorite meals! I think of them kind of like a cheese pizza, but with extra mushrooms and cheese—and in this case, an awesome balsamic dressing. Don't be shocked if your family starts asking for these all the time!

6 large portabella mushrooms, stems removed

¼ cup plus 1 tablespoon extra-virgin olive oil

Fine pink Himalayan salt and freshly ground black pepper

3 tablespoons balsamic vinegar

1 tablespoon raw honey

1 shallot, chopped

2 garlic cloves, finely chopped or grated

1 tablespoon chopped fresh oregano

1 tablespoon chopped fresh basil

¼ to ½ teaspoon crushed red pepper flakes

8 ounces low-moisture mozzarella cheese, torn

¼ cup crumbled blue cheese (optional)

2 tablespoons roughly chopped toasted walnuts (see page 53)

2 cups orzo

1 cup fresh basil leaves

1. Preheat the oven to 400°F. Bring a large pot of salted water to a boil.

2. Rub the mushrooms all over with 1 tablespoon of the olive oil and season with salt and pepper. Place the mushrooms cap-side up on a baking sheet. Bake until slightly softened, about 10 minutes.

3. Meanwhile, make the dressing. In a medium bowl, whisk together the remaining ¼ cup olive oil, the vinegar, honey, shallots, garlic, oregano, basil, red pepper flakes, and a pinch each of salt and pepper.

4. Remove the mushrooms from the oven and carefully flip them over on the baking sheet. Spoon 1 tablespoon of the dressing over each mushroom. Stuff the mushrooms with the mozzarella and blue cheese (if using), dividing evenly. Top with the walnuts. Bake until the mushrooms are tender, about 10 minutes. Turn on the broiler and cook until the cheese is melted and bubbling, 2 to 3 minutes more.

5. Meanwhile, add the orzo to the boiling water. Cook according to package directions until al dente. Drain the orzo, add 3 tablespoons of the dressing, and toss to coat.

6. To serve, spoon the orzo onto plates, then add the mushrooms. Top each plate with fresh basil and serve with any additional dressing alongside.

green curry
with sesame and broccoli

PREP 10 MINUTES
COOK 20 MINUTES
TOTAL 30 MINUTES
SERVES 4

When I was growing up, my mom always made a serious effort to have the best-stocked pantry around. She had backups for her backups, and she never ran out of anything. (Whenever inventory on her Nestlé Toll House chocolate chips dipped below four bags, she ran out to Sam's Club to restock. She always had her priorities in order.) This particular trait definitely rubbed off on me. I'm not as good at it as she is, but I try. And toward the end of the week, when my fresh groceries are dwindling, I love to make a pantry recipe. This green curry is a favorite. It uses a mix of those pantry staples, along with broccoli and a handful of fresh herbs. It's good with whatever vegetable you've got on hand—cauliflower, broccoli, zucchini, sweet potatoes, anything goes. And if you want to add a protein, you can toss in some shrimp or cubed chicken and simmer it along with the broccoli. Either way, it's flexible, easy, and always delicious.

2 tablespoons coconut oil

1 medium yellow onion, chopped

4 garlic cloves, finely chopped or grated

1 (1-inch) piece of fresh ginger, peeled and grated

3 tablespoons sesame seeds

3 tablespoons roasted, salted peanuts

3 tablespoons Thai green curry paste

1 (13.5-ounce) can full-fat coconut milk

1 tablespoon low-sodium soy sauce or tamari

1 tablespoon fish sauce (optional)

2 teaspoons raw honey

3 cups broccoli florets (from 2 medium heads)

Zest and juice of 1 lime

FOR SERVING

Seasoned Coconut Rice (page 227) or steamed rice

¼ cup fresh cilantro, roughly chopped (optional)

¼ cup fresh Thai basil, roughly chopped

Sliced jalapeño

Sliced green onion (optional)

Lime wedges

1. Melt the coconut oil in a large skillet over high heat. Add the onion and cook, stirring occasionally, until soft, about 5 minutes. Add the garlic, ginger, sesame seeds, and peanuts and cook, stirring constantly, until the seeds are golden and toasted, 4 to 5 minutes. Stir in the curry paste and cook until fragrant, about 2 minutes more.

2. Reduce the heat to medium. Stir in ⅓ cup of water and the coconut milk, soy sauce, fish sauce (if using), and honey. Add the broccoli. Bring to a simmer and cook until the sauce thickens slightly and the broccoli is tender, 8 to 10 minutes. Remove the skillet from the heat and stir in the lime zest and juice.

3. Spoon the curry over bowls of rice. Top with the cilantro (if using), Thai basil, jalapeño, and green onion (if using), and serve the lime wedges alongside for squeezing.

spice-roasted cauliflower
with burrata and herbs

PREP 15 MINUTES
COOK 1 HOUR 30 MINUTES
TOTAL 1 HOUR 45 MINUTES
SERVES 4

Whether covered in buffalo sauce or roasted with yummy seasoning, I have found that even the pickiest of eaters enjoy a charred piece of cauliflower—and even request it on a regular basis. I love to core it and cut it into florets, but to try something a little more impressive-looking, I left it whole and roasted it just like that! It's different, but also the same—and feels so much more like a meal you could serve your family for dinner, or even guests at a party. I throw it in a big Dutch oven just like you would a traditional roast. To be honest, I might think it's even more delicious than a meaty dish. You'll have to try it and see!

1 large head of cauliflower, leaves trimmed

2 teaspoons smoked paprika

2 teaspoons chili powder

1 teaspoon ground cumin

1 teaspoon garlic powder

1 teaspoon onion powder

¼ to ½ teaspoon cayenne pepper

¼ to ½ teaspoon crushed red pepper flakes

Fine pink Himalayan salt and freshly ground black pepper

⅓ cup plus 2 tablespoons extra-virgin olive oil

¼ cup sherry

3 tablespoons fresh lemon juice

1 cup chopped mixed herbs, such as basil, dill, and/or cilantro

¼ cup mixed toasted nuts or seeds, chopped (see page 53)

1 garlic clove, finely chopped or grated

8 ounces burrata cheese, at room temperature

1. Preheat the oven to 375°F.

2. Cut away and discard the cauliflower stalk so the cauliflower can sit flat on its underside, then cut a cross into the base. Place the cauliflower in a large Dutch oven.

3. In a small bowl, stir together the paprika, chili powder, cumin, garlic powder, onion powder, cayenne, red pepper flakes, and a pinch each of salt and pepper. Rub the spice mix all over the cauliflower. Drizzle the cauliflower with ⅓ cup of the olive oil, the sherry, and the lemon juice. Pour ¼ cup water into the bottom of the pot.

4. Cover the cauliflower and bake for 1 hour or until fork tender. Remove the lid and bake for another 25 to 30 minutes, until lightly charred on top.

5. Meanwhile, in a small bowl, stir together the herbs, nuts, garlic, remaining 2 tablespoons olive oil, and a pinch each of red pepper flakes and salt.

6. To serve, arrange the burrata on a serving platter. Place the blackened cauliflower alongside. Spoon the herb mixture all over the cauliflower and cheese.

sweet potato nachos

with the works

PREP 15 MINUTES

COOK 45 MINUTES

TOTAL 1 HOUR

SERVES 6

When I was growing up, my dad would often make nachos on the weekends, especially in the fall, because nachos and football go hand in hand. We'd go for a family hike in the Cleveland metro parks—the weather was usually cold and rainy, but his nachos were something to look forward to afterward. He piled them high with cheddar cheese and, um, more cheddar cheese. I'm sure there were other toppings, too, but all I remember is A LOT of cheese. Well, I love his nachos, but I also love reinventing an old favorite. So what I did here was replace the tortilla chips with roasted sweet potato slices. They're definitely different but delicious and much healthier than fried tortilla chips. The potatoes are topped with, yes, cheese, but lots of other bright favorites, plus a homemade spicy jalapeño ranch to finish it all off. Serve these up right out of the pan so everyone can dig in and go to town. They're fun for family dinner, game night with friends, or watching football, of course!

2 pounds sweet potatoes (4 to 5 sweet potatoes), cut lengthwise into wedges

2 tablespoons extra-virgin olive oil

Fine pink Himalayan salt

2 teaspoons onion powder

2 teaspoons smoked paprika

1 to 2 teaspoons chipotle chile powder

1 teaspoon ground cumin

1 teaspoon garlic powder

½ teaspoon dried oregano

¼ teaspoon crushed red pepper flakes

1 (15.5-ounce) can black beans, drained and rinsed

¾ cup shredded sharp cheddar cheese

½ cup shredded pepper Jack cheese

1 large avocado

Juice of 1 lime

2 tablespoons chopped fresh cilantro, plus more for serving

FOR SERVING

Quick Greek Yogurt Ranch (page 113) or store-bought ranch dressing (optional)

Sliced green onion (optional)

Crumbled feta cheese (optional)

1. Preheat the oven to 425°F.

2. On a baking sheet or in a cast-iron skillet, toss together the sweet potatoes and 1 tablespoon of the olive oil. Season with salt. Arrange the sweet potatoes in a single layer, being sure not to crowd the baking sheet. Bake until the potatoes are slightly softened, 15 to 20 minutes.

3. Meanwhile, in a small bowl, stir together the remaining 1 tablespoon olive oil with the onion powder, paprika, chipotle powder, cumin, garlic powder, oregano, and red pepper flakes. Drizzle the spice mix over the potatoes and toss to coat. Continue baking until the sweet potatoes are crisp on the outside and tender, 15 to 20 minutes. Remove the baking sheet from the oven, leaving the oven on.

4. Scatter the black beans over the sweet potatoes, then cover with the shredded cheeses. Return the baking sheet to the oven and bake until the cheese is melted and bubbly, 5 to 10 minutes.

5. In a small bowl, combine the avocado, lime juice, and cilantro. Mix well, mashing up the avocado. Taste and add salt as desired. Top the nachos with the avocado mixture. Top with the dressing, green onion, and crumbled feta as desired. Sprinkle with more cilantro before serving.

bbq grilled zucchini

with rice and avocado herb salad

PREP 15 MINUTES
COOK 10 MINUTES
TOTAL 25 MINUTES
SERVES 4

This combination sounds weird, I know, but hear me out because this is such a delicious recipe. First off, everyone loves BBQ chicken, especially my mom. She prefers it very simply served over—yup, you guessed it—steamed rice. It's a summer staple recipe anytime my dad is grilling. But my dad isn't so into it. He loves BBQ sauce, but not with chicken, for whatever reason. So I made this version for him—with rice for my mom—and I threw in a few extras. By extras I mean a damn good homemade sweet and spicy sauce and an insanely delicious avocado salad. The sauce works on any vegetable you want to grill up. Portobello mushrooms would be great, or in the chillier months, toss it with cauliflower that you then roast in the oven. Since the avocado in the salad will brown over time, I recommend mixing the salad together just before you grill the squash so it doesn't lose any color.

NOTE
Don't skip crosshatching the zucchini and letting it sit with the salt for a few minutes. This easy step draws out all the excess moisture the zucchini holds, which will make for a more flavorful (less watery!) dish.

ZUCCHINI

- 4 zucchini or yellow summer squash, halved
- 1 teaspoon fine pink Himalayan salt
- ½ cup ketchup (I like Primal Kitchen)
- 2 tablespoons raw honey or pure maple syrup
- 1 tablespoon apple cider vinegar
- 1 tablespoon low-sodium soy sauce or tamari
- 2 teaspoons smoked paprika
- 1 teaspoon chili powder
- ½ teaspoon garlic powder
- ½ teaspoon onion powder
- ½ teaspoon ground cayenne pepper
- Freshly ground black pepper
- Extra-virgin olive oil, for brushing
- 1 cup steamed white or brown rice, for serving

SALAD

- ¼ cup fresh lime juice
- 3 tablespoons extra-virgin olive oil
- 2 teaspoons raw honey or pure maple syrup
- 1 jalapeño, seeded, if desired, and chopped
- 1 small shallot, thinly sliced
- Fine pink Himalayan salt
- 4 large avocados, quartered
- ½ cup chopped fresh herbs, such as cilantro, parsley, basil, or dill, plus more for serving
- ½ cup toasted pepitas (see Note on page 53)

- Flaky sea salt and freshly ground pepper

1. Heat a grill to medium-high or a grill pan or large cast-iron skillet over medium-high heat.

2. **MAKE THE ZUCCHINI.** Halve each zucchini lengthwise. Using a paring knife, score the zucchini flesh in a crosshatch pattern (see Note). Sprinkle ½ teaspoon of the salt over the cut sides of the zucchini, dividing evenly. Let sit for 10 minutes to draw out the excess moisture, then pat dry with a clean kitchen towel.

3. **MEANWHILE, MAKE THE SALAD.** In a large bowl, stir together the lime juice, olive oil, honey, jalapeño, shallot, and a pinch of salt. Add the avocado, herbs, and pepitas. Gently fold to combine.

4. In a small bowl, whisk together the ketchup, honey, vinegar, soy sauce, paprika, chili powder, garlic powder, onion powder, cayenne, the remaining ½ teaspoon salt, and pepper.

5. Brush the zucchini all over with olive oil. Then brush the cut sides with the BBQ sauce. Working in batches as needed, grill the zucchini, cut-side down, until they begin to char around the edges, about 3 minutes, then flip and grill for another 3 minutes. Brush the cut sides with more BBQ sauce, then flip again and grill until tender and lightly charred, 1 to 2 minutes more.

6. Transfer the grilled zucchini to a serving platter. Drizzle the remaining BBQ sauce over the tops. Spoon the avocado salad on the side. Sprinkle everything with flaky sea salt and pepper to taste and fresh herbs. Serve the rice alongside.

spicy tomato basil zucchini involtini

PREP 45 MINUTES

COOK 35 MINUTES

TOTAL 1 HOUR AND 20 MINUTES

SERVES 6

I've always enjoyed zucchini, but I know it can seem a bit boring—especially during the summer when you have sooo much on hand. But there's a ton of fun stuff you can do with it. Enter this zucchini involtini. In Italian tradition, involtini is made using sliced and grilled eggplant, but I love it with my favorite summer veg instead. Basically, it's cheesy zucchini baked in tomato sauce, and it is DELICIOUS. Think stuffed pasta minus the pasta and plus lots of great vegetables. It's perfection—and sure to become a new favorite. You can prepare this dish twelve hours in advance, completing all the steps up until the final bake. Let it cool, then store it in the fridge until you're ready to cook and serve. If any excess water collects on the surface of the sauce, drain it off or blot with a paper towel before baking.

NOTE ————

If your zucchini are on the smaller side, your strips might be a bit narrow. Lay two side by side lengthwise, overlapping slightly. Fill and roll them as one piece.

¼ cup extra-virgin olive oil, plus more for greasing

1 medium yellow onion, chopped

2 garlic cloves, finely chopped or grated

2 tablespoons fresh thyme leaves, plus more for serving, or 2 teaspoons dried

1 tablespoon dried basil

1 tablespoon dried oregano

1 to 2 teaspoons fennel seeds

1 teaspoon smoked paprika

Pinch of crushed red pepper flakes

Fine pink Himalayan salt and freshly ground black pepper

2 tablespoons tomato paste

1 red bell pepper, seeded and chopped

1 (14-ounce) can crushed tomatoes or 2 cups tomato sauce

2 large zucchini or yellow summer squash

1 cup whole-milk ricotta cheese

½ cup shredded fontina cheese

½ cup fresh basil leaves, roughly chopped, plus more for serving

8 ounces low-moisture whole-milk mozzarella, torn

1. Preheat the oven to 425°F. Lightly grease a 9 × 13-inch baking dish.

2. Heat the olive oil in a large skillet over medium heat. When the oil shimmers, add the onion and cook, stirring occasionally, until soft and translucent, about 5 minutes. Add the garlic, thyme, basil, oregano, fennel, paprika, and a pinch each of red pepper flakes, salt, and pepper. Cook until very fragrant, another 5 minutes. Stir in the tomato paste to combine. Reduce the heat to low, then add the bell pepper and tomatoes. Simmer until the sauce thickens slightly, about 10 minutes. Taste and add salt and pepper as needed.

3. Meanwhile, using a mandoline or vegetable peeler, cut the zucchini into ¼-inch-thick strips and lay them flat on clean kitchen towels. You should have around 30 strips. Sprinkle the zucchini with salt.

4. In a medium bowl, combine the ricotta, fontina, and basil.

5. Spoon about ¾ cup of the tomato sauce into the bottom of the prepared baking dish. Working with 1 zucchini strip at a time, spoon about 1 tablespoon of the ricotta mixture onto the center of one of the ends. Roll the strip into a coil and place seam-side down in the baking dish. Repeat with the remaining zucchini. Spoon the remaining tomato sauce over the zucchini. Scatter the mozzarella over the top.

6. Bake until the mozzarella is melted and lightly browned on top, 15 to 20 minutes. Remove the baking dish from the oven and let cool for 5 minutes.

7. Serve hot, topped with fresh basil and thyme.

cheesy tortilla skillet

PREP 15 MINUTES
COOK 35 MINUTES
TOTAL 50 MINUTES
SERVES 6

My sister-in-law Lyndsie is obsessed with tortilla soup. I swear, every winter she asks me to create a new recipe for it. Well, I already have (a delicious) one on HBH, but this dish is my compromise. It is basically the toppings of tortilla soup in a skillet, lots and lots of vegetables, and just a touch of cheese. Lynds is a BIG fan of this one! I love to use Siete Foods tortilla chips for this dish. They come in really delicious flavors like jalapeño lime . . . and nacho cheese, which I swear taste just like the Doritos of my childhood. Use any flavor you love!

2 tablespoons extra-virgin olive oil

1 medium yellow onion, chopped

2 poblano peppers, seeded and chopped

2 bell peppers, seeded and chopped

2 teaspoons chipotle chile powder

2 teaspoons smoked paprika

1 teaspoon ground cumin

1 teaspoon dried oregano

Fine pink Himalayan or sea salt and freshly ground black pepper

4 garlic cloves, finely chopped or grated

1¼ cups red enchilada sauce

1 cup cooked rice

1 (15.5-ounce) can black beans, drained and rinsed

½ cup fresh cilantro, chopped, plus more for serving

Juice of 1 lime

1½ cups shredded Mexican cheese blend

2 cups tortilla chips (I like Siete Foods, any flavor)

Sliced avocado, for serving

Plain Greek yogurt, for serving

1.   Preheat the oven to 425°F.

2.   Heat the olive oil in a large oven-safe skillet over medium heat. When the oil shimmers, add the onion, poblanos, bell peppers, chipotle chile powder, paprika, cumin, oregano, and a pinch each of salt and pepper. Cook, stirring occasionally, until very fragrant, 8 to 10 minutes. Add the garlic and cook until fragrant, 1 minute more.

3.   Stir in the enchilada sauce, rice, beans, cilantro, and lime juice. Sprinkle ½ cup of the cheese over the rice. Add the tortilla chips on top, gently pressing them into the cheese. Sprinkle the remaining 1 cup cheese over top. Bake until the cheese is melted, about 10 minutes.

4.   Serve family style topped with more cilantro, sliced avocado, and yogurt.

chicken

lemon harissa chicken

with olives

PREP 15 MINUTES

COOK 45 MINUTES

TOTAL 1 HOUR

SERVES 6

I keep my pantry stocked at all times with harissa, a spicy Moroccan roasted red pepper sauce. Having it on hand allows me to create super-quick and tasty dishes at the last minute—and this chicken is one of them. Inspired by additional flavors of Moroccan cooking, like lemon and olives, it's spicy, sweet, and herby . . . all of my favorites! Plus, this dinner gets thrown together on a sheet pan, so it's pretty darn easy. As soon as the pan comes out of the oven, I serve it up with a simple garlicky yogurt sauce that cuts through the heat.

1½ pounds boneless, skinless chicken breasts or thighs

4 tablespoons plus ¼ cup extra-virgin olive oil

1 medium lemon

2 tablespoons harissa paste

1 teaspoon raw honey

1 teaspoon ground cumin

Fine pink Himalayan salt and freshly ground pepper

½ cup plain Greek yogurt

1 garlic clove, finely chopped or grated

½ cup pitted green olives, preferably Castelvetrano, torn

2 tablespoons chopped salted pistachios

1 pound baby potatoes, cut into 1-inch pieces

1 medium yellow onion, halved and sliced

Mixed tender herbs, such as mint, parsley, and cilantro, for serving

1. Preheat the oven to 425°F.

2. In a medium bowl, combine the chicken, 2 tablespoons of the olive oil, the zest of the lemon, juice of ½ lemon (reserve the rind), harissa, honey, cumin, and a large pinch of salt. Mix to combine well. Let marinate for at least 15 minutes or overnight.

3. Meanwhile, in a small bowl, stir together the juice of the remaining ½ lemon (reserve the rind), the yogurt, the garlic, and a pinch of salt. In a separate small bowl, stir together the olives, pistachios, and ¼ cup of the olive oil.

4. On a rimmed baking sheet, combine the potatoes and the remaining 2 tablespoons olive oil. Season with salt and pepper. Toss to coat well. Add the juiced lemon halves. Roast until the potatoes are fork-tender, 20 minutes.

5. Remove the baking sheet from the oven and nestle the chicken in the potatoes. Arrange the onions around the chicken in an even layer. Roast until the chicken is cooked through, 20 to 25 minutes more.

6. Divide the chicken, potatoes, and onions among plates. Spoon the yogurt mixture onto the chicken and top with the olive mixture. Top with a handful of fresh herbs before serving.

crispy carnitas taquitos

PREP 15 MINUTES
COOK SEE SPECIFIC DEVICE METHOD
SERVES 6

I grew up eating tacos once or twice a week. My brothers and I loved them as kids and still do to this day. But you know? Sometimes it's nice to switch things up, do something familiar just a little differently. Enter these crispy baked taquitos. The first time I made taquitos was back in the day—October 2012, to be exact. It was the first year of HBH and my photos were pretty horrific, but look how far we have come! These taquitos are stuffed with pork in the form of carnitas, which takes a little bit of time but is fairly easy to throw together. The slow-cooked, tender pork is worth the wait. A final broil in the oven crisps some of the meat, and then you just shred it and roll it up with some cheese in a tortilla. As they bake, the tortillas get crunchy. Taquitos are often fried, but it's nice not to deal with the mess of frying. Honestly, these might even be better than if they were fried! Serve them up however you like: you can go simple with some lettuce, avocado, limes, and a dollop of yogurt (or sour cream), or go all out with your sauces (my favorite is the Creamy Poblano Sauce on page 231).

6 garlic cloves, finely chopped

¼ cup light brown sugar

1 tablespoon chipotle chile powder

2 teaspoons smoked paprika

1 teaspoon ground cumin

1 teaspoon dried oregano

Fine pink Himalayan salt

3 to 4 pounds bone-in pork shoulder, trimmed

1 large yellow onion, chopped

1 cinnamon stick

2 oranges, halved

2 limes

16 to 20 (6-inch) corn tortillas

Extra-virgin olive oil

2 cups shredded Mexican cheese

FOR SERVING

Guacamole

Pico de gallo

Quick-Pickled Red Onions (page 221) or store-bought pickled onions

Sliced jalapeños

Shredded lettuce

Orange and lime wedges

SLOW COOKER

COOK 5 HOURS 20 MINUTES TO 10 HOURS 20 MINUTES

1.   In a small bowl, combine the garlic, brown sugar, chipotle powder, paprika, cumin, oregano, and a large pinch of salt. Place the pork in the slow cooker pot and rub the seasoning mixture into the meat. Add the onion and cinnamon stick to the pot. Squeeze in the juice of the oranges and add the halves to the slow cooker. Pour ½ cup of water around the meat. Cover and cook on low for 8 to 10 hours or on high for 5 to 6 hours.

2.   Turn on the broiler. Using tongs, transfer the meat to a baking sheet. Let the meat cool slightly, then shred using two forks. Juice the limes over the shredded meat. Broil until the pork becomes crispy on top, about 10 minutes.

3.   Preheat the oven to 450°F. Warm the tortillas in the microwave until pliable, 30 seconds to 1 minute. Place the tortillas on a baking sheet and rub with olive oil. Spoon 2 tablespoons of the carnitas down the center of each tortilla. Sprinkle about 2 tablespoons of cheese on each tortilla, roll them up and turn them seam-side down. Bake for 5 to 8 minutes. Flip and bake until the tortillas are crisp, 5 minutes more.

4.   Serve the taquitos warm with guacamole, pico de gallo, pickled red onions, jalapeños, lettuce, and citrus wedges on the side.

OVEN

COOK 3 HOURS 50 MINUTES TO 4 HOURS 20 MINUTES

1.   Preheat the oven to 325°F. In a small bowl, combine the garlic, brown sugar, chipotle powder, paprika, cumin, oregano, and a large pinch of salt. Place the pork in a Dutch oven and rub the seasoning mixture into the meat. Add the onion and cinnamon stick. Squeeze in the juice of the oranges and add the halves. Pour in 1 cup of water. Cover and cook until the meat is falling off the bones, 3½ to 4 hours.

2.   Finish as directed for the slow cooker.

saucy, spicy, creamy
cashew butter chicken

PREP 10 MINUTES

COOK 25 MINUTES

TOTAL 35 MINUTES

SERVES 6

Cashew chicken curry is an Indian restaurant-style dish very similar to butter chicken, but, of course, made with cashews, too. Most of the time, they are toasted and tossed in with the chicken and sauce. Inspired by that dish, I cooked up a recipe that takes all of those notes but also includes cashew butter. It not only brings a deep flavor to the sauce but also makes it extra creamy. It's a small addition, but one that I think really sets this dish apart. Serve it with steamed rice and fresh naan (always) for a quick dinner that will satisfy everyone in the family.

¼ cup plain Greek yogurt

6 garlic cloves, finely chopped or grated

2 tablespoons freshly grated ginger

1 tablespoon plus 2 teaspoons garam masala

1 to 2 teaspoons ground cayenne pepper

1 teaspoon fine pink Himalayan salt, plus more as needed

2 pounds boneless, skinless chicken breasts or thighs, cut into bite-size pieces

2 tablespoons extra-virgin olive oil

2 tablespoons ghee or salted butter

3 medium shallots, finely chopped or grated

1 teaspoon ground cumin

½ teaspoon ground turmeric

½ teaspoon ground cinnamon

½ teaspoon ground cardamom

Freshly ground black pepper

2 tablespoons tomato paste

1 (13.5-ounce) can full-fat coconut milk

⅓ cup creamy cashew butter

½ cup fresh cilantro, roughly chopped, plus more for serving

½ cup toasted cashews (see Note on page 53)

Steamed rice and/or naan, for serving

1.   In a large bowl or plastic zip-top bag, combine the yogurt, half of the garlic, 1 tablespoon of the ginger, 2 teaspoons of the garam masala, ½ teaspoon of the cayenne, and the salt. Add the chicken and toss to coat. Let sit for 5 minutes.

2.   Heat the olive oil in a large skillet over medium-high heat. When the oil shimmers, add the chicken and sear until lightly browned, about 2 minutes per side. Add 1 tablespoon of the ghee, and when it is melted, turn the chicken to coat. Transfer the chicken to a plate.

3.   To the same skillet over medium-high heat, add the shallots. Cook, stirring occasionally, until soft, about 5 minutes. Add the remaining 1 tablespoon ghee, the remaining garlic, 1 tablespoon ginger, 1 tablespoon garam masala, and ½ teaspoon cayenne pepper (plus more to taste) and the cumin, turmeric, cinnamon, and cardamom. Season with salt and pepper. Stir to combine. Cook until very fragrant, about 5 minutes. Add the tomato paste and continue to cook, stirring to incorporate, until the paste turns dark red, 2 minutes more.

4.   Reduce the heat to low. Add ¼ cup of water, the coconut milk, and the cashew butter. Stir to combine, scraping up the browned bits from the bottom of the pan. Bring the sauce to a simmer and cook until it thickens slightly, about 5 minutes. Stir in the chicken and any collected juices. Cook, stirring occasionally, until the sauce thickens slightly and the chicken is cooked through, 5 to 7 minutes more. Remove the skillet from the heat and stir in the cilantro. Season with salt and pepper.

5.   Scatter the cashews and more cilantro over the chicken and sauce. Serve family style with rice and naan alongside.

nonnie's sticky apricot chicken

PREP 10 MINUTES
COOK 30 MINUTES
TOTAL 40 MINUTES
SERVES 4

My nonnie loved a good dinner party and was a pro at effortlessly entertaining a crowd. I can't say she enjoyed spending much time in the kitchen cooking, but she could conjure up a delicious dinner with minimal effort. One of her tricks was using a mix of store-bought and homemade ingredients, perhaps leaning heavily on the former, but her food always tasted GOOD. Nonnie got this recipe for apricot chicken from her neighbor in Florida. She served it the night we arrived to visit her for Easter one year—she called it "First Night Apricot Chicken." Apparently, she made it the first night any of her many guests arrived. (When you spend the winters in Florida, you get a lot of visitors.) Well, we devoured it. This recipe is really all about the sauce, and it's a combo I never would have dreamed up. The three main ingredients sound odd together but are magic. They create a sticky, sweet, and savory chicken that will satisfy all your cravings. I serve mine with roasted broccoli and rice, but Nonnie often did mashed potatoes and asparagus. Take your pick! Either way, you'll end up with a stress-free dinner that's full of love.

¾ cup high-quality apricot preserves or jam (I like Bonne Maman)

1 cup Billion Island Dressing (page 149) or store-bought Thousand Island or Russian dressing

1 tablespoon balsamic vinegar

½ to 1 teaspoon crushed red pepper flakes

4 boneless, skinless chicken thighs or breasts (1½ to 2 pounds)

1 large head of broccoli, cut into florets

Steamed rice or cauliflower rice, for serving

Fresh herbs, such as basil, parsley, and/or cilantro, for serving

1. Preheat the oven to 400°F.

2. In a cast-iron skillet or 9 × 13-inch baking dish, stir together the apricot preserves, dressing, vinegar, and red pepper flakes. Add the chicken and turn to coat. Arrange the broccoli around the chicken. Bake until the chicken is cooked through and the sauce is bubbling, 25 to 30 minutes.

3. Serve the chicken, broccoli, and sauce over steamed rice and top with the fresh herbs.

spicy pretzel chicken fingers

with hot honey

PREP 20 MINUTES

COOK 20 MINUTES

TOTAL 40 MINUTES

SERVES 4

According to all the men in my life, no meal is complete without meat. And if it's spicy? Even better. Back in the day, when I was still cooking for my family every night, whenever my brother Creighton came to town for a visit I knew I had to make him something GOOD. On one occasion, I tried extra-spicy chicken fingers inspired by the famous Nashville hot chicken. To this day, he requests them whenever he is back in Colorado. Here, I have tweaked my earlier recipe to make it not only easier but healthier, too. There are two secrets to its tastiness: pretzels in the chicken coating and "oven frying." The chicken is a touch crunchy and perfectly salted, but you don't have any of the frying oil taste that usually comes along with real-deal fried chicken. The sauce is spicy, sweet, and buttery, and the real heart and soul of the recipe. You can't skip it—and if you love a lot of sauce, add a creamy ranch and honey mustard for a little triple dip . . . I always do. Serve these up with oven-baked French fries and a BIG side salad to add lots of color to your dinner. And feel free to use gluten-free pretzels!

CHICKEN FINGERS

4 cups salted pretzel twists

1 teaspoon garlic powder

1 teaspoon onion powder

½ teaspoon smoked paprika

Freshly ground black pepper

2 large eggs

2 tablespoons hot sauce (I like Frank's RedHot)

2 pounds boneless chicken tenders

Extra-virgin olive oil, for brushing or misting

HOT HONEY

¼ cup raw honey

3 tablespoons salted butter

1 teaspoon ground cayenne pepper, plus more as needed

½ teaspoon chili powder

½ teaspoon smoked paprika

FOR SERVING

Flaky sea salt

Quick Greek Yogurt Ranch (page 113) or store-bought ranch dressing (optional)

Spicy Honey Mustard Sauce (page 228) or store-bought honey mustard (optional)

1. Preheat the oven to 425°F. Line a baking sheet with parchment paper.

2. **MAKE THE CHICKEN FINGERS.** In a food processor, combine the pretzels, garlic powder, onion powder, paprika, and a pinch of pepper. Pulse a few times to break up the pretzels into crumbs with a few larger pieces remaining (see Note). Transfer the mixture to a shallow bowl.

3. In a separate shallow bowl, whisk together the eggs and hot sauce. Add the chicken to the egg mixture, turning to coat well. Working with one piece at a time, remove the chicken, allowing any excess egg mixture to drip off. Dredge through the pretzel mixture, pressing to adhere. Place the coated chicken on the prepared baking sheet, avoiding crowding (if you're short on space, use two baking sheets). Lightly brush or mist the chicken with oil.

4. Bake for 15 minutes, then flip the chicken and continue baking until the chicken is cooked through and the coating is crisp, 5 to 7 minutes more.

5. **MEANWHILE, MAKE THE HOT HONEY.** In a small saucepan over medium heat, combine the honey, butter, cayenne, chili powder, and paprika. Cook, stirring, until the butter is melted and the sauce is warmed through, 2 to 3 minutes. Taste and add more cayenne as desired.

6. Sprinkle the chicken fingers with the flaky salt. Serve with the hot honey sauce alongside for dipping, as well as ranch and honey mustard, if desired.

NOTE

No worries if you don't have a food processor. You can break up the pretzels with a rolling pin or even by hand! Just be sure to leave a few bigger pieces so they stick well to the chicken. Mix them up with the spices directly in the shallow bowl.

lemon rosemary chicken

with forty garlic cloves

PREP 15 MINUTES
COOK SEE SPECIFIC DEVICE METHOD
SERVES 4

Wait, what? Yes! This recipe has forty cloves of garlic in it. As much as I love the flavor garlic adds, I sometimes find it can overpower a dish, plus you have to deal with my dad's biggest pet peeve: garlic breath. But there's no worry of either of those things here. You can put your toothbrush away—you don't actually EAT the forty cloves here. Instead, they add ample flavor to this one-and-done roast chicken. Smashing the cloves and cooking them in the sauce allows the bite of the garlic flavor to mellow. You end up with just the right amount that only helps highlight the lemon and rosemary. This chicken is especially delicious served with creamy mashed potatoes, or even some simple steamed rice. Bread on the side is great for mopping up that extra sauce, too.

4 tablespoons extra-virgin olive oil, plus more for greasing

2 tablespoons chopped fresh rosemary or 1 tablespoon dried

Zest and juice of 1 lemon

2 pounds bone-in, skin-on chicken thighs, legs, and/or breasts

Fine pink Himalayan salt and freshly ground black pepper

2 (14-ounce) cans white beans, such as cannellini, drained and rinsed

30 to 40 garlic cloves (from about 3 heads), skin-on, lightly smashed

1 cup dry white wine, such as pinot grigio or Sauvignon Blanc

2 tablespoons cognac

1 tablespoon Dijon mustard

Crushed red pepper flakes

2 tablespoons heavy cream or full-fat coconut milk

¼ cup chopped fresh tender herbs, such as thyme, basil, and/or parsley

SLOW COOKER

COOK 3 TO 7 HOURS

1.   In a large bowl, stir together 2 tablespoons of the olive oil, the rosemary, and the lemon zest. Add the chicken and turn to coat well. Season with salt and pepper.

2.   In the slow cooker pot, combine the beans, garlic, wine, cognac, and mustard. Season with salt, pepper, and red pepper flakes. Nestle the chicken on top of the beans, skin-side up. Cover and cook on low for 6 to 7 hours or on high for 3 to 4 hours.

3.   Turn the broiler to high. Grease a baking sheet.

4.   Carefully transfer the chicken to the prepared baking sheet, placing it skin-side up. Drizzle the remaining 2 tablespoons olive oil over the chicken. Broil, rotating the baking sheet once, until the chicken skin is golden and crisp, 2 to 4 minutes. Watch closely; the broiler works fast.

5.   Stir the lemon juice and cream into the saucy beans. Serve the beans and chicken together topped with the herbs and lots of black pepper.

PRESSURE COOKER

COOK 10 MINUTES, PLUS ADDITIONAL TIME TO COME TO PRESSURE

1.   In a large bowl, stir together 2 tablespoons of the olive oil, the rosemary, and the lemon zest. Add the chicken and turn to coat well. Season with salt and pepper.

2.   In the pressure cooker pot, combine the beans, garlic, wine, cognac, and mustard. Season with salt, pepper, and red pepper flakes. Nestle the chicken on top of the beans, skin-side up. Lock the lid in place and cook on high pressure for 8 minutes. Quick or natural release, then open when the pressure subsides.

3.   Finish as directed for the slow cooker.

OVEN

COOK 35 MINUTES

1.   Preheat the oven to 425°F.

2.   In a large bowl, stir together 2 tablespoons of the olive oil, the rosemary, and the lemon zest. Add the chicken and turn to coat well. Season with salt and pepper.

3.   In a large oven-safe braiser or high-sided skillet over high heat, cook the chicken skin-side down, without moving, until the skin is golden and releases easily from the pan, 4 to 5 minutes. Transfer the chicken to a plate.

4.   To the same pan, add the beans, garlic, wine, cognac, and mustard. Season with salt, pepper, and red pepper flakes. Nestle the chicken on top of the beans, skin-side up. Drizzle the remaining 2 tablespoons olive oil over the chicken. Roast until the chicken is cooked through (the internal temperature will reach 165°F on an instant-read thermometer), 25 to 30 minutes.

5.   Remove the pan from the oven and stir the lemon juice and cream into the saucy beans. Top with the herbs and lots of black pepper. Serve family style.

spiced paprika chicken

with sweet potatoes

PREP 15 MINUTES

COOK 50 MINUTES

TOTAL 1 HOUR 5 MINUTES

SERVES 6

Learning about Middle Eastern cooking has opened my eyes to so much. There are many cuisines under this large regional umbrella, and most of them favor bold herbs and spices, which make for dishes full of color and flavor. They also always put a big focus on vegetables . . . and sauces! And you know I love a saucy situation. I have found so much inspiration in Middle Eastern cuisines, and I often gravitate toward them when I want to put together a super-tasty dinner on a busy night, sometimes entirely made of what I have on hand. That's exactly how this dish came together. While the outcome varies depending on what I find in my kitchen, this version is a favorite I have come back to over and over again. I love how hearty this dish is, with the roasted chicken, potatoes, and big ol' smear of hummus. It's satisfying and deeply flavored, but healthy at the same time. And the added bonus? The leftovers are delicious the following day. If you want to meal-prep it, cook and store the chicken and sweet potatoes in advance, and then make the salad just before serving, adding the hummus and feta at the end.

2 pounds boneless, skinless chicken breasts

4 tablespoons extra-virgin olive oil

1 tablespoon raw honey

4 garlic cloves, finely chopped or grated

1 tablespoon smoked paprika

2 teaspoons ground cumin

½ teaspoon crushed red pepper flakes

¼ teaspoon ground cinnamon

Zest and juice of 1 lemon

Fine pink Himalayan salt and freshly ground black pepper

2 medium sweet potatoes, sliced into ¼-inch-thick rounds

2 tablespoons sesame seeds

⅓ cup sun-dried tomatoes packed in olive oil, oil drained and 2 tablespoons reserved, tomatoes roughly chopped

2 tablespoons red wine vinegar

3 cups baby arugula

1 cup mixed fresh herbs, such as parsley, cilantro, and/or dill, roughly chopped

2 Persian cucumbers, chopped

⅓ cup toasted pine nuts, pepitas, and/or sunflower seeds (see Note on page 53)

2 cups plain hummus

6 ounces feta cheese, cubed or crumbled

Naan, warmed, for serving (optional)

1. Preheat the oven to 425°F.

2. In a medium bowl, combine the chicken, 2 tablespoons of the olive oil, the honey, garlic, paprika, cumin, red pepper flakes, cinnamon, lemon zest and juice, and a pinch each of salt and pepper. Toss to coat.

3. On a rimmed baking sheet, toss the sweet potatoes with the remaining 2 tablespoons olive oil, the sesame seeds, and a pinch each of salt and pepper. Arrange in an even layer. Roast for 20 minutes, then remove from the oven, flip the potatoes, and nestle the chicken into the potatoes. Roast until the potatoes are tender and the chicken is cooked through, 20 to 30 minutes more.

4. Meanwhile, in a medium bowl, whisk together the sun-dried tomato oil and red wine vinegar. Add the sun-dried tomatoes, arugula, herbs, cucumbers, pine nuts, and a pinch each of salt and pepper. Toss to coat.

5. To serve, spread the hummus into bowls and top with the arugula salad, sweet potatoes, and chicken. Add the feta and serve with naan alongside.

coq au vin blanc meatballs

PREP 15 MINUTES
COOK 40 MINUTES
TOTAL 55 MINUTES
SERVES 4

Coq au vin is a classic French dish of chicken braised in red wine. It's made in many regions of France, often with local wine, so the sauce is rich and flavorful, and the slow-cooked chicken is always falling-off-the-bone tender. It is wonderful to make when you're entertaining and have time to devote to the traditional recipe, but on busy nights in the fall and winter, I like to make this quick adaptation. I keep the sauce simple but flavorful, using a good dry white wine (which makes it coq au vin blanc) and bacon for extra richness and a delicious depth of flavor. Making meatballs is my addition—they're not traditional, but I think they make for a fun twist, plus they cook up quickly while they simmer. My brothers especially love this French-inspired dinner served with mashed potatoes or fries on the side.

NOTE

I personally love to cook with bacon fat left over in a pan—it adds a ton of flavor, plus it saves you from having to add more oil! If you feel like your skillet is too greasy, you can pour some off. And if you prefer, you can always wipe the skillet clean and use a few tablespoons of olive oil to cook your meatballs.

1 pound ground chicken

1 large egg, beaten

⅓ cup panko bread crumbs

Fine pink Himalayan salt and freshly ground black pepper

1 tablespoon extra-virgin olive oil, plus more for your hands

2 slices thick-cut bacon, chopped

3 cups shiitake or cremini mushrooms, sliced

2 tablespoons salted butter

2 shallots, chopped

1 tablespoon fresh thyme leaves, plus more for serving

Crushed red pepper flakes

3 garlic cloves, finely chopped or grated

1½ cups dry white wine, such as pinot grigio or Sauvignon Blanc

¾ cup milk of your choice or heavy cream

1 tablespoon Dijon mustard

1. In a medium bowl, combine the chicken, egg, bread crumbs, and a pinch each of salt and pepper. Coat your hands with a bit of olive oil, then roll the meat mixture into 1-inch balls, placing them on a plate. You will have 15 to 20 meatballs.

2. Place the bacon in a large skillet over medium heat. Cook, stirring occasionally, until the bacon is crispy and the fat has rendered, about 5 minutes. Using a slotted spoon, transfer the bacon to a plate, reserving the fat in the skillet (see Note).

3. Add the meatballs to the same skillet over medium heat. Cook, turning them a few times, until browned and crisp, about 5 minutes total. Transfer the meatballs to the plate with the bacon.

4. Add the olive oil to the same skillet over medium heat. When the oil shimmers, add the mushrooms and cook, stirring occasionally, until slightly softened, about 3 minutes. Add the butter, shallots, thyme, and a pinch each of salt, black pepper, and red pepper flakes. Cook, stirring occasionally, until the mushrooms are golden brown and the shallots are softened, 3 to 5 minutes. Add the garlic and cook until fragrant, 1 minute more. Transfer the mushrooms to the plate with the bacon and meatballs.

5. Pour the wine and ¼ cup of water into the skillet. Cook, scraping up any browned bits from the bottom, until reduced slightly, about 10 minutes. Stir in the milk and mustard. Return the bacon, meatballs, and mushrooms to the skillet and simmer until the sauce is slightly thickened and everything is warmed through, 5 to 10 minutes.

6. Transfer the meatballs to plates and spoon the sauce over them. Garnish with fresh thyme.

parmesan chicken saltimbocca

with fried lemon caper sauce

PREP 20 MINUTES
COOK 20 MINUTES
TOTAL 40 MINUTES
SERVES 4

Prosciutto-wrapped chicken? Coated in panko bread crumbs? And pan-fried until lightly golden and crisp? Nothing not to love about all that! If you've never had the pleasure of enjoying chicken saltimbocca, it's an Italian breaded chicken dish traditionally made with fresh sage and prosciutto. Saltimbocca translates from Italian to "jumps in your mouth." If that's supposed to mean this meal is extremely flavorful, well, it is! Here I swapped basil for sage, used Parmesan in the breading, and added a quick lemon caper sauce and simple arugula salad that both really lighten and brighten up this otherwise rich chicken. It is a mouthwatering combination . . . so mouthwatering that it may even "jump in your mouth." You can serve this dish with crusty bread on the side for mopping up any extra sauce, or if you're feeling it, a bed of creamy whipped cauliflower mash (see page 199), which is especially delish.

1 large egg

1 cup panko bread crumbs

½ cup grated Parmesan cheese, plus more for serving

½ teaspoon garlic powder

Fine pink Himalayan salt and freshly ground black pepper

4 thin-sliced chicken breasts or 2 boneless, skinless chicken breasts, halved horizontally

8 fresh basil leaves, plus more for serving

4 thin slices prosciutto

3 tablespoons avocado oil

3 tablespoons salted butter

2 tablespoons drained capers

1 tablespoon lemon zest plus 2 tablespoons lemon juice

½ to 1 teaspoon crushed red pepper flakes

3 cups arugula

2 teaspoons red wine vinegar

1. Beat the egg in a shallow bowl. In a separate shallow bowl, stir together the panko, Parmesan, garlic powder, and a pinch each of salt and pepper.

2. Season the chicken all over with salt and pepper. Working with one piece at a time, press 2 basil leaves on top of the chicken. Wrap 1 piece of prosciutto around the center of the chicken, securing the basil in place. Dip the chicken in the egg, allowing any excess to drip off, then dredge in the panko mixture, pressing to adhere.

3. Heat 2 tablespoons of the avocado oil in a large skillet over medium heat. When the oil shimmers, working in batches, add the chicken and cook until golden brown on the bottom, 3 to 4 minutes. Flip the chicken and cook until golden brown on the other side, 3 to 4 minutes more. Transfer the chicken to a plate. Repeat with the remaining chicken.

4. Meanwhile, in a small saucepan over medium heat, combine 1 tablespoon of the butter and the capers. Cook, stirring, until the capers are fried, about 2 minutes. Add the remaining 2 tablespoons butter, the lemon zest and juice, and the red pepper flakes. Whisk to combine and cook until a sauce forms, 1 minute more.

5. In a large bowl, toss the arugula with the remaining 1 tablespoon avocado oil, the vinegar, and a pinch of salt.

6. Divide the chicken among plates and drizzle the fried caper sauce over the top. Garnish with the fresh basil and Parmesan. Serve warm with the arugula alongside.

spicy gingery chicken

PREP 20 MINUTES
COOK 20 MINUTES
TOTAL 40 MINUTES
SERVES 4

Sichuan chicken is one of my brothers' favorite orders at Chinese American restaurants, and it usually consists of fried chicken thighs stir-fried with vegetables, dried red chile peppers, and mouth-numbing Sichuan peppercorns. (The Sichuan province in China is famous for its spicy cuisine.) When we're home in Colorado and far away from a delicious version, I do my best to make a dish with reminiscent flavors using what's in my pantry. Since I don't love deep-frying, I use my favorite "oven-fried chicken" method and bake everything on a sheet pan. The sauce is a little bit sweet, but heavy on the spice and ginger. I order Sichuan peppercorns online, but you can also use red pepper flakes in a pinch. A mix of bell peppers and lots of shallots offer a nice dose of veggies and flavor, and I always serve the chicken over steamed rice.

3 tablespoons extra-virgin olive oil or sesame oil, plus more for greasing

1 large egg

1½ cups panko bread crumbs

1 pound boneless, skinless chicken thighs or breasts, cut into 1-inch pieces

¼ cup arrowroot powder

1 teaspoon ground ginger

2 bell peppers, seeded and thinly sliced (I like red and green)

Fine pink Himalayan salt and freshly ground black pepper

3 shallots, thinly sliced

⅓ cup raw peanuts

⅔ cup low-sodium soy sauce

⅓ cup pomegranate juice

2 tablespoons rice vinegar

¼ cup raw honey

1 (1-inch) piece of fresh ginger, peeled and minced or grated

2 garlic cloves, finely chopped or grated

2 to 3 teaspoons crushed Sichuan peppercorns or crushed red pepper flakes

Steamed rice, for serving

2 green onions, sliced, for serving

1. Preheat the oven to 475°F. Grease a baking sheet.

2. Beat the egg in a shallow bowl. Place the bread crumbs in a separate shallow bowl. In a large bowl, combine the chicken, arrowroot powder, and ground ginger, tossing to coat well. Remove the chicken from the bowl and drop it into the egg, turning to coat. Working in batches, remove the chicken from the egg, allowing any excess to drip off. Dredge the chicken through the bread crumbs, pressing to adhere. Place the chicken on one side of the prepared baking sheet. Repeat with the remaining chicken. Drizzle the chicken with 2 tablespoons of the oil.

3. Arrange the bell peppers on the other side of the baking sheet and toss with the remaining 1 tablespoon oil, and a pinch each of salt and pepper. Roast for 12 minutes, then flip the chicken, toss the peppers, and add the shallots and peanuts to the baking sheet. Return the sheet to the oven and roast until the chicken is cooked through, 3 to 5 minutes.

4. Meanwhile, in a large skillet, whisk together the soy sauce, pomegranate juice, vinegar, honey, ginger, garlic, Sichuan peppercorns, and ¼ cup of water. Set over medium-high heat and bring to a boil. Cook until the sauce thickens and reduces by a third, 5 to 8 minutes. Reduce the heat to low. Remove the skillet from the heat.

5. Remove the baking sheet from the oven. Pour the sauce over the chicken and peppers and toss to coat. To serve, divide the steamed rice among bowls and add the chicken and peppers. Top with the sliced green onions.

slow-roasted sunday chicken

PREP 15 MINUTES
COOK 3 HOURS
TOTAL 3 HOURS 15 MINUTES
SERVES 4 TO 6

If ever there were a dish worthy of a Sunday dinner, this is it. Nothing is cozier than the smell of a slow-roasting chicken. No matter how old I get, it always brings me back to when my mom would roast one on Sundays (in addition to baking her chocolate chip cookies). She served it up with a buttery side dish, usually potatoes but sometimes rice. And bread. Always bread. So that got me thinking—what's the only thing that could possibly make a Sunday chicken better? A side of buttery, lemony orzo cooked directly alongside, making this hearty dinner a complete one-and-done. Yes, it takes a few hours, but that time is almost completely hands-off, nothing fancy, and the outcome is always stunning . . . and, of course, delicious. Serve it Gerard-family style, straight from the pot, for a perfect dinner that impresses and satisfies everyone. Don't worry, no one needs to know how stinkin' easy it was to make.

3 garlic cloves, finely chopped or grated, plus 3 whole cloves

1 tablespoon fresh thyme leaves, plus 1 thyme sprig

2 teaspoons chopped fresh rosemary, plus 1 rosemary sprig

1 teaspoon smoked paprika

2 lemons

1 tablespoon extra-virgin olive oil

Fine pink Himalayan salt and freshly ground pepper

1 (4-pound) chicken

1 large yellow onion, quartered

2 tablespoons balsamic vinegar

3 tablespoons salted butter, cut into ½-tablespoon slices

1½ cups orzo

2 cups baby spinach

½ cup dry white wine, such as pinot grigio or Sauvignon Blanc

2 cups low-sodium chicken broth

1 tablespoon chopped fresh dill, plus more for serving

Chopped fresh basil and/or parsley, for serving (optional)

1. Preheat the oven to 200°F.

2. In a small bowl, combine the chopped garlic, thyme leaves, chopped rosemary, paprika, and 2 teaspoons lemon zest. Add the olive oil and a generous pinch each of salt and pepper and stir to combine. Rub the seasoned oil all over the chicken and under the skin to season the breast. Stuff 2 onion quarters into the cavity of the chicken.

3. Place the chicken, breast-side up, in a large Dutch oven or oven-safe pot with a lid. Cut 1 lemon into wedges. Scatter the lemon wedges, the remaining 2 onion quarters, the whole garlic cloves, and the thyme and rosemary sprigs around the chicken. Drizzle the balsamic vinegar over the chicken breasts, then scatter 2 tablespoons of the butter over them.

4. Cover the pot and roast the chicken for 2 hours and 45 minutes to 3 hours. Remove from the oven. Increase the oven temperature to 425°F.

5. Discard the lemon wedges, onion, and herb sprigs. In the pot, scatter the remaining 1 tablespoon butter and the orzo around the chicken, stirring until the butter is melted. Sprinkle the spinach around the chicken. Pour in the wine and broth and season with salt. Cut the remaining lemon into slices and add the slices to the pot.

6. Return the pot to the oven and roast, uncovered, until the orzo is al dente and the chicken skin is golden brown, 15 to 20 minutes more. It's okay if there is some liquid left in the pot.

7. Stir the dill into the orzo. Serve the chicken straight from the pot, with additional herbs, if you like, for each plate.

NOTE
If you're having trouble stirring the orzo, just lift up the chicken to move it around.

spicy chicken madras

PREP 10 MINUTES
COOK 20 MINUTES
TOTAL 30 MINUTES
SERVES 6

I developed this recipe using as many of the traditional ingredients found in chicken Madras as I have access to, and I made a couple of swaps for what I couldn't find easily. Supposedly, Madras curry was first made in the south of India in 1960. It gets its title from the city of the same name (though it's now called Chennai). However, there is some debate that it was actually created in curry houses in Britain. In part because of this discrepancy, Madras curry has many variations, but the end result is always a very red curry—thanks to chiles, paprika, and tomato puree—with just the right amount of fiery spice. It has a sour-sweet fruitiness from tamarind, but since I can't easily find tamarind where I live, I use apple cider vinegar plus honey. Yogurt is sometimes added to help cut through the heat, but to keep the recipe dairy-free, I like to use coconut milk. Madras curry powder is traditional in this recipe. I can't find this at my grocery store, so I use yellow curry powder and add cayenne pepper. If you're lucky enough to get your hands on some Madras curry powder, use that and reduce the amount of cayenne to your taste.

1 medium yellow onion, quartered

4 garlic cloves, smashed

1 (1-inch) piece of ginger, peeled

1 red Fresno pepper, halved and seeded, if desired

½ teaspoon ground turmeric

1 teaspoon fine pink Himalayan salt, plus more as needed

1 teaspoon freshly ground black pepper, plus more as needed

3 tablespoons ghee or salted butter

2 pounds boneless, skinless chicken breasts, cut into bite-size pieces

3 tablespoons yellow curry powder

2 teaspoons paprika

1 to 2 teaspoons ground cayenne pepper

½ teaspoon ground cinnamon

1 (15-ounce) can tomato puree

2 tablespoons tomato paste

¾ cup full-fat coconut milk

1 tablespoon apple cider vinegar

1 teaspoon raw honey

Turmeric Rice (recipe follows) or steamed rice, for serving

Chopped fresh cilantro, for serving

1. In a blender or food processor, combine the onion, garlic, ginger, Fresno pepper, turmeric, salt, and black pepper. Pulse until a paste forms, about 1 minute.

2. Melt the ghee in a large skillet over medium-high heat. Add the onion paste and cook, stirring, until beginning to brown, about 5 minutes. Add the chicken and cook, stirring, until cooked through, another 5 minutes. Add the curry powder, paprika, cayenne, and cinnamon. Season with salt and pepper. Cook, stirring, until very fragrant, 1 to 2 minutes more. Add the tomato puree and tomato paste, and continue cooking until incorporated and slightly thickened, 3 to 4 minutes.

3. Reduce the heat to low. Pour in the coconut milk, vinegar, and honey. Scrape up the browned bits from the bottom of the pan and stir to combine. Bring to a simmer and cook until the sauce thickens slightly, about 5 minutes.

4. Spoon the chicken and sauce over bowls of rice and top with the cilantro.

turmeric rice

MAKES 2 CUPS

2 tablespoons salted butter

½ teaspoon ground turmeric

Pinch of crushed red pepper flakes

1 cup white basmati rice

Fine pink Himalayan salt

In a medium saucepan over high heat, combine the butter, turmeric, and red pepper flakes. Cook until the butter is melted, stirring in the spices. Add the rice, 2 cups of water, and a pinch of salt. Bring to a boil, then reduce the heat to low, cover, and cook for 10 minutes. Turn the heat off and let the rice sit, still covered, until all the water is absorbed, 15 minutes more (don't peek!). Fluff the rice with a fork.

beef

red wine–braised short ribs

with whipped provolone cauliflower

PREP 20 MINUTES
COOK SEE SPECIFIC DEVICE METHOD
SERVES 6

GF **SF**

ike clockwork, when I see the first signs of fall, I start slow-braising short ribs. It's my favorite dish as soon as the weather turns cold, which for me, up in Colorado, is sometime around September 1. I have made short ribs a lot of different ways, but this version is my favorite—and it's the one I fall back on year after year. The red wine is KEY. It brings out the rich, decadent flavor of the ribs while creating a sauce bold in flavor with just a hint of sweetness. I often serve these over creamy, buttery mashed potatoes, but sometimes I like to lighten things up with whipped cauliflower. Now, hear me out—even though whipped cauliflower might not sound as delicious as mashed potatoes, I can assure you it is every bit as tasty, if not more so. The cauliflower is ultra-smooth and so creamy. My mom will attest that she prefers whipped cauliflower over mashed potatoes. She's a tough critic and she doesn't love her vegetables, so that really ought to tell you something.

SHORT RIBS

5 pounds bone-in beef short ribs

Fine pink Himalayan salt and freshly ground pepper

1 medium yellow onion, thinly sliced

2 shallots, thinly sliced

2 cups dry red wine, such as Cabernet Sauvignon

2 cups low-sodium beef broth

2 tablespoons tomato paste

4 sprigs of fresh thyme, plus more for serving

2 sprigs of fresh rosemary

2 bay leaves

1 head of garlic, unpeeled and halved crosswise

CAULIFLOWER

Pink Himalayan salt

2 large heads of cauliflower, cored and separated into florets (about 6 cups)

4 garlic cloves, smashed

½ cup shredded provolone cheese

4 tablespoons (½ stick) salted butter

OVEN

COOK 3 HOURS

1. Preheat the oven to 325°F.

2. **MAKE THE SHORT RIBS.** Season the short ribs with salt and pepper. Place them in a Dutch oven over medium-high heat and cook until just browned, 3 to 5 minutes per side. Transfer the ribs to a plate.

3. Add the onion and shallots to the Dutch oven. Cook, stirring, until the onion begins to soften, about 5 minutes. Return the short ribs to the pan. Add the wine, broth, tomato paste, thyme, rosemary, and bay leaves. Season with salt and pepper and gently stir to combine. Add the garlic.

4. Cover and roast until the short ribs are tender and falling off the bone, 2½ to 3 hours. Discard the thyme, rosemary, bay leaves, and garlic.

5. **MAKE THE CAULIFLOWER.** Bring a large pot of salted water to a boil. Add the cauliflower and cook until tender, about 10 minutes. Drain, pat dry, and then return to the pot.

6. Add the garlic to the cauliflower. Using an immersion blender, blend the mixture until smooth and creamy, about 1 minute. (Alternatively, transfer the cauliflower to a food processor, add the garlic, and process until combined.) Add the provolone and butter. Taste and season with salt and pepper. Blend until the cheese has melted.

7. Spoon the whipped cauliflower onto plates and add the ribs on top. Drizzle with the pan sauce, top with fresh thyme, and serve.

RECIPE CONTINUES

SLOW COOKER

COOK 4 HOURS 10 MINUTES TO 8 HOURS 10 MINUTES

1.　Season the short ribs with salt and pepper. Heat a large skillet over medium-high heat. Add the ribs and cook until just browned, 3 to 5 minutes per side. Transfer the ribs to the slow cooker pot.

2.　Add the onion, shallots, wine, broth, tomato paste, thyme, rosemary, and bay leaves. Season with salt and pepper and gently stir to combine. Add the garlic. Cover and cook on low for 6 to 8 hours or high for 4 to 6 hours.

3.　Finish as directed for the oven.

PRESSURE COOKER

COOK 1 HOUR, PLUS ADDITIONAL TIME TO COME TO PRESSURE

1.　Season the short ribs with salt and pepper. Heat a large skillet over medium-high heat. Add the ribs and cook until just browned, 3 to 5 minutes per side. Transfer the ribs to the pressure cooker pot.

2.　Add the onion, shallots, wine, broth, tomato paste, thyme, rosemary, and bay leaves. Season with salt and pepper and gently stir to combine. Add the garlic. Lock the lid in place and cook on high pressure for 50 minutes. Quick or natural release and open when the pressure subsides.

3.　Finish as directed for the oven.

mom's pot roast

PREP 15 MINUTES

COOK SEE SPECIFIC DEVICE METHOD

SERVES 8

My dessert-loving mom has a handful of savory recipes up her sleeve, and pot roast is one of them. When my family lived in Cleveland, she'd cook up a roast every so often throughout the fall and winter months. Hers was pretty simple and may or may not have included one of those pot roast starter packets you can pick up at the grocery store. It was a dinner we'd all look forward to. While my brothers loved the meat (obviously), I would devour the baby carrots my mom would add. They'd slowly cook with the roast, and by the time they'd finished, each little carrot was thoroughly glazed in gravy. Sooo delicious. After all these years, I've finally re-created Mom's roast, but minus the old-school ingredient list. It took some time to perfect, but here she is . . . with two thumbs up from all the brothers! Just like Mom did, I cook this all day long and let the smell fill the kitchen. Just two requirements: thoroughly enjoy the gravy and serve it with bread alongside for exactly that purpose—as well as, per my brother Creighton's recommendation, mashed potatoes (the Whipped Provolone Cauliflower on page 199 would also be great!).

1 tablespoon dried parsley

1 tablespoon onion powder

2 teaspoons garlic powder

2 teaspoons dried thyme

1 teaspoon dried oregano

4 pounds beef chuck roast, cut into 3 or 4 pieces

Fine pink Himalayan salt and freshly ground black pepper

1 large yellow onion, quartered

6 medium carrots, cut into 2-inch pieces

3 cups sliced cremini mushrooms

2½ cups low-sodium beef broth

1 cup red wine, such as Cabernet Sauvignon

2 tablespoons Worcestershire sauce

1 tablespoon tomato paste

2 tablespoons arrowroot powder

6 sprigs of fresh thyme

1 sprig of fresh rosemary

Mashed potatoes, for serving

Fresh parsley, for serving

SLOW COOKER

COOK 8 HOURS

1. In a small bowl, combine the parsley, onion powder, garlic powder, thyme, and oregano. Rub the seasoning mix all over the chuck roast. Season generously with salt and pepper.

2. Transfer the meat to the slow cooker pot. Add the onion, carrots, and mushrooms. Pour in 2 cups of the broth, the wine, the Worcestershire sauce, and the tomato paste.

3. In a glass measuring cup, whisk together the arrowroot powder and the remaining ½ cup broth. Pour the mixture around the meat. Add the thyme and rosemary sprigs. Cover and cook on low for 8 hours, until the meat is tender and falling apart.

4. Turn on the broiler. Transfer the meat to a baking dish or Dutch oven. Broil until the top of the meat begins to crisp, 5 to 8 minutes.

5. Spoon the pot roast, vegetables, and sauce over mashed potatoes. Top with fresh parsley and serve.

RECIPE CONTINUES

BEEF

PRESSURE COOKER

COOK 1 HOUR

1.   In a small bowl, combine the parsley, onion powder, garlic powder, thyme, and oregano. Rub the seasoning mix all over the chuck roast. Season generously with salt and pepper.

2.   Heat a Dutch oven over high heat. Add the meat and cook until browned on the bottom, 3 to 4 minutes. Transfer the meat to the pressure cooker pot. Add the onion, carrots, and mushrooms. Pour in 2 cups of the broth, the wine, the Worcestershire sauce, and the tomato paste.

3.   In a glass measuring cup, whisk together the arrowroot powder and the remaining ½ cup broth. Pour the mixture around the meat. Add the thyme and rosemary sprigs. Lock the lid in place and cook on high pressure for 1 hour. Quick or natural release and open when the pressure subsides.

4.   Finish and serve as directed for the slow cooker.

OVEN

COOK 3 TO 4 HOURS

1.   Preheat the oven to 350°F.

2.   In a small bowl, combine the parsley, onion powder, garlic powder, thyme, and oregano. Rub the seasoning mix all over the chuck roast. Season generously with salt and pepper.

3.   Heat a Dutch oven over high heat. Add the meat and cook until browned on the bottom, 3 to 4 minutes. Remove from the heat. Add the onion, carrots, and mushrooms. Pour in 2 cups of the broth, the wine, the Worcestershire sauce, and the tomato paste.

4.   In a glass measuring cup, whisk together the arrowroot powder and the remaining ½ cup broth. Pour the mixture around the meat. Add the thyme and rosemary sprigs. Cover and roast until the meat is tender and falling apart, 3 to 4 hours (see Note).

5.   Finish and serve as directed for the slow cooker.

NOTE
When I make this dish in the oven, I like to remove the lid for the last 15 to 20 minutes of roasting to help the meat brown.

dad's cheesy baked tacos

PREP 15 MINUTES

COOK 25 MINUTES

TOTAL 40 MINUTES

SERVES 6

S ure, you've had tacos before, but you haven't had my dad's tacos. These are the tacos I grew up eating. Well, not the exact ones—these are better, but the same idea. He always made them crispy, using store-bought shells, and you can do it his way if you want. But I make mine with fresh corn tortillas and a homemade seasoning blend—they get crispy when they bake, all while the cheese inside melts over the spicy seasoned taco meat. I call for ground beef, which was Dad's go-to, but ground chicken or turkey are equally great, as is roasted cauliflower for a vegetarian option! When they come out of the oven, you have a crunchy exterior and a gooey interior. They. Are. Delicious. And then the sauce. I do a creamy poblano sauce, which is my dad's favorite. It is smoky from the pureed roasted peppers, and the creaminess is just perfect for pairing with this taco.

1 pound lean ground beef

1 medium yellow onion, chopped

1 medium poblano pepper, seeded and chopped

2 teaspoons chipotle chile powder, plus more to taste

2 teaspoons smoked paprika

1½ teaspoons ground cumin

1 teaspoon garlic powder

½ teaspoon dried oregano

¼ teaspoon crushed red pepper flakes, plus more to taste

¾ teaspoon fine pink Himalayan salt

12 Seasoned Taco Shells, warmed (see below), or store-bought hard taco shells (I like Siete Foods)

1 cup shredded Mexican cheese blend

Creamy Poblano Sauce (page 231), for serving

1. Preheat the oven to 425°F.

2. Place the beef and onion in a large skillet over medium heat. Cook, breaking up the beef with a wooden spoon, until the beef is browned, about 5 minutes. Add the poblano, chipotle powder, paprika, cumin, garlic powder, oregano, red pepper flakes, and salt. Cook, stirring, until the spices are fragrant, 1 to 2 minutes more. Add ¾ cup of water, then bring to a simmer and cook until the liquid has thickened slightly, about 10 minutes. Taste and add more seasoning as needed. Remove the skillet from the heat.

3. If you're making your own hard taco shells, see variation below. If you're using store-bought, stand the taco shells up on a rimmed sheet pan or in a 9 × 13-inch baking dish. Divide the meat evenly among the shells and top each with cheese. Bake for 10 minutes, until the cheese has melted.

4. Serve the tacos drizzled with the Creamy Poblano Sauce and finished with any other desired toppings.

seasoned taco shells

To make your own hard taco shells, warm corn tortillas in the microwave until pliable, 30 seconds to 1 minute. Rub them on one side with a bit of olive oil. This part's optional, but strongly recommended: mix together 1 tablespoon nutritional yeast (if you happen to have it), 1 teaspoon fine pink Himalayan salt, and ½ teaspoon each of onion powder, garlic powder, ground cumin, smoked paprika, and chili powder, plus some cayenne for a kick. Sprinkle the spice mix over the olive oil so it sticks, then flip the tortillas over so the coating is facedown. Layer the cheese and meat on top, fold the tortillas, and gently press so they enclose the filling. Arrange them on a baking sheet. Bake at 425°F for 5 to 8 minutes, then flip and bake until the cheese is melted and the tortillas have crisped up, 5 minutes more. Sprinkle them with more of the seasoning, if you like.

uncle joe's stuffed peppers

PREP 20 MINUTES

COOK 40 MINUTES

TOTAL 1 HOUR

SERVES 6

Peppers are one of my favorite vegetables, but I'd never stuffed them until one Christmas when my brother Creighton convinced me to make our Uncle Joe's version. He texted Joe asking for his recipe, then promptly took a screenshot and sent it directly to me. I am not going to lie . . . I was very, very skeptical. I questioned multiple steps and I wondered whether I should be trusting Creighton and Uncle Joe with anything related to cooking. Well, I changed a few things around, but in the end, these stuffed peppers were one of my family's favorite dinners that Christmas! Uncle Joe uses Devil's Tongue peppers, which are hard to find in my small town, so I usually grab bell peppers, poblanos, or banana peppers. If you want to use Devil's Tongue instead, note that they are hotter, longer, and skinnier than bell peppers, so you'll need more of them. And a tip from my mom? Serve each saucy, cheesy pepper over your favorite pasta. She recommends angel hair, but anything goes!

4 bell, poblano, or banana peppers, halved and seeded

1 pound ground spicy Italian chicken sausage (see Note on page 80)

½ pound lean ground beef

1 medium yellow onion, chopped

4 garlic cloves, finely chopped or grated

1 tablespoon dried oregano

1 tablespoon dried basil

Crushed red pepper flakes (optional)

Fine pink Himalayan salt and freshly ground black pepper

1 (14.5-ounce) can diced tomatoes

2 cups baby spinach, roughly chopped

2 to 3 cups marinara sauce (I like Rao's)

8 ounces low-moisture whole-milk mozzarella cheese, torn or shredded

Fresh basil leaves, for serving

1. Preheat the oven to 400°F.

2. Arrange the peppers, cut-side up, in a 9 × 13-inch baking dish.

3. Combine the sausage, beef, and onion in a large skillet over medium heat. Cook, breaking up the meat with a wooden spoon, until the meat is browned, 5 to 8 minutes. Stir in the garlic, oregano, basil, and a pinch each of red pepper flakes (if using), salt, and pepper. Cook until fragrant, 1 minute more. Add the tomatoes and spinach. Increase the heat to medium-high and cook, stirring occasionally, until the spinach is wilted and most of the liquid has evaporated, about 5 minutes. Remove the skillet from the heat.

4. Divide the meat filling among the peppers, then slather the marinara sauce all over the peppers. Top with the mozzarella. Bake until the cheese is melted and browning, 20 to 25 minutes.

5. Garnish the peppers with fresh basil and serve.

carne asada "crunchwraps"

PREP 30 MINUTES

COOK 20 MINUTES

TOTAL 50 MINUTES,
PLUS MARINATING TIME

SERVES 4

If ever there were a recipe that perfectly embodies my Taco Bell–loving brothers, this wrap is it. These "crunchwraps" are beyond over the top and I put my own twist on them by making mine with homemade carne asada. The folded-up wrap looks impressive, but it's just one tortilla sectioned into quadrants. You divide your fillings among the sections, layer them into a triangle, and pan-fry. The cheese on the outer layer melts out a bit onto the skillet and gets all crispy—almost deep-fried. It's magical. They're crunchy on the outside, cheesy and saucy inside. My brothers weighed in and said these are just as good as the original.

CARNE ASADA

1 medium yellow onion, quartered

5 garlic cloves, roughly chopped

2 tablespoons chipotle chile powder

1 tablespoon smoked paprika

2 teaspoons fine pink Himalayan salt

½ cup fresh cilantro

⅓ cup fresh orange juice

Zest of 1 lime plus ¼ cup fresh lime juice (from 2 limes)

1 tablespoon raw honey

½ cup Mexican beer (I like Modelo Negra)

1½ pounds flank steak, cut into 4 pieces

WRAPS

4 (10-inch) flour tortillas

2 cups shredded romaine lettuce, plus more for serving

1 cup cherry tomatoes, chopped

1 jalapeño, seeded and finely chopped

3 green onions, sliced

¼ cup plain Greek yogurt or sour cream

1 cup shredded Mexican cheese blend

Extra-virgin olive oil

FOR SERVING

Avocado, mashed or diced

Sliced jalapeños

Quick-Pickled Red Onions (page 221) or store-bought pickled onions

1. **MAKE THE CARNE ASADA.** In a blender or food processor, combine the onion, garlic, chipotle powder, paprika, salt, cilantro, orange juice, lime zest, lime juice, and honey. Blend until smooth, about 1 minute. Add the beer and blend again to incorporate. Place the steak in a 9 × 13-inch baking dish and pour in the marinade, rubbing it into the steak. Cover and refrigerate for at least 2 hours or up to overnight.

2. Remove the steak from the refrigerator 30 minutes before cooking. Heat a grill to high or a grill pan over high heat.

3. Remove the steak from the marinade, allowing the excess to drip off. Place the steak on the grill and sear until browned on the bottom, 5 to 8 minutes. Flip and sear for another 5 minutes for medium-rare, or until your desired doneness is reached. Remove the steak from the grill and let it rest for 5 minutes. Slice very thinly against the grain.

4. **MAKE THE WRAPS.** Working with one tortilla at a time, slice the tortilla from its center to one edge. Spread the carne asada in the bottom left quadrant, then layer lettuce, tomatoes, jalapeño, and green onions on the top left quadrant. Spread the yogurt on the top right quadrant, and sprinkle the cheese on the bottom right quadrant. Carefully fold the carne asada over the lettuce. Then, working clockwise, fold those quarters over the yogurt. Finally, fold those quarters over the cheese.

5. Heat a splash of olive oil in a medium skillet over medium heat. When the oil shimmers, add one wrap and cook until crisp and golden brown, 2 to 3 minutes per side. Repeat with the remaining wraps.

6. Serve warm with avocado, jalapeño slices, pickled onions, and more shredded lettuce as desired.

mongolian beef

PREP 10 MINUTES

COOK 20 MINUTES

TOTAL 30 MINUTES

SERVES 4 TO 6

One of my favorite ways to keep weeknight meals exciting is to re-create some of my favorite takeout dinners. Of course, in my little mountain town, we don't have the widest variety of options, so I always make an effort to try new spots whenever I come across them. Enter Mongolian beef. It's probably one of the most beloved items on a lot of restaurant menus. The classic version usually consists of fried steak tossed in a soy-based sauce sweetened with brown sugar. I'm pretty sure it's that delicious sauce that keeps me (and everyone else) coming back for more. When I re-create this one at home, I use a leaner cut of meat and mix up a less-sugary-than-usual sauce. But don't worry, it tastes just as good as anything you'd take out. My family requests this one all the time . . . and the good news for me is that this dish is QUICK. All you need are a few simple ingredients and 30 minutes.

4 (4- to 6-ounce) strip loin steaks, thinly sliced against the grain

3 tablespoons arrowroot powder

4 tablespoons avocado oil

8 to 10 broccolini stalks, halved crosswise

4 garlic cloves, finely chopped or grated

1 (1-inch) piece of fresh ginger, peeled and minced or grated

1 tablespoon crushed red pepper flakes or sambal oelek

½ cup low-sodium soy sauce or tamari

3 tablespoons raw honey

2 green onions, thinly sliced, plus more for serving

Seasoned Coconut Rice (page 227) or steamed rice, for serving

Toasted sesame seeds, for serving (see Note on page 53)

1.   In a medium bowl, combine the steak with the arrowroot powder. Toss to coat.

2.   Heat 2 tablespoons of the avocado oil in a large cast-iron skillet over high heat. When the oil shimmers, working in batches, add the steak and cook until browned, 2 minutes per side. Transfer the steak to a plate.

3.   To the same skillet over high heat, add 1 tablespoon of the avocado oil and the broccolini. Cook, stirring occasionally, until bright green and tender, 4 to 5 minutes. Transfer the broccolini to the plate with the steak.

4.   Reduce the heat under the skillet to medium. Add the remaining 1 tablespoon avocado oil, the garlic, ginger, and red pepper flakes. Cook until fragrant, about 1 minute. Add ¼ cup of water, the soy sauce, and the honey. Increase the heat to medium-high and bring to a boil. Cook until slightly thickened, 3 to 5 minutes. Return the steak and broccolini to the pan, tossing to coat in the sauce. Cook until warmed through, 1 to 2 minutes. Stir in the green onions.

5.   To serve, spoon the beef and broccolini over the rice. Sprinkle with toasted sesame seeds and more green onion.

beef picadillo

PREP 10 MINUTES
COOK 20 MINUTES
TOTAL 30 MINUTES
SERVES 4

30 **1** **DF** **GF** **SF**

Picadillo is a dish popular in Latin American countries. It's usually made with ground or chopped beef, tomatoes, cumin, olives, and, sometimes, raisins. Served with rice, it can be a super quick AND super flavorful dinner that's a great way to spice things up on an average weeknight. I finish the dish with slices of avocado, a squeeze of lime, and plenty of fresh cilantro to brighten it up!

1 pound lean ground beef

1 yellow onion, chopped

1 red bell pepper, chopped

2 garlic cloves, finely chopped or grated

1 (14.5-ounce) can diced tomatoes

1 cup tomato sauce

2 teaspoons ground cumin

1 bay leaf

¼ cup chopped green olives plus ¼ cup olive brine

Fine pink Himalayan salt plus freshly ground black pepper

¼ cup fresh cilantro, chopped, plus more for serving

Steamed rice, for serving

1 avocado, sliced

1 lime, cut into wedges

1. Heat a large skillet over medium-high heat. Place the beef and onion in the skillet and cook, breaking up the meat with a wooden spoon, until the beef is browned and the onions are softened, about 5 minutes.

2. Add the bell pepper and garlic and cook, stirring frequently, until softened, 2 to 3 minutes. Stir in the tomatoes and their juices, the tomato sauce, cumin, bay leaf, and olive brine. Season with salt and pepper. Add ⅓ cup water. Reduce the heat to medium, cover, and simmer until the liquid has evaporated and the flavors are melded, about 15 minutes.

3. Remove the skillet from the heat and stir in the olives and cilantro.

4. Serve the picadillo over rice, topped with the avocado and cilantro, and spritzed with lime juice.

holy grail spaghetti and meatballs

PREP 30 MINUTES

COOK 1 HOUR

TOTAL 1 HOUR 30 MINUTES

SERVES 6

My oldest brother is the biggest meat lover in the world. The day I make him a meatloaf, he will be able to rest in peace. That's dramatic, but man, he's really dying for that meatloaf! Now, meatloaf is NOT my favorite, but I do like meatballs, and these are my compromise. To no one's surprise, Creighton loves, loves, loves them. And everyone else who's tried them has loved them, too. The reason they are the holy grail? Well, there are a couple. First, the pork keeps them tender and juicy. But the fish sauce is real the secret weapon. Its flavor is undetectable, but it adds ten million miles of savoriness. I really encourage you to use it—all you'll taste is delicious meatballs with an extra special touch. Oh, and Creighton highly recommends enjoying your plate of spaghetti and meatballs with garlic bread on the side. We agree on that!

MEATBALLS

2 slices whole-grain or white bread

1 pound lean ground beef

1 pound ground pork

2 large eggs

¼ cup grated Parmesan cheese

2 or 3 garlic cloves, finely chopped or grated

2 tablespoons chopped fresh oregano or 1 tablespoon dried

2 tablespoons chopped fresh basil leaves or 1 tablespoon dried

1 tablespoon fish sauce, low-sodium soy sauce, or tamari

½ teaspoon fine pink Himalayan salt

Freshly ground black pepper

Olive oil, for your hands

SAUCE

¼ cup extra-virgin olive oil

2 shallots, finely chopped

4 garlic cloves, finely chopped or grated

1 tablespoon dried oregano

1 tablespoon dried basil

1 (4.5-ounce) tube or (6-ounce) can tomato paste

1 to 2 teaspoons crushed red pepper flakes

2 (28-ounce) cans crushed tomatoes

1 teaspoon fine pink Himalayan salt

Freshly ground black pepper

Parmesan rind (optional)

1 pound spaghetti, cooked

Grated Parmesan cheese, for serving

Fresh basil leaves, for serving

1. Preheat the oven to 450°F. Line a baking sheet with parchment paper.

2. **MAKE THE MEATBALLS.** Run the bread under water until just dampened, but not soaked. Gently squeeze out any excess water, then crumble the dampened bread into a large bowl. Add the beef, pork, eggs, Parmesan, garlic, oregano, basil, fish sauce, salt, and a large pinch of pepper. Using your hands, mix until combined. Coat your hands with a bit of olive oil, then roll the meat mixture into golf-ball-sized balls and place them on the prepared baking sheet; you will have around 20 meatballs. Roast until the meatballs are crisp on the outside but not yet cooked through on the inside, about 15 minutes.

3. **MEANWHILE, MAKE THE SAUCE.** Heat the olive oil in a large Dutch oven over medium-low heat. When the oil shimmers, add the shallots, garlic, oregano, and basil. Cook, stirring occasionally, until the shallots begin to caramelize, about 5 minutes. Reduce the heat to low, add the tomato paste and red pepper flakes, and cook, stirring, until the mixture turns dark red, 4 to 5 minutes. Stir in the crushed tomatoes and season with salt and pepper. Add the Parmesan rind, if using. Simmer over low heat until thickened, 20 to 30 minutes.

4. Nestle the meatballs into the sauce, partially cover the pot, and cook over medium-low heat until the meatballs are fully cooked through, 20 to 25 minutes.

5. To serve, divide the spaghetti among plates and top with the sauce and meatballs. Garnish with grated Parmesan and fresh basil leaves.

to make cheesy baked meatballs

To make cheesy baked meatballs, continue through step 3 above. Arrange the meatballs in a 9 × 13-inch baking dish, then pour the sauce over the top, covering the meatballs. Sprinkle 4 ounces torn mozzarella cheese and 1 cup shredded provolone cheese over the top. Bake at 425°F until the cheese is melted, about 15 minutes. Garnish with lots and lots of fresh basil and grated Parmesan and serve with Easy Garlic Knots (page 49) for dipping.

cheesy beef, black bean, and rice skillet

PREP 10 MINUTES
COOK 40 MINUTES
TOTAL 50 MINUTES
SERVES 6

When I find myself in a recipe rut, I turn to flavors I know I love but don't cook with day to day. Cuban food is something I don't make a ton of, but every time I do, I say, "Why don't I make more Cuban food? It's GOOD." This quick-cooking dinner is inspired by two dishes: picadillo and the Cuban sandwich. Picadillo is a traditional dish of ground beef cooked with tomato, peppers and onions, and spices, and is often served with rice. (It usually has olives and raisins for salty and sweet pops, too; see page 213 for my version!) I took the beef and rice, combined them into one skillet, and covered everything with a layer of cheese to add an element of coziness. And that cheese on top is where the Cuban sandwich twist comes into play. I love a good Cuban sandwich, and my favorite part is, of course, all the melty Swiss. So I added some on top of the beef and rice, then baked the whole thing in the oven until it was melty and bubbly. I serve this up with avocado and herbs for color and freshness. If you want to take the toppings a step further, I would recommend a pineapple salsa, too. Then add a fun cocktail to liven up your night—the Strawberry Basil Margarita on page 70 would be perfect.

2 tablespoons extra-virgin olive oil

1 medium yellow onion, chopped

1 pound lean ground beef

1 green bell pepper, seeded and chopped

2 garlic cloves, finely chopped or grated

2 teaspoons dried oregano

1 teaspoon ground cumin

½ teaspoon ground allspice

½ to 1 teaspoon ground cayenne pepper

Fine pink Himalayan salt and freshly ground black pepper

1 cup long-grain rice

¼ cup tomato paste

1 bay leaf

1 (15.5-ounce) can black beans, drained and rinsed

Zest and juice of 1 lime, plus lime wedges for serving

1½ cups shredded Swiss or low-moisture whole-milk mozzarella cheese

Sliced avocado, for serving

Fresh oregano, cilantro, and/or watercress leaves, for serving

1. Preheat the oven to 425°F.

2. Heat the olive oil in a large oven-safe skillet over high heat. When the oil shimmers, add the onion and beef. Cook, breaking up the meat with a wooden spoon, until the onion is soft and the meat is browned, 5 to 7 minutes. Add the bell pepper, garlic, oregano, cumin, allspice, and cayenne, and season with salt and pepper. Cook, stirring occasionally, until the bell pepper is soft, 5 minutes more. Push the mixture to one side of the skillet.

3. Add the rice to the open side of the skillet. Cook, stirring, until the rice is lightly toasted and golden, 1 to 2 minutes. Add the tomato paste and stir the beef and bell pepper back in. Cook until dark red, 1 minute more. Add 2 cups of water and the bay leaf. Bring to a boil, then reduce the heat to low. Cover and cook until most (but not all) of the liquid has been absorbed, about 15 minutes.

4. Remove the skillet from the heat. Discard the bay leaf. Stir in the beans and the lime zest and juice. Sprinkle the cheese over the top. Bake until the cheese is melted and lightly browned, about 10 minutes.

5. Top as desired with avocado and herbs. Serve family style with lime wedges on the side.

sheet pan meatball pitas

with garlic fries, tzatziki, and the works

PREP 30 MINUTES
COOK 55 MINUTES
TOTAL 1 HOUR 5 MINUTES
SERVES 6

My brother Creighton LOVES a gyro. Any time I see him, he's asking me to make gyros! He'll take them any which way I serve them up, but his preferred meat is slow-roasted lamb. I thought about the other foods Creigh likes to eat, and, well, the boy LOVES meatballs, too. And that's how I arrived at this recipe. I use a mix of ground beef and ground lamb to make the most delicious, juicy, and tender meatballs, then I stuff them into pitas with all the fixings. For me, the fries and garlicky tzatziki are essential—you just can't skip them if you want to enjoy this recipe to the fullest extent. The dish is great to double, as the meatballs are insanely delicious as leftovers and served up over a quick chopped salad. If beef and/or lamb isn't appealing to you, ground chicken works just as well.

NOTE ⸻

You might need a second baking sheet here; if your pan is too crowded, your potatoes will steam instead of crisp. No one wants a steamy fry!

FRIES

2 large russet potatoes, cut into ¼-inch-thick matchsticks

¼ cup extra-virgin olive oil

4 tablespoons chopped fresh oregano

½ teaspoon crushed red pepper flakes

Fine pink Himalayan salt

2 garlic cloves, finely chopped or grated

MEATBALLS

1 pound ground lamb or lean beef, or a combination

1 small yellow onion, grated

3 garlic cloves, finely chopped or grated

¼ cup chopped fresh parsley

2 teaspoons ground cumin

1 teaspoon dried oregano

¼ teaspoon crushed red pepper flakes

Fine pink Himalayan salt and freshly ground black pepper

Extra-virgin olive oil, for your hands

FOR SERVING

Garlicky Tzatziki (recipe follows) or store-bought tzatziki

6 pitas or naan, warmed

Shredded lettuce

Chopped cherry tomatoes

Chopped fresh parsley

Quick-Pickled Red Onions (page 221) or store-bought pickled onions

1. Preheat the oven to 425°F. Line a baking sheet with parchment paper.

2. **MAKE THE FRIES.** On a separate baking sheet, toss the potatoes with the olive oil, 2 tablespoons of the oregano, the red pepper flakes, and a pinch of salt. Arrange the potatoes in an even layer, spacing them apart (see Note). Roast for 15 to 20 minutes, then flip and roast until the potatoes are crispy but still tender, 15 minutes more. Remove the baking sheet from the oven. Add the remaining 2 tablespoons oregano and the garlic. Toss gently to combine.

3. **MEANWHILE, MAKE THE MEATBALLS.** In a medium bowl, combine the lamb, onion, garlic, parsley, cumin, oregano, red pepper flakes, and a pinch each of salt and pepper. Using your hands, mix well to combine. Coat your hands with a bit of olive oil, then roll the meat mixture into golf-ball-sized balls, placing them on the prepared baking sheet; you will have 12 to 15 meatballs. Bake until the meatballs are crisp on the outside and cooked through, 15 to 20 minutes.

4. To serve, smear the tzatziki onto warmed pitas. Top with lettuce, tomato, and parsley. Add the meatballs. Finish with more tzatziki, pickled onions, and parsley. Serve the fries alongside, with more tzatziki for dipping.

garlicky tzatziki

MAKES 3 CUPS

2 cups plain Greek yogurt

2 Persian cucumbers, grated

4 garlic cloves, finely chopped or grated

½ cup chopped fresh dill

¼ cup fresh lemon juice

½ teaspoon fine pink Himalayan salt

In a medium bowl, stir together the yogurt, cucumber, garlic, dill, lemon juice, and salt. Taste and add more salt as needed. Stored refrigerated in an airtight container for up to 1 week.

spicy basil beef bowl

PREP 15 MINUTES
COOK 15 MINUTES
TOTAL 30 MINUTES
SERVES 6

I am not sure I love any flavors more than those of Thai cooking. My brother Brendan has taken multiple trips to Thailand and was the first person to introduce me to the country's food. A lot of Thai cuisine strives for a balance of hot, sour, salty, and sweet. It's typically saucy and colorful . . . and these are some of my favorite things. This spicy beef dish was inspired by larb, a meat salad originally from Laos that became one of the most-loved dishes in Thailand. My dish isn't traditional—it's a bit sweeter and I serve it with raw vegetables and mango. It can easily come together in thirty minutes—the recipe uses quick-cooking ground meat (often beef, chicken, duck, fish, pork, or mushrooms, for a vegetarian version) and then everything else is assembly! The spicy meat is KEY, but so are plenty of fresh herbs and my additions of sweet coconut rice and mango, which beautifully balance out the heat.

2 tablespoons sesame or peanut oil

1 pound lean ground beef, pork, or chicken

Freshly ground black pepper

2 medium shallots, thinly sliced

4 garlic cloves, finely chopped or grated

1 (1-inch) piece of fresh ginger, peeled and minced or grated

2 tablespoons thinly sliced lemongrass or 1 tablespoon lemongrass paste

1 red or orange bell pepper, seeded and chopped

⅓ cup raw cashews

¼ cup low-sodium soy sauce or tamari

1 tablespoon fish sauce

2 to 3 tablespoons sambal oelek

2 teaspoons raw honey or pure maple syrup

½ cup fresh Thai or sweet basil leaves

FOR SERVING

Seasoned Coconut Rice (page 227) or steamed rice

Quick-Pickled Red Onions (recipe follows) or store-bought pickled onions

1 cup fresh herbs, such as basil, cilantro, and/or mint

2 medium carrots, shredded or shaved

2 Persian cucumbers, thinly sliced

4 green onions, thinly sliced

1 mango, peeled and thinly sliced or diced

2 limes, cut into wedges

1.   Heat the oil in a large skillet over medium heat. When the oil shimmers, add the meat. Season with black pepper and cook, breaking up the meat with a wooden spoon, until browned, about 5 minutes. Add the shallots, garlic, ginger, lemongrass, bell pepper, and cashews. Cook, stirring, until the garlic is fragrant, about 5 minutes more.

2.   Add ¼ cup of water, the soy sauce, fish sauce, sambal oelek, and honey. Increase the heat to medium-high and bring the sauce to a boil. Cook, stirring, until the sauce coats the meat, 5 to 8 minutes. Stir in the basil until just wilted, about 1 minute, and remove the skillet from the heat.

3.   Divide the rice among bowls and spoon the meat over the top. Top the bowls as desired with pickled onions, herbs, carrots, cucumbers, green onions, and mango. Serve with lime wedges for squeezing.

quick-pickled red onions

MAKES ABOUT 2 CUPS

½ cup red wine vinegar

¼ cup apple cider vinegar

1 tablespoon raw honey

1 tablespoon kosher salt

½ teaspoon crushed red pepper flakes (optional)

1 medium red onion, thinly sliced

In a small saucepan, combine the red wine vinegar, apple cider vinegar, honey, salt, red pepper flakes, and ¾ cup of water. Bring to a simmer over high heat and cook until the honey and salt have dissolved, about 1 minute. Remove the pan from the heat and add the onion, submerging it completely. Let sit for at least 20 minutes at room temperature. Store the onions and brine refrigerated in an airtight container for up to 1 month.

herby avocado steak salad
with browned walnuts

PREP 20 MINUTES
COOK 10 MINUTES
TOTAL 30 MINUTES
SERVES 4

If there is one thing everyone in my family really loves, it's a grilled steak—I don't do it often, but anytime I cook them up, everyone gets excited. It doesn't take much to make it delicious, you know? The key is to pick a cut of steak that'll have a really nice flavor: I love a bone-in rib-eye or a lean filet mignon. A great steak is best served simply, with a good side like French fries or roasted potatoes. But I have one exception to that rule: a REALLY good steak salad. We used to order it at restaurants on special occasions—our favorite was from Moose Jaw in Lakewood, Ohio. But now? I make my own version at home!

WALNUTS

6 tablespoons salted butter

¼ cup raw walnuts

2 garlic cloves, smashed

DRESSING

2 tablespoons champagne vinegar

2 teaspoons Worcestershire sauce

2 teaspoons fresh lemon juice

1 teaspoon Dijon mustard

Fine pink Himalayan salt and freshly ground black pepper

SALAD

2 to 3 (8-ounce) rib-eye or filet mignon, at room temperature

Fine pink Himalayan salt

1 tablespoon cold salted butter

1 to 2 avocados, diced

1 English cucumber, chopped

¼ cup fresh basil leaves

¼ cup fresh dill

2 tablespoons fresh oregano

2 tablespoons fresh thyme leaves

4 to 5 cups baby spinach or baby arugula (optional)

⅓ cup crumbled blue or goat cheese

1. **BROWN THE WALNUTS**. In a small skillet over medium heat, melt the butter. Add the walnuts and garlic. Cook, stirring constantly, until the butter begins to brown and the walnuts turn golden, 3 to 4 minutes. Using a slotted spoon, transfer the walnuts to a plate, reserving them for later. Discard the butter and garlic or save for another use.

2. **MAKE THE DRESSING**. In a small bowl, whisk together the vinegar, Worcestershire sauce, lemon juice, and mustard. Season with salt and pepper.

3. **MAKE THE SALAD**. Season the steaks all over with salt and heat a large skillet over high heat. When the skillet is just smoking, add the steak, then add the butter. Swirl the pan so the butter melts around the steaks and cook until a crust forms on the bottom of the steaks, 2 to 3 minutes. Reduce the heat to medium, then flip the steaks and spoon the melted butter over the top. Cook another 2 to 3 minutes for medium-rare or to your liking. Transfer the steaks to a cutting board and let rest for 10 to 15 minutes.

4. Meanwhile, in a serving bowl, combine the avocados, cucumbers, basil, dill, oregano, thyme, greens (if using), and the reserved browned walnuts. Gently toss to combine.

5. Thinly slice the steak against the grain. Add the steak to the serving bowl and drizzle the dressing over the top. Toss to coat. Crumble the blue cheese on top and serve immediately.

fish &
seafood

sesame soy miso-glazed salmon

with seasoned coconut rice

PREP 10 MINUTES
COOK 20 MINUTES
TOTAL 30 MINUTES
SERVES 4

This recipe was inspired by flavors found in Japanese cooking, and it has a bit of a tropical flare to it, too. Let's start with the rice, which was inspired by sushi rice. Usually, for sushi, chewy cooked short grain rice is dressed with a little rice vinegar and sometimes the smallest amount of sugar to create a combination of flavors that is incredible when paired with fish. If you ask me, it's a big part of why we really all love sushi—it's all about that rice! Cooking it with coconut milk instead of water makes for an even richer version that leaves everyone wanting just one more spoonful. This sweet, creamy rice pairs perfectly with the salty, miso-glazed salmon. I like to roast the salmon with broccoli on the side, but you can easily switch it up and use cauliflower, asparagus, or Brussels sprouts instead. The dish comes together effortlessly in just about 30 minutes.

¼ cup raw honey

3 tablespoons low-sodium soy sauce or tamari

2 tablespoons red or white miso paste

2 tablespoons rice vinegar

1 (1-inch) piece of fresh ginger, peeled and minced or grated

½ teaspoon crushed red pepper flakes, plus more for serving

1 large bunch broccolini

1 tablespoon sesame or extra-virgin olive oil

Fine pink Himalayan salt and freshly ground black pepper

4 (5-ounce) salmon fillets

Seasoned Coconut Rice (recipe follows) or steamed rice, for serving

1 tablespoon toasted sesame seeds (see Note on page 53)

3 green onions, sliced

½ cup pomegranate seeds (optional)

1. Preheat the oven to 425°F. Line a baking sheet with parchment paper.

2. In a small saucepan, combine ¼ cup of water with the honey, soy sauce, miso, vinegar, ginger, and red pepper flakes. Bring to a boil over high heat, then reduce the heat to medium. Cook until the sauce thickens slightly, about 5 minutes. Remove the pan from the heat.

3. On one side of the prepared baking sheet, toss the broccolini with the sesame oil and a pinch each of salt and pepper. Place the salmon on the other side. Spoon 1 tablespoon of the glaze evenly over each salmon fillet.

4. Roast for 5 minutes. Spoon another tablespoon of the glaze over each salmon fillet. Continue roasting until the broccolini is tender and the salmon reaches your desired doneness, 3 to 5 minutes more.

5. Divide the rice among bowls. Add the salmon and broccolini. Spoon some of the remaining glaze over the salmon. Garnish with sesame seeds, green onions, and pomegranate seeds, if desired. Serve with any remaining glaze alongside.

seasoned coconut rice

MAKES 3 CUPS

1 (13.5-ounce) can full-fat coconut milk

1 cup sushi or jasmine rice

½ teaspoon fine pink Himalayan salt

1 tablespoon rice vinegar

1 teaspoon raw honey

In a medium saucepan, combine the coconut milk and ½ cup of water. Bring to a boil over high heat. Stir in the rice and salt. Reduce the heat to low, cover, and cook for 10 minutes. Turn off the heat and let sit, covered, for 15 to 20 minutes more (don't peek!). In a small bowl, whisk together the vinegar and honey. Remove the lid, fluff the rice with a fork, and then stir in the vinegar mixture. Serve warm.

coconut shrimp
with double the sauce

PREP 20 MINUTES
COOK 10 MINUTES
TOTAL 30 MINUTES
SERVES 6

This shrimp is breaded in coconut, oven-baked, then served up with a peppery honey sauce full of mango chunks AND a spicy honey mustard. If you know me, and you maybe know my dad (or know about my dad), you'll know this is our kind of shrimp recipe. Actually, it's my brother Brendan's, too. SO MUCH FLAVOR. And crispy, crunchy TEXTURE. Am I being dramatic? Absolutely, but this shrimp is so delicious and even healthier than ordering coconut shrimp out at a restaurant, because they're baked, not fried, which helps to balance out the fact that these are addicting. But those two honey sauces steal the show. Don't skip them either. You need ALL the sauce, and these shrimps go from tasty to BEYOND DELICIOUS with them.

SHRIMP

Extra-virgin olive oil, for greasing and brushing or misting

2 large eggs

1½ cups shredded unsweetened coconut

½ cup panko bread crumbs

2 tablespoons all-purpose flour

2 tablespoons sesame seeds

½ teaspoon smoked or sweet paprika

Fine pink Himalayan salt

2 pounds large, raw tail-on shrimp, peeled and deveined

HONEY PEPPER SAUCE

½ cup raw honey

Zest and juice of ½ lemon

1 teaspoon freshly ground black pepper

¼ cup chopped mango or pineapple

Fresh lemon or lime wedges, for serving

Spicy Honey Mustard Sauce (recipe follows) or store-bought honey mustard, for serving

1. Preheat the oven to 425°F. Grease two baking sheets.

2. **MAKE THE SHRIMP.** In a shallow bowl, beat the eggs. In a separate shallow bowl, stir together the shredded coconut, bread crumbs, flour, sesame seeds, paprika, and a pinch of salt.

3. Add the shrimp to the egg and toss well to coat. Working with one shrimp at a time, remove from the egg, allowing the excess to drip off. Dredge the shrimp through the coconut mixture, pressing gently to adhere. Place on the prepared baking sheets. Repeat with the remaining shrimp. Lightly brush or mist the shrimp with olive oil. Bake, rotating the baking sheets halfway through, until the coating is light golden and crisp, 8 to 12 minutes.

4. **MEANWHILE, MAKE THE HONEY PEPPER SAUCE.** In a small bowl, combine the honey, lemon zest and juice, and pepper. Stir in the mango.

5. Arrange the shrimp on a serving platter with lemon wedges for squeezing. Serve with both sauces alongside for dipping.

spicy honey mustard sauce
MAKES ⅔ CUP

⅓ cup avocado oil mayonnaise

¼ cup Dijon mustard

2 tablespoons raw honey

Juice of ½ lemon

1 teaspoon curry powder

¼ to ½ teaspoon ground cayenne pepper

Fine pink Himalayan salt

In a small bowl, combine the mayonnaise, mustard, honey, lemon juice, curry powder, and cayenne. Season with salt. Store refrigerated in an airtight container for up to 2 weeks.

crispy chipotle fish tacos

with creamy poblano sauce

PREP 15 MINUTES
COOK 15 MINUTES
TOTAL 30 MINUTES
SERVES 4

Picture this: It was Christmas Eve and my brother Red requested a Mexican-inspired dinner for the next day. I was feeling a bit bored of our usual lasagna, so I happily revamped the menu. Come Christmas morning, I woke up early to plot out our dinner. It had all the things: queso fundido, cilantro-lime rice, tacos, enchiladas, chorizo-stuffed poblano peppers, and every salsa, crema, and sauce I could conjure up. One of those sauces was meant to be a spicy charred jalapeño-cilantro situation, but at some point during the day, I ran out of jalapeños, so I switched gears to use some poblano peppers I had in the fridge. Turns out it was the best ingredient swap of the night. The fire-roasted sauce is a game-changer and inspired these tacos. I built the dish around the sauce, seasoning the fish with a little chipotle pepper and serving up each taco with a quick mango salsa tossed with Tajín, a hot-tart Mexican spice blend of chili powder and lime. I love keeping Tajín on hand to add a quick hit of flavor to sweet mango or pineapple. So delish. And while most tacos in Mexico are made with soft corn tortillas, I love hard taco shells here, which add crunch to every bite. There's a lot to love about these tacos. Just. So. Delicious.

3 tablespoons extra-virgin olive oil

6 garlic cloves, finely chopped or grated

1 tablespoon chipotle chile powder

1 tablespoon smoked paprika

2 teaspoons onion powder

Fine pink Himalayan salt

2 pounds mahi-mahi fillets

1 mango, peeled and diced

Zest and juice of 1 lime

1 teaspoon Tajín seasoning or chipotle chile powder

12 Seasoned Taco Shells (page 205) or store-bought hard taco shells, warmed (I like Siete Foods)

Creamy Poblano Sauce (recipe follows)

Shredded cabbage, for serving

Chopped fresh cilantro, for serving

1. In a 9 × 13-inch baking dish, combine the olive oil, garlic, chipotle chile powder, paprika, onion powder, and a pinch of salt. Add the fish and turn to coat, rubbing the mixture into the fish. Set aside to marinate for 10 minutes.

2. Heat a grill to medium-high or a grill pan or skillet over medium-high heat. Add the fish and cook until cooked through, 3 to 4 minutes per side. Remove the fish from the heat and flake into bite-size pieces.

3. In a medium bowl, toss together the mango, lime zest and juice, and Tajín. Taste and add salt as needed.

4. Stuff the fish into the taco shells, drizzle with poblano sauce, and finish with shredded cabbage, cilantro, and the seasoned mango. Serve immediately.

creamy poblano sauce

MAKES 1½ CUPS

1 poblano pepper

2 garlic cloves, skin on

2 cups fresh cilantro

1 avocado, halved

¼ cup fresh lime juice

1 teaspoon ground cumin

Fine pink Himalayan salt

1. Turn on the broiler.

2. Arrange the poblano and garlic cloves on a baking sheet. Broil for 3 to 5 minutes, watching closely, until darkened on top. Using tongs, remove the garlic cloves. Flip the pepper and broil until charred, 2 to 3 minutes more.

3. Remove the baking sheet from the oven. Remove the garlic skins and the poblano seeds. Transfer the poblano and garlic to a blender or food processor and add the cilantro, avocado, lime juice, cumin, and a pinch of salt. Blend until smooth and creamy, scraping down the sides as needed, about 1 minute. If necessary, add water, 1 tablespoon at a time, to thin. Taste and add more salt as needed.

4. Store refrigerated in an airtight container for up to 1 week.

spicy tuna roll stack

PREP 30 MINUTES

TOTAL 30 MINUTES

SERVES 4

My younger brother Red is constantly traveling from one town to the next, one country to another, always on the move to wherever his snowboarding takes him. He's rarely home in Colorado, but when he does happen to make an appearance, his first dinner request is almost always a sushi night. You know I am a sucker when it comes to my brothers, aiming to please them with their favorite dishes. But I draw the line at sushi. Sushi is great and all, but I'll be honest: I am NOT a master, and making enough to feed my large, hungry family is just not going to happen. But then I came across the seafood stack. While it looks impressive—and maybe even complicated—it couldn't be simpler to create. All you do is layer into a cup the ingredients that would normally go in a roll: fish, rice, seaweed, and all. When you flip over the cup, you've got yourself a sushi stack. It's super easy, fun, and, in my opinion, the best way to have a sushi night in our home. Red gives this dish his seal of approval. Now it's pretty much tradition that I make spicy tuna stacks every time he comes around.

2 (4- to 6-ounce) sushi-grade tuna steaks, cubed

3 tablespoons plus 2 teaspoons low-sodium soy sauce or tamari, plus more for serving

1 tablespoon toasted sesame oil

1 to 2 teaspoons crushed red pepper flakes

1 green onion, thinly sliced

1 tablespoon toasted sesame seeds, plus more for serving (see Note on page 53)

1 cup cooked sushi rice or other short-grain white or brown rice

2 tablespoons rice vinegar

1 teaspoon sugar

½ teaspoon fine pink Himalayan salt

⅓ cup avocado oil mayonnaise

1 to 2 tablespoons sriracha

1 toasted nori sheet, cut into thin strips

1 cup diced cucumber (3 to 4 Persian cucumbers)

1 cup mashed avocado (3 to 4 avocados)

Microgreens, for serving

½ cup wonton crisps (optional)

1. In a medium bowl, combine the tuna, 3 tablespoons of the soy sauce, the sesame oil, red pepper flakes, green onion, and sesame seeds. Toss to mix well.

2. In a separate medium bowl, combine the rice with the rice vinegar, sugar, and salt. Toss to mix well.

3. In a small bowl, stir together the mayonnaise, sriracha, and the remaining 2 teaspoons soy sauce.

4. In a dry 1-cup measure, layer ¼ cup of the tuna, then a quarter of the nori. Add ¼ cup each of the cucumber, then the avocado. Pack in ¼ cup of the seasoned rice. Invert the cup onto a plate and tap the bottom of the cup to release the stack, then carefully wiggle the cup off the stack. Repeat with the remaining ingredients to create 4 stacks total.

5. Top each stack with microgreens, wonton crisps, if desired, and sesame seeds. Serve with the spicy mayo and more soy sauce alongside for dipping.

slow-roasted salmon

with baby potatoes and goddess sauce

PREP 15 MINUTES

COOK 35 MINUTES

TOTAL 50 MINUTES

SERVES 4

In the dead of winter, I gravitate toward all those cozy pasta and pizza and short rib and roast chicken recipes I love so much. Sometime midseason, I realize I am cooking the same dishes over and over again. And that's when I think about what I haven't made in a while. To get out of the rut, more times than not I turn to this slow-roasted salmon. It's just the right combination of light and healthy, but still super cozy. Slow-roasting the salmon really locks in its flavor and turns out a luscious, buttery fillet that flakes perfectly every time. You can use skin-on or skinless salmon—I personally love the additional healthy omega-3 fatty acids and flavor in the skin. I roast some baby potatoes right alongside, and then serve everything with Goddess Sauce, an herby avocado-yogurt sauce that you'll want to scoop up into every bite.

1 pound baby potatoes, halved if large

⅓ cup plus 2 tablespoons extra-virgin olive oil

Fine pink Himalayan salt and freshly ground black pepper

Juice of 2 lemons

1 tablespoon raw honey

2 teaspoons smoked paprika

2 teaspoons ground cumin

1 to 2 teaspoons crushed red pepper flakes

1 (2-pound) salmon fillet

3 Persian cucumbers, chopped

4 ounces feta cheese, cubed or crumbled

Goddess Sauce (page 153) or store-bought green goddess dressing

Roughly chopped fresh dill and fresh basil leaves, for serving

1. Preheat the oven to 425°F.

2. On a rimmed baking sheet, toss the potatoes with 2 tablespoons of the olive oil. Season with salt and pepper. Roast until tender, about 25 minutes.

3. Meanwhile, in a small bowl, combine the remaining ⅓ cup olive oil with the lemon juice, honey, paprika, cumin, red pepper flakes, and a pinch each of salt and pepper.

4. Remove the potatoes from the oven and reduce the oven temperature to 300°F. Push the potatoes to one side of the baking sheet and add the salmon (skin-side down if leaving the skin on) to the other side. Pour the olive oil sauce all over the salmon. Bake until the salmon reaches your desired doneness, 10 to 20 minutes more.

5. To serve, arrange the potatoes, salmon, cucumbers, and feta on plates. Drizzle any oil left in the pan over the top. Dollop the goddess sauce onto the potatoes and salmon. Sprinkle with the dill and basil and serve.

white fish
with fried olive and caper dressing

PREP 10 MINUTES
COOK 15 MINUTES
TOTAL 25 MINUTES
SERVES 4

I don't cook a ton of white fish—we've got some pretty picky eaters in the family, especially when it comes to seafood. But in an effort to squeeze in something new, I took a sauce I knew they'd love and tried it on a mild-flavored, delicious fish: Chilean sea bass. I had a feeling I could get them hooked on the garlicky goodness with tangy fried olives, no matter what it was on. Spoiler alert: It worked! This combination is pretty hard to beat. The dish always turns out pretty, feels kind of fancy, and yet is so simple—it doesn't even take 30 minutes to make and requires just one skillet. Feel free to use whatever white fish you like. Chilean sea bass is my personal favorite because, when prepared properly, it melts in your mouth like butter. But halibut or tilapia would also be great! The only other thing I'd add is a good piece of crusty bread or some oven-baked fries for mopping up every bite of briny deliciousness.

⅓ cup plus 2 tablespoons extra-virgin olive oil

½ cup pitted green olives, roughly chopped if large

2 tablespoons capers, drained

1 garlic clove, finely chopped or grated

½ cup fresh parsley, chopped

½ cup fresh basil leaves, chopped

2 tablespoons fresh oregano leaves, chopped

2 tablespoons champagne vinegar

2 teaspoons lemon zest plus 1 tablespoon fresh lemon juice

Crushed red pepper flakes

Fine pink Himalayan salt and freshly ground black pepper

4 (6-ounce) Chilean sea bass, halibut, or tilapia fillets

1. In a large skillet over medium heat, combine 1 tablespoon of the olive oil, the olives, and capers. Cook, stirring occasionally, until the capers are beginning to crisp, 4 to 6 minutes. Add the garlic and cook until fragrant, about 1 minute more. Transfer the mixture to a medium bowl. Add ⅓ cup of the olive oil, the parsley, basil, oregano, vinegar, and lemon zest and juice. Season with red pepper flakes, salt, and pepper. Stir to combine well and set aside.

2. Pat the fish dry and season it all over with salt and pepper. Heat the remaining 1 tablespoon olive oil in the same skillet over medium-high heat. When the oil shimmers, add the fish and cook until browned and cooked through, 3 to 4 minutes per side.

3. Divide the fish among plates and drizzle any oil from the skillet over the top. Spoon the olive and caper dressing over the fish. Serve.

spicy shrimp tacos

with jalapeño-mango salsa

PREP 15 MINUTES
COOK 15 MINUTES
TOTAL 30 MINUTES
SERVES 4

Obviously, I care a lot about how things taste. But I am also a visual person—before I started HBH, I was going to school to be a fashion stylist! So sometimes when I'm cooking a new dish, how I imagine the photo will look leads the way. It's no surprise then that the bright, colorful ingredients popular in Caribbean cooking inspire me. I love the flavors of this tropical cuisine—the dishes often have spice mixed with sweetness, sometimes from fruits. Spice and pineapple are two of my favorite tastes, so all my senses led me to these fun tacos with seasoned shrimp, pineapple, and a super-special gingery coconut sauce. The tacos are layered with so much flavor, color, and texture that you'd think they might take a long time to make, but they are actually the easiest. Everything is roasted together on one sheet pan and then assembled. And while you might not think you need both a pineapple salsa and an additional cilantro sauce, trust me, you do. Tacos are all about the toppings, and these two are essential for the maximum tropical color and taste we are going for.

TACOS

1½ pounds large, raw shrimp, peeled and deveined

2 tablespoons extra-virgin olive oil

2 teaspoons chipotle chile powder

1 teaspoon smoked paprika

1 teaspoon garlic powder

1 teaspoon onion powder

¼ teaspoon ground cinnamon

Fine pink Himalayan salt and freshly ground black pepper

1 or 2 medium jalapeños

1 cup diced fresh pineapple

1 cup diced fresh mango

¼ cup fresh cilantro, roughly chopped

Juice from 1 lime

Juice from ½ orange

3 cups shredded cabbage

SAUCE

1 cup fresh cilantro

½ cup coconut cream

2 garlic cloves, finely chopped or grated

1 (1-inch) piece of fresh ginger, peeled and finely chopped or grated

Juice of 1 lime

Fine pink Himalayan salt

FOR SERVING

Corn or flour tortillas, warmed

Crumbled feta

Sliced avocado

Fresh cilantro leaves

1. Preheat the oven to 425°F.

2. **MAKE THE TACOS.** On a baking sheet, toss together the shrimp, olive oil, chipotle chile powder, paprika, garlic powder, onion powder, cinnamon, and a pinch each of salt and pepper. Arrange in a single layer on one side of the sheet. On the other side, add a jalapeño (or two, if you like your salsa spicy). Roast together until the shrimp is pink and cooked through, 10 to 12 minutes. Remove the baking sheet from the oven and turn on the broiler.

3. Using tongs, return the jalapeño directly to the oven rack. Broil until charred, about 1 minute, and then remove from the oven. When the jalapeño is cool enough to handle, remove the seeds, if desired, then roughly chop the pepper. In a medium bowl, combine the chopped jalapeño with the pineapple, mango, cilantro, lime juice, orange juice, and a pinch of salt.

4. **MEANWHILE, MAKE THE SAUCE.** In a blender or food processor, combine the cilantro, coconut cream, garlic, ginger, lime juice, and a pinch of salt. Blend until smooth. Taste and add more salt as needed.

5. In a large bowl, toss the cabbage with ¼ cup of the sauce to coat well.

6. Stuff the cabbage and shrimp into the warmed tortillas. Top as desired with the remaining sauce, the salsa, feta, avocado, and cilantro.

creamy bacon and tuscan shrimp

PREP 10 MINUTES
COOK 15 MINUTES
TOTAL 25 MINUTES
SERVES 6

Anything with garlic, butter, Parmesan, and basil has me ALL in. Usually I do chicken this way—a lot of restaurants will call it Tuscan chicken—because that's my family's go-to protein, but when I have guests in town visiting or I travel back to Ohio to see my more adventurous family, I make an effort to have fun and play around with seafood recipes. Fresh faces mean new palates to please, and that's always very exciting for me! Well, I swapped in shrimp for chicken, and the verdict? It's even more delicious. But the bacon is really the secret here. It adds a salty, savory, rich flavor that takes this dish to the next level. Serve it over pasta or polenta, or do as I do: scoop the sauce and shrimp up on toasted pieces of crusty ciabatta bread with a sprinkle of fresh basil on top. It's a simple 25-minute recipe that feels special enough to take you to the idyllic Tuscan countryside of your dreams. Yum.

2 slices thick-cut bacon, chopped

1 tablespoon extra-virgin olive oil

1½ pounds jumbo raw shrimp, peeled and deveined

Fine pink Himalayan salt and freshly ground black pepper

4 garlic cloves, finely chopped or grated

1 teaspoon dried rosemary

1 teaspoon dried oregano

1 teaspoon paprika

Crushed red pepper flakes

½ cup sun-dried tomatoes packed in olive oil, drained and chopped

½ cup dry white wine, such as pinot grigio or Sauvignon Blanc

1 cup full-fat coconut milk or heavy cream

3 cups baby spinach

¼ cup grated Parmesan cheese

Juice of 1 lemon

Fresh basil leaves, for garnish

Crusty bread or cooked pasta, for serving (optional)

1. Place the bacon in a large skillet over medium heat. Cook until the bacon is crispy and the fat has rendered, about 5 minutes. Using a slotted spoon, transfer the bacon to a paper towel–lined plate.

2. Add the olive oil to the bacon fat in the skillet and heat over medium heat. Pat the shrimp dry. When the oil is shimmering, add the shrimp and a pinch each of salt and pepper. Cook, flipping once, until the shrimp are pink and opaque, about 2 minutes per side. Add the garlic, rosemary, oregano, paprika, and a pinch of red pepper flakes. Continue cooking, stirring, until the garlic is fragrant, 1 to 2 minutes. Add the sun-dried tomatoes and cook until their oils release, about 1 minute.

3. Pour in the wine, scraping up any browned bits from the bottom of the pan, and bring to a simmer. Cook until the liquid is reduced slightly, 2 to 3 minutes. Stir in the coconut milk, spinach, and Parmesan. Return to a simmer and cook until the spinach is wilted, 2 to 3 minutes more. Remove the skillet from the heat. Stir in the lemon juice. Sprinkle the bacon and basil over the top.

4. Serve with crusty bread or your favorite cut of pasta.

ginger-pepper salmon

with garlic rice noodles

PREP 10 MINUTES

COOK 15 MINUTES

TOTAL 25 MINUTES

SERVES 4

When it comes to fish, a sticky sauce and a little kick are always my go-to accompaniments. This salmon was inspired by a black pepper chicken that I make all the time, especially when my older brother Creighton is around, since it's one of his favorite dinners. One day he asked for that dish, but I just had salmon in the fridge. I gave it a try, and let me tell you, I love this version even more. The fish sits in a sweet, spicy sauce and turns crispy and caramelized after a few minutes under the broiler. Each fillet is served over rice noodles tossed in a garlicky coconut mixture. And then I always add fresh basil and extra lime. When everything is put together, it's the perfect combination of flavors and texture.

8 ounces vermicelli rice noodles

4 (6-ounce) skin-on salmon fillets

1 teaspoon ground turmeric

1 teaspoon ground ginger

Fine pink Himalayan salt and freshly ground black pepper

¼ cup raw honey

¼ cup low-sodium soy sauce or tamari

2 tablespoons rice vinegar

½ teaspoon crushed red pepper flakes, plus more to taste

3 tablespoons sesame oil or extra-virgin olive oil

2 medium shallots, sliced or chopped

1 small head of broccoli, cut into florets

2 tablespoons salted butter

4 garlic cloves, finely chopped or grated

⅓ cup full-fat coconut milk

Fresh basil and/or cilantro, for serving

Lime wedges, for serving

1. Bring a large pot of water to a boil over high heat. Turn off the heat, add the noodles, and cook according to the package directions. Drain.

2. Meanwhile, turn the oven to broil.

3. Rub the salmon all over with the turmeric, ginger, and a pinch each of salt and black pepper.

4. In a small bowl, combine the honey, soy sauce, vinegar, red pepper flakes, and ¼ cup of water.

5. Heat the oil in a large oven-safe skillet over medium heat. When the oil shimmers, add the shallots and broccoli and cook, stirring, until the broccoli is beginning to soften slightly, 2 to 3 minutes. Pour in the honey–soy sauce mixture. Increase the heat to medium-high and bring to a boil. Add the salmon, skin-side up, and cook until it is opaque two-thirds of the way up the sides, about 2 minutes. Transfer the skillet to the oven and broil until the salmon is medium-rare and the skin is crispy, 3 to 4 minutes.

6. In a medium skillet over medium heat, combine the butter, garlic, and a pinch of red pepper flakes. Cook, stirring, until the butter is melted and the garlic is light golden brown, 1 to 2 minutes. Stir in the coconut milk and cook to warm through, 3 to 5 minutes. Remove the skillet from the heat, add the noodles, and toss to coat.

7. Divide the noodles among bowls and place the salmon on top. Spoon the sauce over the salmon. Top with basil and serve with lime wedges for squeezing.

the florida vacation sandwich

PREP 20 MINUTES
COOK 20 MINUTES
TOTAL 40 MINUTES
MAKES 4 SANDWICHES

You know the dishes you get only while on vacation? The ones you look forward to every year when you visit your favorite spot in your favorite getaway town? Well, my cousin Maggie's family has been visiting Naples, Florida, since she was a kid. One of the restaurants they always hit up is Buzz's Lighthouse. The grouper sandwich on their menu is famous, and when she told me about it, I knew I had to create my own version. They do theirs with American cheese, coleslaw, fried or blackened grouper, Thousand Island dressing, and rye bread. Mine is a bit different, but oh so good. I opted for slightly spicy pepper Jack cheese, a homemade coleslaw, and my Spicy Honey Mustard Sauce to complement the delicious pan-seared grouper. It's easy to make at home, but the outcome is top-notch restaurant quality. You might even feel like you're on vacation. To get the real experience of this sandwich, Maggie says you have to add a side of fries and pickles. No problem!

SLAW

1 (14-ounce) bag coleslaw mix
2 tablespoons apple cider vinegar
2 tablespoons Dijon mustard, smooth or grainy
1 tablespoon raw honey
Fine pink Himalayan salt

SANDWICHES

1 tablespoon smoked paprika
2 teaspoons chili powder
2 teaspoons dried oregano
2 teaspoons dried thyme
1 teaspoon garlic powder
1 teaspoon onion powder
½ teaspoon ground cayenne pepper
Fine pink Himalayan salt and freshly ground black pepper
4 (6-ounce) grouper fillets
1 tablespoon extra-virgin olive oil
8 slices rye bread
2 tablespoons salted butter, at room temperature
Billion Island Dressing (page 149) or store-bought Thousand Island dressing
2 slices pepper Jack cheese
2 slices sharp cheddar

1. **MAKE THE SLAW.** In a medium bowl, toss the coleslaw mix with the vinegar, mustard, honey, and a generous pinch of salt. Let the slaw sit while you prepare the sandwich, or cover and refrigerate it for better flavor—the longer it sits, the stronger the flavor will become.

2. **MAKE THE SANDWICHES.** In a small bowl, stir together the paprika, chili powder, oregano, thyme, garlic powder, onion powder, cayenne pepper, and a pinch each of salt and pepper. Rub the spice mixture all over the grouper.

3. Heat the olive oil in a large skillet over medium-high heat. When the oil shimmers, add the fish and cook until opaque and cooked through, 3 to 4 minutes per side. Transfer the fish to a plate.

4. Spread one side of each slice of bread with butter. Spread the other side of each slice with the Billion Island Dressing, then add ½ slice of each cheese on top of four of the bread slices. Layer on the slaw and 1 fish fillet on top of each slice of cheese. Top with the remaining slices of bread, buttered-side up.

5. Wipe out the skillet from the fish and return it to medium-low heat. Add two of the sandwiches to the skillet and cook until the bread is golden and the cheese is a bit melty, 3 to 5 minutes per side. Repeat with the remaining two sandwiches.

6. Transfer the sandwiches to a cutting board, halve, and serve warm.

sweet, spicy, saucy
honey garlic shrimp

PREP 10 MINUTES

COOK 20 MINUTES

TOTAL 30 MINUTES

SERVES 4

What I love most about shrimp is just how versatile it can be. I always keep it in my freezer because it's quick to defrost and can do, well, pretty much anything. It can take on so many flavor profiles from all over the world. I love cooking up a saucy shrimp dish on a busy weeknight because it always satisfies my craving for something that hits all the right notes—salty, tangy, spicy, sweet—and is even quicker than it would be for takeout to get to me. That brings me to this dish, which, surprise, surprise, is really all about the sauce. If I'm being honest, it is truly hard to stop eating . . . but in a good way. One trick: I like to remove the shrimp shells, but leave the tails on for easier eating. Leaving the tails on during cooking adds flavor, too, so I often recommend it!

3 slices thick-cut bacon, chopped

1 pound jumbo, raw, tail-on shrimp, peeled and deveined

2 tablespoons sesame oil

1 shallot, chopped

3 garlic cloves, finely chopped or grated

2 tablespoons raw honey

2 tablespoons fish sauce

1 tablespoon low-sodium soy sauce or tamari

1 Fresno pepper, seeded and sliced, or ½ teaspoon crushed red pepper flakes

1 teaspoon freshly ground black pepper

Steamed white or brown rice, for serving

4 green onions, thinly sliced

Fresh Thai basil or sweet basil leaves, for serving

1. Place the bacon in a large skillet over medium heat and cook, stirring occasionally, until the bacon is crispy and the fat has rendered, about 5 minutes. Using a slotted spoon, transfer the bacon to a paper towel–lined plate. Drain off all but 1 tablespoon of the bacon fat (see Note on page 186).

2. Pat the shrimp dry. Add the sesame oil and shallot to the same skillet over medium heat. Cook, stirring occasionally, until the shallot is softened, 2 to 3 minutes. Add the garlic and cook until fragrant, another 1 to 2 minutes. Add the honey, fish sauce, soy sauce, Fresno pepper, and black pepper. Cook until the sauce is slightly reduced, 2 to 3 minutes. Add the shrimp and cook, tossing, until pink and opaque, 5 to 7 minutes.

3. Spoon the shrimp and sauce over bowls of rice. Add the bacon, dividing evenly. Top with the green onions and basil and serve.

seafood florentine

PREP 10 MINUTES
COOK 15 MINUTES
TOTAL 25 MINUTES
SERVES 4

One of the dishes my mom would make often when I was growing up—and that she still makes to this day—is her Chicken Florentine. Her recipe is so simple, but she really does it up with lots of butter and Parmesan as the base of a creamy spinach sauce. It's always delicious and such a treat whenever she makes it. Since I love the flavors so much, I wondered what would happen if I swapped the chicken for a fillet of fish. As it turns out, I like it with mild white fish even better! Coating the fish in a bit of flour before searing gives you a perfectly crisped fillet. And I spoon the sauce on top so each fillet is sitting in a buttery puddle of goodness. Whenever I serve this to my dad, he says, "You couldn't get this at a restaurant. It's so much better than any restaurant."

4 (5- to 6-ounce) white fish fillets, such as mahi-mahi, sea bass, or halibut

Fine pink Himalayan salt and freshly ground black pepper

¼ cup flour of your choice

2 tablespoons extra-virgin olive oil

2 tablespoons salted butter

1 shallot, thinly sliced

3 garlic cloves, finely chopped or grated

1½ cups cherry tomatoes

2 tablespoons fresh thyme leaves

Crushed red pepper flakes

¾ cup milk of your choice

2 ounces cream cheese, cubed

¼ cup grated Parmesan cheese

4 cups baby spinach, roughly chopped

Juice of 1 lemon

2 tablespoons chopped fresh parsley

1. Pat the fish dry and season all over with salt and pepper. Place the flour in a shallow bowl. Dip the fish into the flour to coat on both sides.

2. Heat the olive oil in a large skillet over medium heat. When the oil shimmers, add the fish and cook until lightly browned on the bottom, 2 to 3 minutes. Flip and continue cooking until lightly browned and cooked through, 2 to 3 minutes more. Transfer the fish to a plate.

3. To the same skillet over medium heat, add the butter, shallots, garlic, tomatoes, and thyme. Cook, stirring occasionally, until the garlic is fragrant, about 2 minutes. Add a pinch of red pepper flakes, the milk, and cream cheese. Season with salt and pepper. Reduce the heat to low and cook, stirring constantly, until smooth and creamy, about 3 minutes. Add the Parmesan and spinach and cook until the spinach is wilted, 3 to 5 minutes more. Stir in the lemon juice and parsley. Slide the fish back into the sauce, and cook until warmed through, 2 to 3 minutes.

4. To serve, divide the fish among plates and spoon the sauce over the top.

blackened salmon skewers

with feta caprese

PREP 20 MINUTES

COOK 10 MINUTES

TOTAL 30 MINUTES

SERVES 4

The very first salmon recipe I ever made was a blackened salmon taco, which still lives online on my website (the photos are pretty horrendous—I've come a long way!). I haven't made that dish in a looong time, but I remember it being delicious. And to this day, it's still my brother Brendan's favorite recipe (it was his idea, after all!). Those tacos gave me the inspiration for these skewers. And you know what? I'm really not sure which I like more. These skewers are incredible and SO EASY. I toss the fish with a good amount of spices and herbs for really great flavor. The feta-instead-of-mozzarella spin on caprese salad on the side adds a nice layer of freshness with some richness, too. But here's what you can't skip: the spicy honey mustard sauce for dipping. It's a creamy touch to balance out that cayenne on the salmon.

SALMON SKEWERS

3 tablespoons extra-virgin olive oil, plus more for brushing

1 tablespoon light brown sugar

1 tablespoon smoked paprika

2 teaspoons ground cumin

2 teaspoons dried thyme

2 teaspoons dried oregano

1 teaspoon cayenne pepper

¼ to ½ teaspoon crushed red pepper flakes

½ teaspoon fine pink Himalayan salt

4 garlic cloves, finely chopped or grated

1 tablespoon lemon zest

2 pounds skinless salmon fillets, cut into 1-inch cubes

CAPRESE

¼ cup extra-virgin olive oil

2 tablespoons balsamic vinegar

2 teaspoons raw honey

¼ to ½ teaspoon crushed red pepper flakes

Fine pink Himalayan salt and freshly ground black pepper

2 cups cherry tomatoes, halved

4 ounces feta cheese, cubed

¼ cup fresh basil leaves, chopped

¼ cup shelled pistachios, finely chopped

Spicy Honey Mustard Sauce (page 228) or store-bought honey mustard, for serving

1. Heat a grill to medium-high or a grill pan or large skillet over medium-high heat.

2. **MAKE THE SALMON SKEWERS.** In a medium bowl, combine the olive oil, brown sugar, paprika, cumin, thyme, oregano, cayenne, red pepper flakes, salt, garlic, and lemon zest. Add the salmon and toss to coat. Thread the salmon onto skewers (you'll need 4 to 6 skewers). Cook, brushing with olive oil and turning every few minutes, until the salmon is cooked through and blackened a bit, 8 to 10 minutes total.

3. Meanwhile, make the caprese. In a large bowl, whisk together the olive oil, vinegar, honey, red pepper flakes, and a pinch each of salt and pepper. Add the tomatoes, feta, basil, and pistachios. Toss to combine.

4. Transfer the caprese to a serving platter. Lay the salmon skewers on top. Serve with the honey mustard alongside for dipping or drizzling.

dessert

salty chocolate pretzel rye cookies

PREP 15 MINUTES

COOK 10 MINUTES

TOTAL 25 MINUTES, PLUS CHILLING TIME

MAKES 24 COOKIES

By now you know the story of my mom having dessert on the table before anything else was even considered. You also probably know cookies were her number one and still are to this day. When my brothers and I were growing up, she could bake them completely by memory. Always crisp on the edges and doughy in the middle. Her not-so-secret recipe? The one on the back of the Nestlé Toll House chocolate chip bag. But her special touch was extra chocolate chips. I'd share the recipe with you, but it's probably sitting on a shelf in your pantry right now. You know me, though . . . I love to add to a favorite. Just like Mom's, these are crisp on the edges, doughy in the middle, and loaded with chocolate. The differences? Rye flour, pretzels, brown butter, and chocolate chunks. The rye adds unexpected flavor. It's nutty and rich, and when combined with the salty pretzels and brown butter, it makes for a cookie that really does melt in your mouth like Mom's. Even Asher loves them, and let me tell you, that girl is picky about her cookies. She says the pretzels with the chocolate chunks really get her excited—that salty-sweet thing that makes every dessert better.

1 cup (2 sticks) salted butter, at room temperature

¾ cup packed dark brown sugar

¼ cup granulated sugar

2 large eggs, at room temperature

2 teaspoons pure vanilla extract

1½ cups dark rye flour

¾ cups all-purpose flour

½ teaspoon baking soda

¼ teaspoon fine pink Himalayan salt

1½ cups chopped dark chocolate chunks or chips

1 cup mini pretzel twists, roughly crushed

Flaky sea salt

1. Preheat the oven to 350°F. Line a baking sheet with parchment paper.

2. Melt ½ cup of the butter in a small saucepan over medium heat. Cook, stirring, until the butter begins to brown, 3 to 4 minutes. Transfer the butter to a heatproof bowl and place the bowl in the freezer to chill for 10 to 15 minutes.

3. In a large bowl, using an electric mixer, beat together the cooled brown butter, the remaining ½ cup butter, the brown sugar, and the granulated sugar on low, then slowly increase the speed to high and beat until fluffy, about 2 minutes. Add the eggs, one at a time, beating until each is combined, about 1 minute per egg. Add the vanilla and beat until creamy, 1 minute more. Add both flours, the baking soda, and the salt, and beat until just combined. Fold in the chocolate chunks.

4. Roll the dough into 1-tablespoon balls. Arrange the balls on the prepared baking sheet, spacing them 2 inches apart. Gently press a few crushed pretzel pieces all over each dough ball, firmly sticking them in.

5. Bake the cookies for 7 minutes. Remove the baking sheet from the oven and tap it firmly against the counter a few times to flatten the cookies. Return to the oven and bake until the cookies are just beginning to set around the edges but are still doughy in the center, 1 to 3 minutes more. Remove the baking sheet from the oven and tap it firmly against the counter to flatten the cookies again. Sprinkle the cookies with flaky salt and let them cool on the baking sheet; they will continue to cook slightly. Enjoy the cookies warm or at room temperature. Store at room temperature in an airtight container for up to 4 days.

creamy vegan coconut chocolate pudding

PREP 5 MINUTES

COOK 15 MINUTES

TOTAL 20 MINUTES, PLUS SETTING TIME

SERVES 6

Who doesn't love a classic chocolate pudding? I feel like it's what we all want the most when we're craving something comforting and sweet. My nonnie used to buy those chocolate pudding cups with the peel-off tops. My brothers and I would hunt them down every time we entered her house, but I later learned she was buying the sugar-free, fat-free kind, which have zero flavor. I didn't know what I was missing out on until I made my first batch of pudding in high school. While the fact that the homemade stuff is a million and one times better than store-bought isn't shocking, the experience still knocked me off my feet. This version is dairy-free, using creamy coconut milk. Do up each bowl of the stuff with a dollop of coconut cream and some chocolate shavings. It feels fancy, and is, of course, delicious, but so, so easy. Once you make this, you'll never go back to the store-bought stuff again. I swear.

⅔ cup unsweetened cocoa powder

¼ cup arrowroot powder

3 (13.5-ounce) cans full-fat coconut milk

¼ cup pure maple syrup (more or less to taste)

Flaky sea salt

½ cup dark chocolate chunks or chips or 3.2 ounces chopped dark chocolate

1 tablespoon pure vanilla extract

Coconut whipped cream, for serving (optional)

Chocolate shavings (optional)

1.   In a medium saucepan, whisk together the cocoa powder and arrowroot powder. Whisk in 1 can of coconut milk until fully combined and smooth. Add the remaining coconut milk, the maple syrup, and a pinch of salt.

2.   Set the pan over medium-high heat and bring the mixture to a boil. Cook, whisking continuously, until the mixture thickens, 8 to 12 minutes. Whisk in the dark chocolate until melted and smooth, about 1 minute. Remove the pan from the heat. Whisk in the vanilla.

3.   Transfer the pudding to a serving bowl or into individual serving dishes. Serve warm, or press plastic wrap directly onto the pudding and refrigerate until set, about 1 hour. Top with whipped cream and chocolate shavings, if desired.

old-school peanut butter bars

with fudge icing

PREP 15 MINUTES

COOK 15 MINUTES

TOTAL 30 MINUTES, PLUS COOLING AND SETTING TIME

MAKES 16 BARS

In grade school, pizza day was always the most exciting of the month. Pizza for lunch with a side of "lunchroom-style" desserts baked by the members of the PTA . . . what's not to love about that? Everyone always looked forward to chocolate chip cookies, but my favorites were the peanut butter bars. They were doughy, heavy on the peanut butter, and topped with the most delicious fudgy chocolate icing that surely contained an entire bag of confectioners' sugar. While I loved those so much, I wanted to make a more grown-up version. Most important to me was getting that chocolate on the top just right. The verdict? I can't say they are an exact replication of the lunchroom bars we grew up with, but this version is GOOD. The almond flour makes them tender and keeps them gluten-free. The icing . . . well, I figured why load it up with extra sugar when chocolate can just do its thing? Trust me, the icing will make your eyes roll back with that peanut butter underneath. These bars are easy—SO easy. Bring them to your next party—they'll be the first dessert to disappear.

PEANUT BUTTER BARS

¼ cup coconut oil

1 cup creamy peanut butter

¼ cup raw honey

1 large egg, at room temperature

1 teaspoon vanilla extract

1½ cups almond flour

½ teaspoon baking powder

¼ teaspoon fine pink Himalayan salt

FUDGE ICING

1½ cups semisweet chocolate chips

2 tablespoons coconut oil

Fine pink Himalayan salt

1. Preheat the oven to 350°F. Line an 8 × 8-inch baking dish with parchment paper, leaving a 1-inch overhang on either side.

2. **MAKE THE PEANUT BUTTER BARS.** In a large microwave-safe bowl, melt together the coconut oil and ¼ cup of the peanut butter in the microwave, stirring every 30 seconds, until combined, about 1 minute total. Stir in the honey, egg, and vanilla. Add the almond flour, baking powder, and salt. Transfer the dough into the prepared baking dish and use a spatula to spread it into an even layer.

3. Bake until golden brown, 12 to 15 minutes. Remove from the oven and let cool for 10 minutes.

4. Dollop the remaining ¾ cup peanut butter over the bars, lightly spreading in an even layer. Let cool completely, about 30 minutes.

5. **MEANWHILE, MAKE THE ICING.** In a large microwave-safe bowl, melt the chocolate chips and coconut oil together with a pinch of salt in the microwave, stirring every 30 seconds, 1 to 2 minutes. (Alternatively, you can do this in a small saucepan over medium-low heat.) Spread the icing over the bars. Let set for about 1 hour.

6. Using the parchment overhang, remove the bars from the baking dish. Slice into 2-inch squares and enjoy! Store leftovers in an airtight container at room temperature for up to 5 days.

lemon tart with vanilla sugar

PREP 20 MINUTES

COOK 25 MINUTES

TOTAL 45 MINUTES, PLUS CHILLING TIME

SERVES 8

This tart is hands down one of the best things to make throughout the winter and early spring, when Meyer lemons are in season. It showcases this gorgeous winter citrus, which is around for only a short time—though, of course, the recipe works as well with regular lemons throughout the year! It's like your favorite lemon bars, but in an extra-creamy tart that's silky smooth and just sweet enough, using honey and only a smidge of refined sugar. The crust is gluten-free, but still rich and tender. And you know I had to add an extra special touch—blueberries are basically "nature's sprinkles," and this vanilla sugar is really something special. The presentation is super fancy, but in reality, this perfect dessert is super simple.

CRUST

¼ cup melted coconut oil, plus more for greasing

1 cup finely shredded unsweetened coconut

1 cup almond flour

2 tablespoons raw honey

½ teaspoon fine pink Himalayan salt

FILLING

5 large egg yolks

1 cup sweetened condensed milk

1 tablespoon lemon zest

½ cup fresh lemon juice

1 teaspoon pure vanilla extract

½ teaspoon fine pink Himalayan salt

VANILLA SUGAR

¼ cup granulated sugar

⅛ teaspoon vanilla bean powder

Whipped cream, for serving (optional)

Fresh blueberries, for serving (optional)

1. Preheat the oven to 350°F. Grease a springform pan or pie dish.

2. **MAKE THE CRUST.** In a food processor, combine the coconut oil, shredded coconut, almond flour, honey, and salt. Process, scraping down the sides of the bowl as needed, until a soft dough comes together, about 1 minute. Press the mixture into the prepared pan, going halfway up the sides. Bake until lightly golden brown, 12 to 15 minutes. Keep the oven on.

3. **MEANWHILE, MAKE THE FILLING.** Meanwhile, make the filling. In a medium bowl, beat the egg yolks until smooth. Add the sweetened condensed milk, lemon zest, lemon juice, vanilla extract, and salt. Beat to combine. Carefully pour the filling into the baked crust.

4. Bake until the filling is just set on top, 12 to 14 minutes. Let cool slightly, then cover and chill in the fridge until completely set, at least 1 hour and up to 5 days.

5. **MEANWHILE, MAKE THE VANILLA SUGAR.** In a small bowl, whisk together the sugar and vanilla bean powder.

6. Top the tart as desired with whipped cream and blueberries. Sprinkle the vanilla sugar over the top.

brown sugar tahini shortbread

PREP 15 MINUTES

COOK 15 MINUTES

TOTAL 30 MINUTES, PLUS CHILLING TIME

MAKES 24 COOKIES

These cookies are DELICIOUS. And I really mean *delicious*. The tahini is the special ingredient that MAKES them. It's not that you really even know it's there, but it adds a richness that's truly something special. Also, dark brown sugar. Trust me. It works very well with the tahini and vanilla and makes a perfectly sweet, slightly maple-y cookie that is roll-your-eyes-back good. They're as buttery as a classic shortbread, but with a nice amount of nuttiness and crunch from the sesame seeds on the edge. And the chocolate, well, to me it seals the deal, but you can also leave it out if you'd rather focus on all that buttery, nutty deliciousness. Hard to beat these! And the best part? Once the dough log is in the fridge, it can hang out in there for days (up to 5, to be specific, and sliced cookies will keep for a couple of months in the freezer; see Notes). That means you can make the dough on, say, a Sunday, and then have warm baked tahini cookies in just minutes any day of the week.

½ cup plus 2 tablespoons (1¼ sticks) salted butter, at room temperature

½ cup packed dark brown sugar

1 cup tahini

2 teaspoons pure vanilla extract

¾ cup all-purpose flour, plus more as needed

¾ cup whole-wheat pastry flour

4 ounces dark chocolate, chopped (optional)

1 large egg, beaten

¼ cup turbinado or demerara sugar

2 tablespoons sesame seeds (optional)

Flaky sea salt

1.   In a large bowl, using an electric mixer, beat together the butter and brown sugar on medium speed until fluffy, scraping down the sides as needed, about 2 minutes. Add the tahini and vanilla and beat on low for about 1 minute, then increase the speed to high and continue beating until combined, 2 minutes more. Add both flours and mix until completely combined, scraping down the sides of the bowl as needed, 1 to 2 minutes. If the dough seems too sticky, add more all-purpose flour as needed, 1 tablespoon at a time, up to ¼ cup. Fold in the chocolate (if using).

2.   Turn out the dough on a large piece of parchment paper or plastic wrap. Using your hands, shape it into a log about 12 inches long and about 2 inches in diameter. Wrap the dough up in the parchment and refrigerate for at least 4 hours or up to 5 days.

3.   Preheat the oven to 350°F. Line two baking sheets with parchment paper.

4.   Unwrap the chilled dough and brush with the beaten egg. In a small bowl, stir together the turbinado sugar and sesame seeds (if using). Sprinkle the mixture all over the dough, turning to coat and pressing to adhere. Cut the dough into ½-inch-thick slices (see Notes). Arrange the cookies on the prepared baking sheets, spacing them 1 inch apart. Bake until the edges of the cookies are golden brown, 12 to 14 minutes.

5.   Remove the cookies from the oven and immediately sprinkle with sea salt. Let cool on the baking sheet for about 10 minutes. Enjoy or let cool completely, and then store at room temperature in an airtight container for up to 4 days.

NOTES

A very sharp chef's knife is the best choice for slicing this dough. It is important to cut in a quick forward motion rather than sawing back and forth. If the dough cracks, just push the rounds back together. The cookies will be okay—I promise!

These are perfect make-ahead cookies to have on hand when you need something sweet in a pinch. After you slice the cookies, you can rewrap them in parchment and freeze in an airtight container for up to 3 months. When you're ready to bake, let the cookies thaw on the baking sheet for 5 to 10 minutes, then bake as directed, adding an additional minute or two if needed.

coconut cake

with chocolate frosting

PREP 30 MINUTES
COOK 30 MINUTES
TOTAL 1 HOUR, PLUS COOLING TIME
SERVES 8 TO 10

I am sure you know by now that I adore a layer cake. I love baking them, assembling them, decorating them, and then photographing them. Oh yeah, and eating them, too! I am always looking for excuses to bake them up, whether it's for a birthday, a holiday, or even a random Friday night. A layer cake just feels special and exciting every time. Usually I go for chocolate-on-chocolate since I was raised by a true chocoholic, but this sweet coconut cake with heavy hints of vanilla hits all the right notes. It's light and fluffy, and that honey keeps it ultra-moist and the perfect amount of sweet. And using coconut oil instead of butter also boosts the coconut flavor. But of course, there's still chocolate, because I'm still me. That fudgy frosting is, well, it's the true icing on the cake. Here's a tip: If you love frosting, make twice as much. You can never have too much . . . am I right?

CAKE

¾ cup melted coconut oil, plus more for greasing

1 cup full-fat coconut milk

½ cup plain Greek yogurt

½ cup raw honey

3 large eggs, at room temperature

1 cup granulated sugar

1 tablespoon pure vanilla extract

3 cups all-purpose flour

1½ teaspoons baking powder

1½ teaspoons baking soda

1 teaspoon fine pink Himalayan salt

1 cup sweetened shredded coconut, plus more for layering

FROSTING

½ cup (1 stick) salted butter, at room temperature

2 ounces cream cheese, at room temperature

1 cup confectioners' sugar

½ cup unsweetened cocoa powder

2 teaspoons pure vanilla extract

¼ cup full-fat coconut milk

1. Preheat the oven to 350°F. Grease three 6-inch round cake pans or two 8-inch round cake pans. Line the pans with parchment paper, then grease the parchment.

2. **MAKE THE CAKE.** In a stand mixer fitted with the paddle attachment, beat together the coconut oil, coconut milk, yogurt, honey, eggs, sugar, and vanilla on low speed until combined, about 1 minute. Add the flour, baking powder, baking soda, and salt. Mix until just combined, 1 minute more. Fold in the shredded coconut. Pour the batter into the prepared cake pans, dividing evenly.

3. Bake until the tops are just set and the cakes are no longer jiggly in the center, 30 to 35 minutes. Remove and let cool for 5 minutes. Run a knife around the edges of the pans and turn the cakes out onto a cooling rack. Let cool completely.

4. **MEANWHILE, MAKE THE FROSTING.** In a stand mixer fitted with the paddle attachment, combine the butter and cream cheese. Beat on low speed until light and fluffy, about 2 minutes. Add the confectioners' sugar, cocoa powder, and vanilla. Beat, scraping down the sides of the bowl as needed, until the frosting is light and fluffy, 2 to 4 minutes. Beat in the coconut milk until combined, about 30 seconds more.

5. To assemble, place one cake layer on a serving plate or cake stand. Spread one-quarter of the frosting over the top of the cake and sprinkle a handful of shredded coconut over the frosting. Repeat with the remaining cake layers, taking care not to overfill the layers. Spread the remaining frosting evenly over the top and down the sides of the cake. Serve or store refrigerated for up to 3 days.

maple oatmeal lace cookies

PREP 15 MINUTES

COOK 15 MINUTES

TOTAL 30 MINUTES, PLUS COOLING TIME

MAKES 18 COOKIES OR 9 COOKIE SANDWICHES

Lace cookies are traditional at the holidays, but I love baking them year-round. If you've never experienced a lace cookie, get ready for something good. They're crisp, buttery, and perfectly sweet, with hints of caramel throughout. To make a near-perfect thing even better, I sandwich a generous dollop of sweet and creamy maple frosting in between two of them, then give them a little dip in melted chocolate. They look amazing, and they taste it, too. You could also use the melted chocolate to fill the sandwiches, or even drizzle it over the cookies. There are lots of options, and every one of them will taste good and look beautiful if you want to package them up and gift them. My recipe uses rye flour because it pairs so nicely with the brown sugar and vanilla, creating a truly special cookie. If you don't keep rye flour on hand or if you want a gluten-free cookie, you can swap in almond flour.

COOKIES

½ cup (1 stick) salted butter

⅔ cup packed light brown sugar

2 teaspoons vanilla extract

1 large egg

1½ cups old-fashioned rolled oats

2 tablespoons rye flour

FILLING

3 tablespoons salted butter

3 tablespoons pure maple syrup

¾ cup confectioners' sugar

½ teaspoon ground cinnamon

Fine pink Himalayan salt

4 ounces melted dark chocolate (optional)

1. Preheat the oven to 350°F with racks positioned in the upper and lower thirds of the oven. Line two baking sheets with parchment paper.

2. **MAKE THE COOKIES.** In a medium saucepan, melt the butter over medium heat. Cook, stirring often, until the butter is browned, about 3 minutes. Transfer to a medium bowl. Whisk in the brown sugar and vanilla until combined. Stir in the egg, oats, and rye flour. Let sit for 10 minutes to thicken and cool slightly.

3. Drop the cookie dough onto the prepared baking sheets in scoops of 1 scant tablespoon each, placing them 3 inches apart. Use the back of a spoon to slightly flatten the top of the dough to form a disk.

4. Bake, rotating halfway through, until the cookies are golden brown around the edges, 7 to 9 minutes. The butter will be bubbling up around the cookies—this is okay. Remove the cookies from the oven and let cool on the baking sheet for 5 minutes. Transfer to a wire rack and let cool completely, about 30 minutes.

5. **MEANWHILE, MAKE THE FILLING.** In the same saucepan, melt the butter over medium heat. Cook, stirring often, until the butter is browned, about 3 minutes. Remove the pan from the heat. Whisk in the maple syrup, confectioners' sugar, cinnamon, and a pinch of salt. Let sit for 5 to 10 minutes to thicken and cool slightly.

6. Spread the filling and/or the melted chocolate on the bottoms of half of the cookies. Top with the remaining cookies to create sandwiches. Refrigerate for 30 minutes to set.

7. If desired, dunk one half of each cookie sandwich into the melted chocolate, allowing any excess to drip off. Place on a piece of parchment paper and let set in the refrigerator for 20 to 30 minutes or in the freezer for 15 minutes. Store refrigerated in an airtight container for up to 4 days.

almond cake
with rosemary-lemon sugar

PREP 25 MINUTES

COOK 40 MINUTES

TOTAL 1 HOUR 5 MINUTES, PLUS COOLING TIME

SERVES 8

This cake might just be my favorite. I know, I know, you would probably expect chocolate cake to be my favorite. While I do always love chocolate, this cake is something new and different . . . and DELICIOUS. It's definitely light and airy, but a smidge denser than your typical cake. The olive oil makes it moister than any butter cake out there, and the almond flour adds an extra special touch—plus protein and healthy fats. And then there are the preserves. I use fig preserves because they're my favorite and I think they pair incredibly with the other flavors here, but you can use strawberry or any other fruit jam you love. When the cake comes out of the oven and is still piping hot, a sprinkle of rosemary-lemon sugar melts right into the top as it cools. That sweet ricotta makes a perfect bed for sliced, honeyed strawberries. Try swapping in figs for the berries, if you can find them, or really any other fruit you have on hand. Make the cake work for you!

CAKE
- ¾ cup plus 1 tablespoon granulated sugar
- 3 large eggs, at room temperature
- 3 teaspoons lemon zest plus 2 tablespoons fresh lemon juice
- 2 teaspoons orange zest
- 1 cup extra-virgin olive oil, plus more for greasing
- 1 cup milk of your choice, at room temperature
- ¼ cup fig preserves (I like Dalmatia)
- 1 tablespoon pure vanilla extract
- 1 cup all-purpose flour
- 1 cup almond flour
- 2 teaspoons baking powder
- 1 teaspoon fine pink Himalayan salt
- 3 teaspoons finely chopped fresh rosemary
- ¼ cup raw honey
- 1½ cups fresh strawberries, sliced

WHIPPED RICOTTA
- 2 cups whole-milk ricotta cheese
- 2 tablespoons raw honey

1. Preheat the oven to 375°F. Grease a 9-inch round cake pan. Line the pan with parchment paper, then grease the parchment.

2. In a stand mixer fitted with the paddle attachment, beat ¾ cup of the sugar, the eggs, 2 teaspoons of the lemon zest, and the orange zest on high speed until the mixture is pale and fluffy, about 5 minutes. With the mixer still running, slowly drizzle in the olive oil and beat until combined, about 2 minutes. Add the lemon juice, milk, fig preserves, and vanilla, beating to combine. Reduce the speed to low. Slowly add both flours, the baking powder, and the salt, beating until just combined. Transfer the batter to the prepared pan and tap it against the counter to smooth out the batter.

3. Bake until a tester inserted into the center comes out clean, 40 to 50 minutes. Let cool for 5 minutes.

4. Meanwhile, in a small bowl, combine the remaining 1 tablespoon sugar, 1 teaspoon lemon zest, and 2 teaspoons of the rosemary. Run a knife around the edge of the cake, invert the cake onto a plate, and then flip it back over onto a serving plate. Immediately sprinkle the rosemary-lemon sugar mixture over the hot cake. Let cool completely, about 30 minutes.

5. Meanwhile, in a small saucepan, bring the honey to a gentle boil over medium-high heat. Cook for 1 minute, then remove from the heat. Stir in the remaining 1 teaspoon rosemary. Let cool, then add the strawberries, tossing to combine.

6. **MAKE THE RICOTTA.** In a food processor, combine the ricotta and honey. Pulse until smooth and creamy, 2 to 3 minutes.

7. Just before serving, dollop the whipped ricotta on top of the cake and spoon the honeyed strawberries over the top. Store any leftovers refrigerated in an airtight container for up to one week.

malted milk cookie dough cups

PREP 20 MINUTES

TOTAL 20 MINUTES, PLUS CHILLING TIME

MAKES 12 COOKIE DOUGH CUPS

I think we probably all have similar stories when it comes to chocolate chip cookie dough. Most of us grew up stealing swipes out of the bowl with our fingers as we helped grown-ups in the kitchen. Some of us even prefer the dough to the actual cookie. I love the dough and the cookies equally—I can't pick a favorite, you know? When my brothers and I were kids, my mom would always mix up a batch and a half of dough. That extra half was specifically meant for snacking because my mom knew that between her and her five kids (more of us would come later), she'd need more—she's smart like that. Well now, what if we made cookie dough the whole dessert? And what if we wrapped it in chocolate? These cups are exactly what—and they're a perfectly healthy (mostly nuts and chocolate) and safe (no raw egg or flour here!) way to satisfy that craving. The malted milk powder takes the dough up a notch and adds even more sweet vanilla-ish flavor. If you don't have any on hand, just skip, or use more almond flour. These are so full of protein and antioxidants, I'd even consider calling them a "protein bite" for when you're in need of a pick-me-up . . . but that just wouldn't be as much fun, now would it?

SHELL

1 (12-ounce) bag semisweet chocolate chips

2 tablespoons coconut oil

FILLING

¼ cup cashew butter

1 tablespoon raw honey

1 teaspoon pure vanilla extract

¼ cup almond flour

2 tablespoons malted milk powder

2 tablespoons mini semisweet chocolate chips

Flaky sea salt, for sprinkling

1. Line a 12-cup muffin tin with paper liners.

2. **MAKE THE SHELL.** In a medium microwave-safe bowl, melt the chocolate chips and the coconut oil together in the microwave, stirring every 30 seconds. (Alternatively, you can do this in a small saucepan over medium-low heat.)

3. Drop 1 tablespoon of the melted chocolate mixture into each paper liner, then use the back of a spoon to brush the chocolate halfway up the sides of the liners. Freeze until firm, about 10 minutes.

4. **MEANWHILE, MAKE THE FILLING.** In a medium bowl, stir together the cashew butter, honey, and vanilla. Add the almond flour and malted milk powder. Stir to combine well. Fold in the mini chocolate chips.

5. Spoon 2 teaspoons of the cookie dough filling into each cup and use a wet finger or the back of a spoon to flatten it down. Freeze for another 10 minutes, then spoon the remaining melted chocolate over the tops, covering the cookie dough completely. Smooth the chocolate as needed. Sprinkle with flaky sea salt.

6. Freeze until firm, 20 to 30 minutes. Store refrigerated in an airtight container for up to 2 weeks.

peanut butter cups

To make peanut butter cups, in step 4, stir together ½ cup creamy peanut butter, 2 to 3 tablespoons raw honey, and 1 teaspoon vanilla (omit the almond flour and malted milk powder). Melt the chocolate and coconut oil together as directed in step 2 and finish the recipe as directed in steps 3 through 6.

strawberry rye shortcakes

with honey-vanilla cream

PREP 30 MINUTES

COOK 20 MINUTES

TOTAL 50 MINUTES, PLUS CHILLING AND COOLING TIME

MAKES 6 SHORTCAKES

Extra-juicy, extra-jammy strawberry shortcakes all done up with a splash of bourbon and buttery rye biscuits: Can you think of a better way to celebrate summer? Truth is, I didn't grow up eating shortcakes, but now that I'm an adult, they are one of my favorite sweets. They're always easy to throw together, but these are special. Instead of using just any ol' biscuit recipe, I worked in some rye flour. The brightness of strawberries works so well with the heartier rye, and while the biscuits are still buttery and flaky, they really hold up against the super-juicy berries. That splash of bourbon ties everything together in a beautiful, warming way, though you can easily leave it out if you prefer. If you have strawberries on hand and don't know what to do with them, you NEED to make these shortcakes. You just do. You can also swap out the strawberries for any other berry you love, or use a mix of all your favorites!

BISCUITS

1¼ cups all-purpose flour, plus more for dusting

1¼ cups rye flour

1 tablespoon baking powder

¼ teaspoon fine pink Himalayan salt

¾ cup (1½ sticks) cold salted butter, cubed

¾ cup cold buttermilk, plus more for brushing

Demerara or turbinado sugar, for sprinkling (optional)

BERRIES

3 cups fresh strawberries, sliced, or 3 cups fresh blueberries

2 tablespoons raw honey

1 tablespoon bourbon (optional)

Flaky sea salt

HONEY-VANILLA CREAM

1¼ cups heavy cream

1 teaspoon pure vanilla extract

⅔ cup crème fraîche or plain Greek yogurt

3 tablespoons raw honey

1. Preheat the oven to 425°F. Line a baking sheet with parchment paper.

2. **MAKE THE BISCUITS.** In a food processor, combine both flours, the baking powder, the salt, and the butter. Pulse a few times until pea-size pieces begin to form. Drizzle in the buttermilk and continue pulsing until the dough is shaggy; it will be a bit dry.

3. On a floured work surface, turn out the dough and pat it into a 1-inch-thick square, about 6 inches wide. Cut the dough into 4 equal pieces. Stack the pieces, then press down to flatten them together. Dust the surface with flour and roll out the dough into a 1-inch-thick square, about 6 inches wide, adding more flour as needed. Using a very sharp knife or a pastry cutter, cut the dough into 6 rectangular biscuits, about 2 × 3 inches each. Brush the tops of the biscuits with buttermilk and sprinkle with the sugar (if using). Transfer to the prepared baking sheet and chill in the freezer for 10 minutes.

4. Remove the biscuits from the freezer and bake until the tops are lightly golden and bottoms are deeper golden, 15 to 20 minutes. Let cool for 20 to 30 minutes.

5. **MEANWHILE, MAKE THE BERRIES.** In a medium bowl, toss together the berries, honey, bourbon (if using), and a pinch of flaky salt. Let sit until the berries release their juices, 15 to 20 minutes.

6. **MAKE THE HONEY-VANILLA CREAM.** In a stand mixer fitted with the whisk attachment, beat together the cream and vanilla on medium-high speed until soft peaks form, 2 to 3 minutes. Add the crème fraîche and honey and beat until incorporated, about 30 seconds more. Refrigerate until ready to use.

7. To assemble the shortcakes, slice each biscuit horizontally. Dollop ½ cup of the cream onto the bottom half of each biscuit. Spoon on about ½ cup of the berries, then top with the other biscuit halves. Enjoy immediately!

crinkle-top
roasted banana bread

PREP 15 MINUTES

COOK 1 HOUR 25 MINUTES

TOTAL 1 HOUR 40 MINUTES, PLUS COOLING TIME

MAKES 1 9 × 5-INCH LOAF

W e were still living in Cleveland the first time I ever baked banana bread. On a typical rainy day, I pulled a recipe from one of my mom's cookbooks, and while I don't remember all the details, I do remember that it called for walnuts. I didn't understand why, and so I did what any normal thirteen-year-old would do: I swapped in an equal amount of chocolate chips for the walnuts. Since then, loaf after loaf of banana bread, I've been adding *all* the chocolate. And while, sure, you've made banana bread before, you've never made it quite like this. Other than the chocolate, it has two secrets: roasted, caramelized bananas and a crinkly-crackly topping. Roasting the bananas brings out their natural sweetness, which allows you to use much less sugar in the cake. In fact, other than a touch of honey, the only sugar is in that sprinkle on top, which adds tons of craveable texture. You can skip the topping, but trust me, it's a special touch worth adding. If you can't wait for the cake to cool, I get it—just eat it piping hot with a smear of butter and a drizzle of honey.

¼ cup melted coconut oil, plus more for greasing

6 medium ripe bananas, unpeeled

¼ cup raw honey or pure maple syrup

2 large eggs

2 teaspoons pure vanilla extract

1½ cups whole-wheat pastry flour

1½ teaspoons baking soda

2 teaspoons fine pink Himalayan salt

1 cup semisweet or dark chocolate chunks or chips

2 tablespoons granulated sugar

1 teaspoon ground cinnamon

1. Preheat the oven to 350°F. Grease a 9 × 5-inch loaf pan.

2. Line a baking sheet with parchment paper and arrange the bananas on it. Roast until the banana peels have blackened on top, 20 to 25 minutes. Remove from the oven and let cool slightly. Peel the bananas and mash them. You should have about 2 cups of roasted mashed banana.

3. In a medium bowl, stir together the mashed banana, coconut oil, honey, eggs, and vanilla to combine. Add the flour, baking soda, and salt, and mix until just combined. Fold in the chocolate chips. Transfer the batter to the prepared pan.

4. In a small bowl, stir together the sugar and cinnamon. Sprinkle the mixture evenly over the top of the batter.

5. Bake until the center of the banana bread is set and doesn't move when you shake the pan, about 1 hour. Let cool for at least 30 minutes before slicing. Store in an airtight container at room temperature for up to 5 days.

pumpkin spice latte cake

with coffee frosting

PREP 30 MINUTES

COOK 30 MINUTES

TOTAL 1 HOUR, PLUS COOLING TIME

SERVES 4

Everybody knows about pumpkin spice latte season come fall. It's a celebrated time of year. Well, I like to make my own version of the beloved latte at home so I don't have to wait, with a mix of the warming spices found in chai, pumpkin puree, and a tiny shot of espresso. It's literally fall in a mug and so warm *and* warming that all you want to do is cozy up in a giant sweater by the fire all day. While that's pretty unbeatable, I took all of those flavors and baked them into this cake. You know I am a cake girl through and through, so I might be biased, but I think I love this version even more than the drink. Every bite contains sweet pumpkin and light, fluffy frosting with just a hint of coffee—you're going to want to take a little taste of it every time you walk by. My thought process is this: fall is a short season, so we'd better live it up while it's here and enjoy every sweet minute of it . . . preferably with a yummy drink and a slice of (generously) frosted cake in hand.

CAKE

½ cup melted coconut oil, plus more for greasing

⅔ cup packed light or dark brown sugar

1 tablespoon pure vanilla extract

2 large eggs, at room temperature

1 (15-ounce) can pumpkin puree

1½ cups all-purpose flour

1¼ teaspoons baking powder

½ teaspoon baking soda

1 teaspoon ground cinnamon

½ teaspoon ground ginger

½ teaspoon ground cardamom

¼ teaspoon freshly grated nutmeg

¾ teaspoon fine pink Himalayan salt

FROSTING

½ cup (1 stick) salted butter, at room temperature

2 ounces cream cheese, at room temperature

1½ cups confectioners' sugar

1 tablespoon instant espresso powder

1 tablespoon vanilla extract

1. Preheat the oven to 350°F. Line an 8-inch square baking pan with parchment paper, leaving a 1-inch overhang on two opposite sides. Grease the parchment.

2. **MAKE THE CAKE.** In a stand mixer, beat together the coconut oil, brown sugar, vanilla, eggs, and pumpkin on low until combined, about 1 minute, scraping down the sides of the bowl as needed. Add the flour, baking powder, baking soda, cinnamon, ginger, cardamom, nutmeg, and salt. Mix on low speed until completely smooth with no lumps remaining, about 2 minutes. Pour the batter into the prepared pan.

3. Bake until the center is just set, 25 to 30 minutes. Use the parchment paper overhang to remove the cake from the pan and place on a cooling rack. Let cool for about 30 minutes.

4. **MEANWHILE, MAKE THE FROSTING.** In a stand mixer, beat together the butter and cream cheese until light and fluffy, about 2 minutes. Add the confectioners' sugar, espresso powder, and vanilla. Beat until the frosting is light and fluffy, 2 to 4 minutes more.

5. Spread the frosting over the cake. Slice, snack, and enjoy! Store in an airtight container at room temperature for up to 5 days.

dark mocha lava cakes

PREP 10 MINUTES

COOK 25 MINUTES

TOTAL 35 MINUTES

SERVES 4

½ cup coconut oil, plus more for greasing

8 ounces dark chocolate, chopped

½ cup strong black coffee or espresso

3 large eggs

3 egg yolks

¾ cup granulated sugar

½ cup all-purpose flour

4 squares semisweet or dark chocolate (from 1 chocolate bar)

Ice cream or whipped cream, for serving (optional)

Cocoa powder and/or chocolate shavings, for serving

Two things I love: really good chocolate and really damn good coffee. When you put the two together? I am very, very happy. If you're not already on board, let me be the person to sell you on the idea of putting coffee in your chocolate desserts. It helps to highlight those incredible flavors of the chocolate—and I promise they will not taste like coffee. They'll just be delicious! That is especially true with these individual lava cakes. Dark chocolate makes for a rich cake and a gooey center. Every bite is true perfection. I like to really do it up with ice cream or whipped cream and fancy-looking chocolate curls on top. And if you prefer them dairy-free, you can use coconut cream or just leave off the whip. Whatever you do, just make sure you enjoy these guys warm, straight out of the oven. P.S.: These are my mom's and little sister's FAVORITE. They ask me to make them all the time.

1. Preheat the oven to 375°F with a rack in the center position. Grease four 8-ounce ramekins with coconut oil.

2. In a small saucepan, melt the dark chocolate and coconut oil together over low heat, stirring often, until well combined and smooth, about 5 minutes. Remove the pan from the heat and stir in the coffee.

3. In a medium bowl, whisk together the eggs, egg yolks, sugar, and flour until combined. Stir in the melted chocolate mixture. Divide the batter evenly among the prepared ramekins. Place 1 square of chocolate into the center of each ramekin and gently push it into the batter. Place the ramekins on a baking sheet.

4. Bake until the sides of the cakes are set but the centers are still slightly loose, 15 to 20 minutes. Let the cakes cool in the ramekins for 1 minute, then run a knife around the sides and invert them onto plates. Top each cake with a scoop of ice cream and dust with cocoa powder. Serve immediately.

double-crusted apple cobbler

with cinnamon sugar

PREP 30 MINUTES

COOK 50 MINUTES

TOTAL 1 HOUR 20 MINUTES, PLUS CHILLING TIME

SERVES 8

One of the very first desserts I ever baked up was an apple pie. The family was coming over for a party, and I knew a classic slice was my grandpa's favorite. I think I wanted to impress him. Even though I'd never baked a pie in my life, I set out to make a double-crusted version—I was pretty fearless in the kitchen, and the truth is, I am grateful for it. To this day, I believe that very first apple pie was the best one I've ever baked. I haven't made that many since, mostly because that one was a real project and I want to let the memory stay amazing. But . . . I do make a *lot* of apple cobblers. They're much simpler and always delicious. My biggest hang-up, however, is the crust. Do I use biscuits or a crumble? Well, you know me. Eventually I said to myself, "Why not just do both?" And here we are. Two times the crust is the perfect solution to pretty much any problem. It might be a little less traditional than that first pie, but I'm pretty sure my grandpa would love this one, too.

BISCUITS

2½ cups all-purpose flour, plus more for rolling

1½ teaspoons baking powder

¼ teaspoon fine pink Himalayan salt

¾ cup (1½ sticks) cold salted butter, cubed, plus melted butter, for brushing

¾ cup cold buttermilk

2 tablespoons granulated sugar (optional)

½ teaspoon ground cinnamon (optional)

FILLING

5 to 7 medium apples (about 2¼ pounds), cored and cut into ¼-inch slices (I like Honeycrisp)

2 tablespoons arrowroot powder

1 tablespoon ground cinnamon

Flaky sea salt

¾ cup Maple Apple Butter (page 20) or store-bought apple butter

½ cup pure maple syrup

1 tablespoon fresh lemon juice

2 teaspoons pure vanilla extract

CRUMBLE

½ cup all-purpose flour

2 tablespoons packed dark brown sugar

½ teaspoon ground cinnamon, plus more for dusting

4 tablespoons (½ stick) salted butter, at room temperature

Ice cream, for serving (optional)

1. Preheat the oven to 400°F. Line a baking sheet with parchment paper.

2. **MAKE THE BISCUITS.** In a food processor, combine the flour, baking powder, salt, and butter. Pulse until pea-size pieces begin to form. With the motor running, drizzle in the buttermilk until the dough is shaggy; it will be a bit dry.

3. On a floured work surface, turn out the dough and pat it into a 1-inch-thick square. Cut the dough into 4 equal pieces. Stack the pieces on top of each other, then press down to flatten them together. Dust the surface with flour and roll the dough into a 1-inch-thick rectangle, about 6 × 10 inches. Using a very sharp knife, cut the dough into about 15 square biscuits, about 2 inches wide. Transfer to the prepared baking sheet and chill in the freezer for 10 minutes.

4. **MEANWHILE, MAKE THE FILLING.** In a 12-inch oven-safe skillet, toss together the apples, arrowroot, cinnamon, and a pinch of flaky salt. Add the apple butter, syrup, lemon juice, and vanilla, and toss to combine.

5. **MAKE THE CRUMBLE.** In a small bowl, stir together the flour, brown sugar, and cinnamon. Add the butter and combine well with your hands until the mixture is moist and crumbly. Sprinkle the crumble evenly over the apples.

6. Arrange the biscuits on top of the apples and the crumble. Brush with melted butter. If desired, in a small bowl, stir together the sugar and cinnamon and sprinkle the mixture over the biscuits. Place the skillet on the parchment-lined baking sheet.

7. Bake until the biscuits have risen and are golden, 50 to 55 minutes. Let cool for 5 minutes.

8. Serve warm or at room temperature with ice cream, if desired. Store covered at room temperature for up to 3 days.

chocolate olive oil cake

PREP 15 MINUTES

COOK 40 MINUTES

TOTAL 55 MINUTES, PLUS
COOLING TIME

SERVES 10

I grew up on my mom's chocolate layer cake. She is a pro baker, and no Gerard family celebration was complete without her cake. While it's *so* delicious and I still adore it, there is always, always room for more cake—especially chocolate cake. I love this recipe because it's as easy as piling the ingredients into one bowl, stirring, and baking. It reminds me of the old-school "dump it" cake recipes my grandma would cut out of magazines back in the day. I took that simple formula and elevated the taste with an olive oil twist, which adds warmth and healthy fats. It's all about that balance. And the only thing that could make a chocolate cake better is, yup, chocolate frosting. I used a base of the soft Italian cheese mascarpone, which has the perfect amount of tang to highlight and set off all that richness. With a pinch of flaky salt at the end, this cake has got it all going on. My mom even asked for it for her next birthday. It's that frosting that really does it for her . . . and everyone else, too.

CAKE

½ cup extra-virgin olive oil, plus more for greasing

3 large eggs, at room temperature

1 cup granulated sugar

½ cup plain Greek yogurt

1 tablespoon vanilla extract

1 cup all-purpose flour

½ cup unsweetened cocoa powder

1½ teaspoons baking powder

½ teaspoon fine pink Himalayan salt

¾ cup strong brewed coffee, cooled

FROSTING

1½ cups semisweet chocolate chips (I recommend 60% cocoa)

1½ cups mascarpone, at room temperature

1 teaspoon pure vanilla extract

Flaky sea salt, for serving (optional)

Chocolate shavings, for serving (optional)

1. Preheat the oven to 350°F. Lightly grease a 9-inch round cake pan and line the bottom with parchment paper.

2. **MAKE THE CAKE.** In a large bowl, whisk together the olive oil, eggs, sugar, yogurt, and vanilla until smooth. Add the flour, cocoa powder, baking powder, and salt. Whisk to combine well. Pour in the coffee and whisk until just incorporated. Transfer the batter into the prepared pan and use a spatula to smooth out the top.

3. Bake until a tester inserted into the center comes out clean, 40 to 50 minutes. Remove the cake from the oven and let cool for 5 to 10 minutes. Run a knife around the edge of the cake, invert the cake onto a plate, and then flip it back over onto a serving plate. Let cool completely, about 30 minutes.

4. **MEANWHILE, MAKE THE FROSTING.** Place the chocolate chips in a medium microwave-safe bowl. (Alternatively, you can do this in a small saucepan over medium-low heat.) Microwave, stirring every 30 seconds, until completely melted. Let cool for 10 minutes.

5. Stir in the mascarpone, a dollop at a time, until the mixture is smooth. Stir in the vanilla. Whisk until glossy and smooth.

6. Swirl the frosting onto the top of the cake. Just before serving, top the cake with flaky salt and chocolate shavings, if desired. Store, covered, in the refrigerator for up to 4 days.

acknowledgments

Writing a cookbook is no small task. I could never have completed this one without a huge network of support and many helpers along the way. If not for my team, this book wouldn't have become a reality!

Thank you first to my incredible editors, Francis Lam and Amanda Englander. Francis, this was our first book together, and even though we struggled to complete it, we made it. You really helped make the book great!

Amanda, well, you've been here with me since book number one. How you've managed to put up with me this long is beyond me. Thank you for pushing me daily to keep creating; for making sense of my writing (so that it's . . . actually readable); and for helping me through all of the obstacles that came our way—there sure were many! Once again, we somehow did it, and I think we did an amazing job.

An enormous thank-you to the entire team at Clarkson Potter, for making this book what you see today! A special thank-you to Erica Gelbard and Stephanie Davis, for creating tons of happy buzz around this book and always giving me so much of your valuable time. Your ideas are the best in the business. To Mia Johnson and Stephanie Huntwork, for the hours of work you spent designing the pages of this book. It turned out to be more beautiful than I ever pictured. To Terry Deal, Derek Gullino, and Jill Flaxman, thank you for all your behind-the-scenes work to make this book happen!

To my manager, Alix Frank. Wow, you've been through it all with me, and the support you've given me with not only this book, but just about every other project we have going on, is incredible and doesn't go unnoticed. I really couldn't do any of it without you. Thank you for being a sounding board, an advocate, and a friend through it all.

And to Andrea Barzvi, thank you for pushing through this process and always speaking up for what I want. This book wouldn't have come together without you!

A big thank-you to Kristen Kilpatrick, my wonderfully kind and talented lifestyle photographer. Your good mood is infectious, and our time together never feels like work. Your photos capture something inside of me I didn't know existed, and you're somehow always able to bring out my happiest, smiley self. I'm thankful to call you a friend.

Thank you to our incredible recipe testers, Casey Elsass and Grace Rosanova. You tested countless recipes over and over to make sure they were perfected before being printed in these pages. I really could not have made this cookbook without you.

And finally, to my family—the most important people in my life. My brothers, my sister, my cousins . . . everyone has played a part in helping this book come together. From wild ideas to taste-testing to general everyday support, all I can say is thank you.

Lastly, a special thank-you to both of my parents, without whom I really couldn't do any of what I do. You have both been constant supports and a huge help throughout not only the making of this book, but also throughout my career. I couldn't ask for a better set of parents, and I wouldn't trust any two people more to help me run and grow HBH.

index

Note: Page references in italics indicate photographs.

Copyright © 2022 by Tieghan Gerard
All rights reserved.

All interior photographs are copyright © 2022 by Tieghan Gerard except pages 6, 10, 16–17, 44–45, 78–79, 104–5, 140–41, 170–71, 196–97, 224–25, 252–53, which are copyright © 2022 by Kristen Kilpatrick.

Published in the United States by Clarkson Potter/Publishers, an imprint of Random House, a division of Penguin Random House LLC, New York.
clarksonpotter.com

CLARKSON POTTER is a trademark and POTTER with colophon is a registered trademark of Penguin Random House LLC.

Library of Congress Cataloging-in-Publication Data is on file with the publisher.

ISBN 978-0-593-23255-2
Ebook 978-0-593-23256-9

Printed in Italy

Contributing Editor: Amanda Englander
Lifestyle Photographer: Kristen Kilpatrick
Editor: Francis Lam
Art Director: Mia Johnson
Production Manager: Derek Gullino
Production Editor: Terry Deal
Composition: Merri Ann Morrell
Copy Editor: Laura Cherkas
Indexer: Thérèse Shere
Marketer: Stephanie Davis
Publicist: Erica Gelbard

10 9 8 7 6 5 4 3 2 1

First Edition